# Humanity, Environment and God

# Humanity, Environment and God

Glasgow Centenary Gifford Lectures

Edited by Neil Spurway

BLACKWELL
Oxford UK & Cambridge USA

Copyright © University of Glasgow 1993

First published 1993

Blackwell Publishers
108 Cowley Road
Oxford OX4 1JF
UK

238 Main Street, Suite 501
Cambridge, Massachusetts 02142
USA

*British Library Cataloguing in Publication Data*
A CIP catalogue record for this book is available from the British Library.

*Library of Congress Cataloging-in-Publication Data*

Humanity, environment and God: Glasgow centenary Gifford lectures/edited by
   Neil Spurway.
      p.    cm.
      ISBN 0–631–17495–8
      1. Human ecology—Religious aspects—Christianity.    2. Religion and
science—1964–    3. Natural theology.    I. Spurway, Neil, 1936–  .
BT695.5.H86    1993    261.8′362—dc20    92–35259    CIP

Typeset in 10 on 12 pt Baskerville by Pure Tech Corporation, Pondicherry, India
Printed in Great Britain by Biddles Ltd, Guildford, Surrey

This book is printed on acid-free paper

# Contents

# List of Contributors

**John Barrow** Professor of Astronomy, University of Sussex
**Don Cupitt** Dean of Emmanuel College, Cambridge
**Richard Dawkins** Reader in Zoology, University of Oxford
**John Habgood** Archbishop of York
**Anthony Kenny** Warden of Rhodes House, Oxford
**John Roberts** Warden of Merton College, Oxford
**Neil Spurway** Senior Lecturer, University of Glasgow

# Preface

As an earnest teenager, drawn to both science and religion, I devoured Gifford Lectures. Eddington and Sherrington, Whitehead, Raven, Temple and Dixon were my gurus. Their thoughts soared; their learning was prodigious, their writing majestic. If understanding was to be had, of 'Life, the Universe and Everything', it would surely be found through them?

Perhaps the success of my adolescent quest seems, in the perspective of forty years, to have been less total than I had hoped; this, however, would have surprised few of the lecturers. The great majority were healthily aware of the limits of what humankind could say about its own situation. (Cynics, who assume that Gifford lecturers lack this humility, have usually not read them.)

The quest itself remains. It can be ignored, much of the time, but cannot be dismissed:

> Just when we are safest, there's a sunset-touch,
> A fancy from a flower-bell, someone's death...

As stimulators, counsellors, companions upon the way, the company of Gifford lecturers must surely be the most notable group of scholarly thinkers ever assembled by the fiat of a single man. And, in expression of a lifetime's debt to these great figures, what finer privilege could one enjoy than to edit a Centenary Celebration series of Gifford Lectures?

Planning this celebration, the Gifford Lectureships Committee of the University of Glasgow identified five major, and still-active, areas of scholarship from which lecturers had been drawn during the hundred years since the inception of the series: physical science, biology, history, philosophy and theology itself. The Committee then invited one leading exponent of each of the first four disciplines to give up to three lectures each, and two churchman-theologians, both of modern yet of very different casts of mind, respectively to introduce and to round off the series. To give unity and a contemporary focus to the six contributions, a suggestion by Principal Sir Alwyn Williams was adopted: each speaker was invited to address in his own terms the overall theme of 'Environment'. Texts, written for or following the lectures which resulted, make up the main part of this book.

In counterpoint to the modern sections, however, I have placed between them short excerpts from Glasgow's first Gifford lecturer, Max Müller, who held the position from 1888 to 1892. Müller's core discipline was philology, which he had been applying for many years to the study of comparative religion. He built an extraordinarily wide-ranging *tour de force* upon this framework, and within his four substantial volumes there are perspicacious comments relating to themes re-addressed by each of our Centenary contributors.

Introducing the whole is a chapter (not given as a lecture) which attempts to place the Centenary contributions in the contexts of the main challenges confronting Natural Theology in Lord Gifford's time and now, and to relate the mosaic of thought, constructed in the hundred years over which these Lectureships have so far extended, to the magnificent benefaction which began them.

Neil Spurway
*For the Gifford Lectureships Committee*
*of the University of Glasgow*

# 1
# Introduction: 100 Years (and More) of Natural Theology

## Neil Spurway

### The Bequest

21 August, 1885: Granton House, Edinburgh – in the garden, overlooking the Firth of Forth, Adam, Lord Gifford, sometime Senator of the College of Justice, is signing his Will. His witnesses are his doctor and his regular cab driver. The latter's involvement has been described by one late twentieth-century commentator, Stanley Jaki,[1] as 'almost defiantly un-propitious'. However, our own sense of the matter may perhaps be rather different. His doctor and his driver are two people upon whom, in long-term widowerhood and now deeply encroaching paralysis, Lord Gifford greatly, and almost equally, depends; they are probably the two closest of his helpers and confidants who are not to be beneficiaries. Furthermore, though now extremely wealthy (his bequest would be worth several million pounds at 1990s rates), Adam Gifford is not high-born. In any case there is, one suspects, more sense of fundamental human equality on the Scottish bench in this late nineteenth century than is likely to be found at the same period among judges in Professor Jaki's country of origin, Hungary.

Be this as it may, Lord Gifford's Will itself is almost defiantly propitious – humane in its concern for named individuals, but at the same time visionary and munificent in its central provision. This is for the foundation, in the four Scottish universities extant at this time (Aberdeen, Edinburgh, Glasgow and St Andrews), of Lectureships or Popular Chairs for 'Promoting, Advancing, Teaching and Diffusing the study of Natural Theology'. That term is to be taken in its 'widest sense... in other words, "The Knowledge of God, the Infinite, the All, the First and Only Cause...

and the Knowledge of... the Relations which men and the whole universe bear to Him, the Knowledge of the Nature and Foundation of Ethics or Morals, and of the Obligations and Duties thence arising." ' Strong stuff! However, as subsequent clauses reveal, this is a self-taught yet deeply-read philosopher writing, not a dogmatic churchman. 'The Lecturers appointed... shall not be required to... subscribe any declaration of belief... they may be of any religion or way of thinking, or... of no religion... provided only that they be able and reverent men, true thinkers... and earnest inquirers after truth...' for, Lord Gifford believes, 'nothing but good can result from free discussion.' Finally, he requires that the lectures be 'public and popular... open not only to students of the Universities, but to the whole community without matriculation'. Doctor and driver equally must symbolize the audience.

Adam Gifford died on 20 January, 1887, and the first lectures on the bequest were given the following year. We will consider their story later. Before that, let us look closer at the man, his concept of Natural Theology, and the intellectual climate in which such thinking would have been undertaken in his time.

## Lord Gifford

Adam West Gifford was born in 1820, the eldest child of a small leather-work maker. Serious and scholarly even in youth, he was nicknamed 'the philosopher'. But there was recreation too: his brother John[2] records chess (with pieces the two boys had carved), home-made model boats and, when they were older, early morning skating.

The family were committed Christians, but must have been flexible in sectarian matters, for they worshipped at churches of different denominations (within Scottish Protestantism) when they moved house. Adam was very much a part of these activities, and as a young professional man taught in more than one Sunday School.

When the time came to choose a career Adam Gifford trained in the Law, combining university studies with clerkship in the office of one of his uncles, a solicitor. In 1849 he advanced to the status of advocate (barrister) – a role in which he was highly successful and acquired considerable wealth. In parallel with this he assumed in 1865 the Sheriff-dom of Orkney and Shetland (a visiting, not residential, office). Finally, in 1870, at the rather early age of 49, he was appointed a judge of Scotland's most senior court, the Court of Session – thereby acquiring the title 'Lord Gifford'. It is recorded that he refused to judge criminal cases, believing that those guilty before the law were too often people who had themselves previously been wronged by society. Instead, he specialized in commercial actions, handing down judgements based more on commonsense equity than legalism.

Already, however, the first of two devastating misfortunes had befallen him. His dearly-loved wife, whom he had only married in 1863, died less than five years later. They had one son.

The second misfortune was cumulative. From 1872 till his death 15 years later, Lord Gifford suffered what appears to have been an inexorable series of ever-more-debilitating strokes. In January, 1881, he was struck by one of the most severe of these while presiding over a case. Though realizing that he could not move, he completed the hearing, and only after the court had risen did he call for help. He never walked again, and resigned his judgeship within weeks.

His fortitude and faith at this time are indicated by some of the utterances his brother quotes:

> I have often wished for leisure to read and to think; now I have it!
>
> I will never walk again, but it doesn't matter. I need no crutches; there are wings ready for me to bear me home to God.

According to John Gifford's fond and admiring account, the elder brother had even in boyhood shown quiet strength and yet warmth of character: now it was evident how marvellously fortified he was by a total, though undogmatic, faith:

> I think I have seen more clearly many things about God since I have been laid aside; in the night I often can't sleep, and I follow out new trains of thought about Him.
>
> To be happier or wiser, that just means to have more of God.

Yet not only was Adam Gifford a man of deep faith; he was also a man of towering ability and wide learning. While practising law he had been a particularly avid reader and memoriser (yet at the same time a stern critic) of poetry. Now, deeply paralysed but with his mind (until his very last year) still acute, he enthusiastically immersed himself in the more structured insights of philosophical theology, which he could read in German and French as well as Latin and Greek. According to John's memoir, he particularly delighted at this period in the writings of Spinoza on the one hand, and in the Gospel of St John on the other. It is possible to see the latter balancing the former in his thought: 'Spinoza holds that everything is God. I hold that God is everything.' Without God, nothing would exist: 'In Him we live and move and have our being.' Putting the same insight another way: 'The Infinite cannot be infinite if it does not include everything.'

These cameo recollections of Adam Gifford's mind are telling in relation to the lectures we shall soon discuss; and one other comment, on the same page (p. 98) of his brother's memoir is perhaps even more so. John notes that, in the Bible, Adam Gifford 'ever sought and found the highest and purest thoughts this world contains,' yet (here is the crux) 'he did not hold the doctrine of a verbal inspiration.'

## Lord Gifford as a Lecturer

Until physical disability advanced too far, Lord Gifford was himself in wide demand as a lecturer to literary groups, philosophical societies and Christian associations, as well as to legal gatherings. Seven of his texts were published by one of his nieces and his son[3] and a further sample of his titles is recorded in the memoir by his brother. He lectured (in addition to the legal subjects) on the writings both of Elizabeth Barrett Browning and of Charles Darwin; on the thought of Erasmus and that of Emerson, yet also on the life of St Bernard of Clairvaux; on the Metaphysics of Substance, but again – with no less an admixture of impressive learning and sensitive perception – on the Avatars of Vishnu.

Here I shall quote from three of the published lectures. Page references are to the original edition, where the texts are complete.

Let us begin with the piece *Ralph Waldo Emerson*, delivered in 1872. First, a sentence praising the genius of the past, in a metaphor suggesting that Lord Gifford would not have been unhappy with lectures taking the theme of 'Environment' 116 years later:

> Exalt not the genius of today above the lessons of experience or the words of ancient wisdom, but remember that the greenness of earth's latest beauty rests on the rocks and the ashes which it took milleniums to form. (p. 14)

Next, a provocative counterpoint to Wittgenstein's claim that 'whatever can be said can be said clearly':

> It is a great mistake to suppose it the only test of genius to be always clear and distinct and lucid. It is only very narrow genius that is always that. The great man, like the great painter, is great both in light and in shadow. Nature lives in both, and is perfect in *chiaro-oscuro*. (p. 24)

And last, from this lecture, a long passage closely germane to our main theme:

Emerson is not distinctively a religious writer, that is to say he does not profess to teach or to enforce religion, but his tone is eminently religious. The truth is, that although in education and elsewhere we may try to separate secular from sacred, and provide time-tables and conscience clauses and so on, religion will not be separated from anything whatever! It will penetrate every cranny and pervade every space, and it will flow around and through every subject and every substance like electricity. You cannot produce and you cannot maintain religious vacuum, and if you could, even secularism would die in it...

It is very difficult to gather from any of Emerson's writings what are his precise religious beliefs. He nowhere announces them, and it is only from scattered hints and implications that an approximation can be reached. He is still claimed as a Unitarian, although probably his true position is rather that of a philosophic Theist. I imagine he would not classify himself as either a Unitarian or a Trinitarian or a Polytheist; but that he would rather stand along with such men as his great contemporary Theodore Parker, who thought that *one* and *three* and many were just man's arithmetic of Deity, modes of human reckoning, finite aspects which can only have a figurative application to the Infinite. I gather also that he rather inclines to the higher or subjective pantheism; but he will not limit, and he cannot define. Before all such questions he stands uncovered and reverently silent. No proud denial, no cynic scoff, no heartless sneer escapes him; and without a theory of the universe he clings to its moral meaning. I believe he seems to say that the universe exists hospitably for the weal of souls. 'I will bate no jot of heart or of hope though I cannot see the end of transgression. I know that there is a permanent behind everything that is mutable and fleeting; and though abyss open under abyss, and opinion displace opinion, all are contained in the Eternal Cause'. (pp. 28–30)

Second, let us quote from the somewhat dauntingly named lecture, *Substance. A Metaphysical Thought*, (1876). The text early indicates Lord Gifford's vigorous (though healthily sceptical) awareness of the sciences:

What are proudly though not quite justly called the *Physical Sciences* are perhaps now in the ascendant, (and very self-asserting some of them are); and there are not wanting among their votaries and champions those who arrogantly claim for them alone the name of '*Sciences*', as if the polar collocations and the whirling vortices of enchanted atoms were all that ultimately man could really know! There are some who say and think that they could find in the grey matter of the brain the very essence of the soul; and love and reverence and hope and faith and joy they call only the measured cadences of its tremulous vibrations. Now to such materialists, if any such there be, the proper answer is to be found in the truths and in the intuitions of ultimate metaphysics. Only go deep enough, and press analysis far enough, and the most obstinate materialist may be made to see that matter is not *all* the universe, and that there is something below and above and around and within it. Mind is not the outcome of trembling or rotating atoms. Neither qualities of matter nor thoughts of mind are self originated or self sustained. There are other spirits than volatile alcohols or irresolvable gasses, and forces far more etherial and dominant than the expansion of steam or the explosion of gunpowder or of nitroglycerine; and vast as is the astonishing magnificence of the universe of suns and their mere material attendants, one soul outweighs them all! (pp. 130–1)

Now we see where he is going – and go he most confidently does:

The force behind and in all forces, the energy of all energies, the explanation of all explanations, the cause of all causes and of all effects, the soul that is within and below and behind each soul, the mind that inspires and animates and thinks in each mind, in one word the substance of all substances, the substance of all forms, of all phenomena, of all manifestations, is *God*...

Said I not that the word *substance* was perhaps the grandest word in any language? There can be none grander. It is the true name of *God*. Every line of thought meets here. Every eager question is answered here. Every difficulty and perplexity is resolved here. Here the philosopher must rest. Here the ignorant must repose...

The universe and all its phenomena, suns and galaxies – with their inconceivable dependences, other universes, countlessly unthought, because unthinkable by finite minds, all, – all, – are but the forms of the Infinite, the shadows of the Substance that is One for ever. (pp. 154–5)

And if God be the substance of our souls, He must also be the substance of our thoughts and of all our actions. Thoughts and actions are not self-sustaining and self-producing any more than worlds. They are mere manifestations first of our soul, but next and far more truly manifestations of God who is our ultimate Substance. 'In Him we live and move and have our being.' Observe the emphasis and the force of the *in*. '*In Him*.' It is not said 'by him' or 'from him' or 'through him' or 'by his power.' These may be all true, but not the truth declared here. It is *in Him* that we *have our being*. We are parts of the Infinite, literally, strictly, scientifically so. A human soul or a human thought outside of God would be a rival deity!

I pause here for a moment to remind you that I am not here to-night as a preacher, to teach theology, or even to teach religion, in the common sense of the word. I am here simply and solely as a scientific lecturer, trying to point out to you strict rigid scientific metaphysic and mental truth. I have not gone a single step out of my way as a student of metaphysic and mental science, and if I have had to speak to you of God, frankly and freely, that is only because God is necessarily found by all who fairly follow up the scientific idea of *substance* to its deepest roots and to its highest sources. The highest science always becomes religious, – nay, religion itself.

Let me also ask you, as an humble but thorough-going disciple of science, to take nothing on my word, nothing on my authority or on the authority of any other man. Science knows no authority but the intuition of truth. (pp. 157–8)

We may suspect that the word 'science' has, by this stage of the argument, assumed a somewhat more ambitious meaning even than that represented by statistical mechanics and neuro-anatomy – the disciplines passingly alluded to in the opening lines of our first quotation from this lecture. Lord Gifford includes within 'science' the metaphysical conclusions which may be drawn from science. Nevertheless, the cast of his mind is clear.

In a last quote from this source, Lord Gifford reveals the fertile interaction between Spinoza and St John to which his brother was later to draw our attention:

If God be the *substance* of all forces and powers and of all beings, then He must be the *only substance*, the only substance in the universe or in all possible universes. This is the grand truth on which the system of Spinoza is founded, and his whole works are simply drawing deductions therefrom.

'I am and there is none besides me,' – no being, no thing, no existence, – I *am*, and nothing else *is*. (p. 158)

To conclude this section, let us finally consider some excerpts from Lord Gifford's address *The Ten Avatars of Vishnu* (1880).

There is an apostolic precept, the neglect or nonobservance of which, not only miserably narrows our minds and degrades us in selfishness, but wholly deprives us of the highest and purest pleasure of which our nature is susceptible. The precept is, – 'Look not, every man on his own things, but every man also on the things of others'. It is difficult, it is impossible, to say how much nobler and how much happier we should be if we constantly gave this precept our implicit obedience. (p. 203)

In this spirit, Gifford sets about introducing his audience to

...the immense and vastly complicated system of religion known as Brahmanism or Hinduism. Originally, so far as can now be gathered, strictly theistic, it has become in the lapse of ages almost all embracing, and now it is not so much one religion as a vast congeries and mixture of almost all forms of religion and almost all aspects of faith. (p. 206)

In Hinduism there will be found spiritualism the most refined for the spiritualist, and materialism the grossest for the modern atomist or the ancient Epicurean. There is theism for the theist and atheism for the atheist. The mystic and the metaphysician may find mists and atmospheres teeming with congenial shadows, and the sensual and the earthly may grovel upon the ground! Hinduism offers culture to the educated and wisdom to the wise, while with equal hand she gives superstitions and charms to the ignorant and to the foolish. To the philosophic monotheist is presented an ideal of deity too lofty for expression, dimly indicated as the unthinkable and the for ever unknown; while to the idolator is thrown open the vastest pantheon, crowded and populous with Superstition's nameless and innumerable brood. The ritualist and the devotee may find ceremonies and penances which would consume a thousand lives, while the holy and devout may spend unconscious centuries in the extasies of absorption. (pp. 206–7)

Whatever Hinduism, or Brahmanism, may have latterly or in its bulk become, still in its purest and highest essence it was (indeed I think it still is, and I am glad to think so) a monism, a monotheism and in one aspect a pantheism of a pure and noble kind...

Pure Brahmanism knows only one God, indeed only one Being, in the universe, – 'Brahm,' or 'Brahman,' in whom all things consist and exist, apparently for ever. Observe, this Brahm or Brahman is quite different from *Brahmâ* the *Father*, to whom we shall come immediately, and who is supposed to have made all things. Brahm never made anything. Brahm is neither a person nor a thing. He or It is of neuter gender, or of no gender at all, not even of the lifeless gender...

He, It, has no name; to name him at all is to name him wrong; to conceive of him at all, is to misconceive him... he should not be named and he cannot be thought of.

From this inconceivable and unnameable Brahm there issue (issue is the word, and it is an eternal procession) the Trinity or Triad of the Hindus, with whom really begins their theology. The doctrine of a Trinity, though not the earliest, is one of the most prominent doctrines of Hinduism, and this itself is a very striking fact. The Hindu Trinity are these.

1 *Brahmâ*, the Creator, the Father.
2 *Vishnu*, the Preserver.
3 *Siva*, the Destroyer,

with whom is indissolubly connected the function of *reproduction*. (Very curious this. He only destroys by making new, by reproducing.)

These are the Trinity, and all these are males. They have names and they have gender, contrasting strikingly with the primeval neuter, the unutterable 'Brahm'!

I have said that the Trinity issue from Brahm, and 'issue' is the word, and the thought. Brahm does not create the Trinity. He is not creator and they are not his creatures. Perhaps 'Manifestation' best conveys the idea. God is manifested in the Trinity! Three essences in one God! Three aspects of the Infinite! (pp. 209–11)

...all the persons of the Hindu Triad are objects of worship. But the great neuter Brahm whence they issue *is not*... men seldom or never worship the abstract. (p. 215)

And so finally to the incarnations, the Avatars themselves:

In all religions incarnations are known. Ever and again man's spirit tells him – 'The gods are come down to us in the likeness of men'. In the crowd or in the solitude, by night or by day, ever still the heavens are opened, the dazzling smites us to the ground, and 'deep calleth unto deep'. Whence this inextinguishable belief? From the felt possibility, nay the certain truth, that the Infinite can come down, has come down, and is manifest upon earth. Where is the soul so dead and so lost as not to have had its avatar, and not often to await the visitor from on high? Vishnu in Brahminical mythology is the Preserver, and has often come down, made a descent, an avatar, to vindicate and to save. (p. 217)

## Natural Theology

Having acquired some feel for the man, his thought and his prose, let us look at what Lord Gifford meant by the specific term 'Natural Theology'. His definition in the Will is full and impressive, when cited entire. Natural Theology is

The Knowledge of God, the Infinite, the All, the First and Only Cause, the One and the Sole Substance, the Sole Being, the Sole Reality, and the Sole Existence,

together with

the Knowledge of His Nature and Attributes, the Knowledge of the Relations which men and the whole universe bear to Him, the Knowledge of the Nature and Foundations of Ethics or Morals, and of all Obligations and Duties thence arising.

Thus far, the definition might be considered to encompass the whole of both metaphysical and moral theology, as expressed within a culture imbued by the influence of Aristotle. Nevertheless, there are already significant omissions. Note that there is no mention of Christ or even the general concept of a Messiah; nothing of salvation, nothing of eternal life, nothing of worship, nothing of the Holy Spirit.

At first, as one reads, one assumes these omissions imply merely that Lord Gifford, the impassioned expositor of Hinduism, does not wish to tie his benefaction simply to Christianity among the world's religions. But he has lectured on Emerson too, so he is about to go further in his openness. The Will instructs the University Senates, as patrons and administrators of the Lectureships, that

> The Lecturers appointed shall be subjected to no test of any kind, and shall not be required to take any oath, or to emit or subscribe any declaration of belief, or to make any promise of any kind; they may be of any denomination whatever, or of no denomination at all (and many earnest and high-minded men prefer to belong to no ecclesiastical denomination); they may be of any religion or way of thinking, or as is sometimes said, they may be of no religion, or they may be so-called sceptics or agnostics or freethinkers, provided only that they be able, reverent men, true thinkers, sincere lovers of and earnest inquirers after truth.

Thus, within the ambit of theology, Lord Gifford is extremely flexible as to subject-matter and as liberal as it is possible to be with regard to viewpoint. In the sentences which immediately follow, however, he is quite specific in his prescription of the approach to be adopted. It is to be his own approach to the Metaphysics of Substance:

> I wish the lecturers to treat their subject as a strictly natural science, the greatest of all possible sciences, indeed, in one sense, the only science, that of Infinite Being, *without reference to or reliance upon any supposed special exceptional or so-called miraculous revelation.* I wish it considered just as astronomy or chemistry is.

The references to science, and particularly to astronomy and chemistry, would have made almost all professional scientists who encountered it in the late nineteenth century smile, and make (if this is possible) an even higher proportion smile today. It is hard to imagine doing laboratory experiments, or making instrumental observations, in any useful sense, upon the Absolute. Yet, having earlier seen his own example, we know what Lord Gifford intends. Furthermore, the interpolated clause eschewing revelation (my italics) is crucial – and totally in the traditional spirit of Natural Theology. From Aquinas on, the contrast has always been between the theology based upon observation of the world and experience of life in it and the theology based upon what has been identified as revelation.

At some length, therefore, the Victorian Law Lord has arrived at a position totally compatible with that of the seventeenth century Chancellor who, 260 years earlier, had succinctly and beautifully defined Natural Theology as

> That spark of knowledge of God which may be had by the light of nature and the consideration of created things.[4]

## Victorian Thought and Natural Theology

As a last step before turning to the lectures elicited by the Gifford bequest, it will be constructive to recall something of the intellectual climate in which Adam Gifford had matured his mind – and of which, one hopes, the University Senators who constituted the first generation of the Will's administrators were corporately no less conscious.

We have seen that Lord Gifford was not ignorant of physics; and in his time physics was extremely strong. No cracks would be evident in its classical edifice until the turn of the century. Perhaps even more important, in terms of impact upon the non-professional, the engineering based upon physics had, throughout the preceding 50-60 years, been making huge strides. Furthermore, two Scots, Maxwell and Kelvin, were at the forefront. For the most part, the effects of both physics and engineering were to increase human confidence, in respect not only of power over nature but understanding of nature. (Bacon had contrasted these, believing that the achievement of power need not imply understanding: but one suspects that few Victorians shared this cautious view). Hubris apart, theirs was not a necessarily anti-religious confidence, but it was clearly more compatible with the God of the Grand Design than with an interventionist, miracle-working deity. Debates about determinism versus free will were certainly stimulated by late nineteenth-century physics, but at least two philosophical resolutions were available – Hegelian idealism (or one of its offshoots) and an essentially-Cartesian dualism. Adam Gifford's own outlook, indeed, seems to have combined elements of both.

There was, however, one respect in which the physics of the time *was* pessimistic. The newly-matured science of thermodynamics (which had originated in France and Germany, but to which both Maxwell and Kelvin contributed – the latter massively) predicted the running down of everything: it made clear that the everyday experiences

> That no life lives forever;
> That dead men rise up never;

That even the weariest river
Winds somewhere safe to sea

are all embracing, and point ineluctably to the ultimate degradation of all energy, the 'heat death' of the universe. Furthermore, the urgency of this process, at least within our solar system, was seriously exaggerated by Kelvin who, knowing nothing of atomic physics, underestimated the life-span of the sun by several orders of magnitude.

Clearly, this concept lent itself (in the minds of those who were aware of it) to one mode of religious interpretation – suggesting a not-unimaginably-distant Armageddon. But it did challenge simplistic ideas of a Design for ever-continuing progress, with which other scientific findings and outlooks seemed highly compatible. Biology, in particular, appeared to many mid-Victorians to point to such progress.

At the start of the century, Paley's *Natural Theology* and in the 1830s the series of Treatises written on the bequest of the Earl of Bridgewater, had topped a long tradition of writing by devout naturalists: naturalists who, in successive generations, had perceived in the forms of plant and animal life – the 'Book of God's Works' – ever more evidence of a beneficent, omnipotent and infinitely wise Designer. The idea that different species were not individually created, but evolved, was one which developed gradually, particularly in France and Britain, with many great names from Geology and Zoology associated. In particular, Sir Charles Lyell's landmark work, *Principles of Geology* (1830–3), established once-for-all in mainstream science the chronological interpretation of the stratigraphic record, though Lyell himself still believed in the independent Divine creation of each species. Scottish involvement in the next 15 years was remarkable rather than glorious. Robert Chambers, an Edinburgh publisher, elicited a storm of both religious and scientific protest when (at first anonymously) he proclaimed progressive transmutation – evolution, up to and including man, though without yet a scientifically-comprehensible mechanism – as the expression of the Laws of God; Hugh Miller, the stonemason-geologist from Cromarty averred that, on the contrary, each phylum could be seen from the fossil record to have fallen from an original, Divinely-fashioned perfection. It was, of course, Charles Darwin's *The Origin of Species* (1859) which irresistably documented the course of evolution *and*, within the limits of the developmental biology of the day, proposed the mechanism of it – Natural Selection, from a vast diversity of spontaneous variations.

Such an account need not be interpreted as a denial of the hand of God, only denial that it was an endlessly fussy hand. Darwin himself (though his sense of Divine involvement was to diminish in old age) at the time of writing *The Origin* suggested that he was showing, not that God was not at work, but how He was at work. And Charles Kingsley, known to most of us nowadays as a polymathic author, but more importantly in this context one of the naturalist clerics, wrote to thank Darwin for a copy of *The Origin* in these terms:

> I have gradually learned to see that it is just as noble a conception of Deity, to believe that He created primal forms capable of self-development into all forms needful *pro tempore* and *pro loco*, as to believe that He required a fresh act of intervention to supply the *lacunas* which he himself had made. I question whether the former be not the loftier thought.

And again, more strongly:

> Now that they have got rid of an interfering God, a master-magician as I call it – they have to choose between the absolute empire of accident and a living immanent, ever-working God.

Many of us at the present day would consider that these words of Kingsley's embody what is still the essential religious response to Darwin and, *mutatis mutandis*, to other scientific revolutionaries.

Yet a number of eminent Victorians went even further. Thus Frederick Temple, who had contributed to the impactful multi-author work of biblical criticism *Essays and Reviews* (1861), and was later to become Archbishop of Canterbury, argued in 1884 that the world's imperfections were those of 'a half completed picture, not yet ready to be seen'. The prospect of heat death was ignored, or unencountered. In Temple's eyes the doctrine of evolution implied perpetual progress, reducing pain and enhancing joy. As John Durant has remarked,[5] this Natural Theology of providential progress actually owed more to Herbert Spencer than to Darwin. Either way, it attracted a large body of liberal Protestant opinion in the 1880s.

Of course, as is well known, this was not the universal view. In the first place, Darwin and Spencer were opposed by many who still wished to take the Bible creation story literally. To one of these, the geologist Sedgwick, the 'transmutation of species' was 'a theory no better than a phrensied dream'. At heart, however, this was one of the great clashes between Natural and Revelation-based Theology; and Natural Theology, in the majority of such clashes, ultimately wins – even if this particular battle is, incredibly, not over even yet in the southern states of the USA.

There were others, however, who found in Darwinism a different flaw. These critics were content to conceive evolution as the working out of

Divine ideas through time, but the concept that variations occurred randomly and their subsequent survival or extinction depended upon competitive struggle – 'Nature, red in tooth and claw / With ravine' seemed utterly at odds with the picture of an all-wise, all-loving and all-powerful God. As such, one suspects this was a view cleaved to primarily by sensitive, retiring souls. Yet somebody vocal, whose thought included these elements, was the Scot, Henry Drummond, who in the 1880s rewrote Darwinism with altruistic cooperation, a struggle not for the individual's survival but for that of others, built into the account.

If, in this sketch of the Victorian intellectual scene, I have given pride of space to evolutionary thinking, this is no doubt partly because I am myself a biologist. But the conflicting strands of Victorian thought about the ascent of man reflect and embody the era's thought-forms about politics, morality and social justice too. Darwin used language gleaned from Malthus, and was himself the source (though he would not have been the approving source) of later 'Social Darwinism', which claimed to justify inequalities of class and race on biological grounds.

The touching of the sacrosanct with the brush of science was reflected also in textual and historical criticism of the Bible, undertaken mostly in Germany, but not ignored in Britain, and supported in both countries by the new findings of archeology. Like evolutionary thinking, the new outlook on the Bible was an affront to some of the faithful, and a vitalizing renaissance to others: everywhere, it disrupted old ways of thought. Rather similar in its consequences was the study of comparative religion, providing yet further indications of the less-than-unique status of biblical revelation.

The Scottish reception of both these forms of scholarship, especially biblical criticism, was characteristically confused. The fate of Robertson Smith epitomises the conflict. A Free Kirk minister and Professor of Old Testament in that Church's College at Aberdeen, he wrote the article 'Bible' in the *Encyclopaedia Britannica* of 1875. In this entry he expounded German arguments which he had studied at first hand, indicating that the Old Testament Prophets chronologically preceded the formal state-ment of their precepts in Deuteronomy's 'Mosaic' Law. In modern eyes, this is the obvious progression – the Law codifies what the Prophets had proclaimed. But, after a six-year battle, the Free Kirk General Assembly voted, by a majority, to dismiss Smith. He was not totally destroyed: Cambridge took him to its bosom. Yet he had been drained, and died young.

Lord Gifford's reaction to the treatment of Smith is not on record, but surely his sympathies must have lain with this earnest enquirer after truth. Even more fascinating would have been to have the text of Lord Gifford's lecture on Darwin; sadly, it does not seem to have been preserved. There are sufficient hints elsewhere for one to be fairly confident that he aligned himself more closely with Kingsley than with Sedgwick. One suspects, however, that he might have approved the standpoint of Drummond – which would appear in print a few years later, but could in the meantime have been known to him personally. On comparative religion, by contrast, there is no need to speculate: we have seen that his response was liberal and warm.

Arguably more important than any of his individual judgements, however, would have been Lord Gifford's awareness of debate. All around him during the period when he must have conceived the idea of his great legacy, there were powerfully conflicting schools of thought. Rationalism vied with conservative faith, metaphysical optimism with sombre doubt. For all its material confidence and success, the age was, in deeper matters, one 'of observance more than assurance' in Asa Briggs' phrase[6] – an age whose most representative poetry is surely that of spiritual struggle; the poetry of Clough (of whom we shall hear more), Arnold and, perhaps most centrally, Tennyson:

> I falter where I firmly trod,
> And, falling with my weight of cares
> Upon the great world's altar-stairs,
> That slope through darkness up to God,
>
> I stretch lame hands of faith, and grope
> And gather dust and chaff, and call
> To what I feel is Lord of all
> And faintly trust the larger hope.

This was the climate in which Adam Gifford, a man of profoundly trusting faith himself, cast his bread upon the waters. Apart from his wish that they be scientific in their approach, the lecturers on his foundation were to be 'under no restraint whatsoever in their treatment of their theme'. They might 'freely discuss... all questions about man's conception of God or the Infinite, their origin, nature, and truth, whether he can have any such conceptions, whether God is under any or what limitations, and so on...', so convinced was Lord Gifford of the merits of untrammelled discussion.

One other hope this master of prose must have entertained: though it cannot feasibly be stated as a condition, I am sure he trusted that his lecturers would not only think well but write well. To cite one more phrase from his own piece on Emerson, what he would have wanted to draw forth were

Thoughts that breathe and words that burn.

## A Century of Lectures

The Will being confirmed, the Senates moved fast. One has a sense perhaps (though there is no explicit record) of competition, as to which university could get the first Gifford lecturer onto the podium. In the event, Edinburgh won, hands down; that Senate had probably received private news of the bequest well before it was published, since not only had Lord Gifford been an Edinburgh man throughout his life, but also the city was then, as it still largely is, the centre for legal affairs in Scotland. Furthermore, as if to press home its advantage, the Edinburgh Senate chose a local figure and, interestingly enough, not an academic but a freelance philosophical writer: James Hutchison Stirling. The other three Senates all looked to Oxford for their inaugural speakers; both distance, and academic calendars, must therefore have added to delays. Stirling gave his first lecture in January, 1888. Max Müller, in Glasgow, did not open till November[7] and Andrew Lang, at St Andrews, in January, 1889. Aberdeen's choice, Edward Tylor, did not even get going until well into the latter year. Whether the Senators of the granite city disdained competitive haste, or Tylor let them down, I have been unable to establish, though as a question mark upon the speaker's professionalism, it is noticeable that his was to become the only one of the nineteenth-century lecture series never to be published.

The matter of starting dates, however, is of minor significance beyond a little healthy rivalry. More substantial interest attaches to the topics chosen, then and later. These have been fully listed up to 1984, both chronologically and alphabetically, by Stanley Jaki. Jaki also offers a critical survey, from his own neo-Thomist standpoint, of the 150 volumes published up to that point. This is a prodigious feat, though Jaki marrs it by treating almost every outlook different from his own as something close to an intellectual sin. Nevertheless, I gratefully acknowledge his scholarship, as I do that of Bernard Jones[8] who amicably anthologized the lectures published up to 1967. The following impressionistic and far from inclusive sketch is not, however, entirely derivative.

Stirling, as the very first Gifford lecturer, was also the first of many advocates, in the early period, of German Idealism. Nevertheless he was also, to his great credit, prepared to be so 'public and popular' as to make jokes. The *Scotsman* newspaper's accounts indicate that there were a great many in the lectures as delivered, but Stirling even permitted quite a number to survive into his published text:

> Our transatlantic brothers, as we hear at this moment, are going to have
> object glasses, or reflectors, or refractors, of ever so many feet; but the very

tallest American, with the very tallest of telescopes, will never be able to say that he spied out God.[9]

Müller, Lang and Tylor could all be classified, in respect of their professional starting-points, as anthropologists of religion though, as will be seen later in this volume, the edifice which Müller built on this foundation was remarkable. What seems in principle, to a modern critic, an unjustified equation between Natural Theology and Natural Religion was commonly made in those early years. It is as if most members of the four Senates were less clear than Lord Gifford had been, what Natural Theology was – or at least what, in the last years of the nineteenth century, was left for it to be. Sir James Frazer's lectures (St Andrews, 1911–13) on the beliefs of aborigines and on nature worship, perhaps represented the extreme of this trend: for this reason, or otherwise, after Frazer it ceased, apart from one resurgence in the thirties. Yet a decade before Frazer, one of the greatest Gifford series ever, William James' 'Varieties of Religious Experience' (Edinburgh, 1900–2) could be seen as taking its spring from naturalistic description of human religious practice. The differences between Frazer and James are: first, that *primitive* practice figures only in small parts of James' discussion; second, that his whole study is structured on the basis of profound psychological insight; and third, that well-derived philosophical conclusions were the purposeful culmination of James' thought, yet had no part in Frazer's.

Several other early accounts were of the religions of Greece and Rome. At least one of the very early lecturers on this subject, Edward Caird, (St Andrews, 1890–2; Glasgow, 1900–2), actually merged the two initial streams of Gifford thought, the descriptive and the metaphysical, by interpreting Greek religion in Hegelian terms. His brother, John (Glasgow, 1894–6), was probably the pre-eminent outright Hegelian, but as many as ten of the early lecturers were Idealist philosophers substantially influenced by Hegel. Among these was Bernard Bosanquet (Edinburgh, 1910–12) who delivered himself of the upstanding assertion that 'We experience the Absolute better than we experience anything else' – surely one of the most extraordinary pieces of scholarly wishful thinking ever uttered! Even when it avoids such excesses, explicitly Hegelian thought is hardly compatible with the modern temper (though Don Cupitt argues, later in this book, that its indirect and implicit influence is of great importance). Nevertheless, we can respect the sustained purpose of several of these philosophers, perhaps the best known of whom, alongside Bosanquet himself, was Andrew Pringle-Pattison (Aberdeen, 1911–13; Edinburgh, 1921–3). Their purpose was to reconcile the importance, attached by both intuition and Christian teaching to the human person, with the idea of God as the Absolute. They argued that although the Absolute could not be an individual it could still be the source of individuation – so that the Many may be regarded as, at the same time, both offshoots and components of the One.

In all, three of these philosophers gave two full series of Gifford Lectures each, under separate invitations, in different universities. Several other lecturers had two bites, but at the same cherry. The best known in the latter group was Arthur Balfour (Glasgow, 1913–15 and 1922–3), the only lecturer also to become Prime Minister, who rather beautifully expressed a more common-sense theism. Such two-full-series feats have not been demanded since the 1920s, but a modern trend towards multi-author series has brought about some shorter repeat billings, Anthony Kenny's contribution to the present series being the latest.

The only nineteenth-century lecturer who was neither a Germanic philosopher nor a student of primitive or classical religion was Edinburgh's second lecturer (1891–3), the physicist, Sir George Stokes. Theologically, Stokes was a latter-day Paley, elegantly restating the argument from design. Many of the scientists who were to follow Stokes would adopt less traditional stances. Nevertheless, the Edinburgh Senate's invitation of a scientist, so early in the history of the Lectureships, was noteworthy: not only did it adhere more closely to the benefactor's intentions than many of the other early choices, but it represented the first step in the direction of some of the greatest twentieth-century series.

To my mind the finest lectures by a physical scientist were Sir Arthur Eddington's (Edinburgh, 1926–7) on 'The Nature of the Physical World'. The published version opens with an unforgettable image[10] of the 'two tables' at which he was writing – the one table coloured, hard, substantial, certain, the other mostly emptiness, the fleeting particles within its space being governed by laws of probability but not of cause. This is one of several lucid and evocative conceptions which remain well known. By contrast Niels Bohr (Edinburgh, 1949–50) was neither lucid nor evocative, according to those who attended (he never published). Werner Heisenberg, also talking about quantum theory (St Andrews, 1955–6), was considerably more accessible. Four years later (1959–61), Carl von Weizsäcker, the Kantian and theistic cosmologist, gave an admirably-rounded series of lectures in Glasgow.

Unaccountably, since cosmology was saying much that should have been of extreme interest to Natural Theology, there was then a gap of 25 years before the next series in this subject-area – the lectures, still to be published, by Carl Sagan (Glasgow, 1985–6). These were, as far as it has been possible to establish, the most popular of all time; drawn initially by memories of Sagan's television performances, audiences which sometimes topped 600 (including those watching video screens in overflow rooms) were held by a pyrotechnic exposition of 'The Search for Who We Are' in the solar system and beyond – sound science and brilliant theatre.

Categorizing Gifford lecturers is of course always rash. Sagan, though normally considered an astronomer, is also a biologist. Many people, eminent purely as biologists, have also been prominent in the Gifford Roll of Honour. The first was Hans Driesch (Aberdeen, 1906–8), the last great exponent of vitalism. This was a concept proper to expound in 1906, but not acceptable to modern thought. Fifteen years later (St Andrews, 1921–2), the psycho-biologist Lloyd Morgan presented a philosophy of evolution and emergent mind which lay half-way, in more than date, between Idealism and Scientific Realism. In my view Morgan did not place sufficient emphasis upon the Darwinian mechanisms of chance variation and natural selection; certainly he did not perceive that they are paralleled by the mental-world processes of conjecture and potential refutation. That insight awaited Karl Popper, who was regrettably never a Gifford lecturer; but Morgan took steps along the way.

The greatest biological lectures yet were surely those of Sir Charles Sherrington, 'Man on His Nature' (Edinburgh, 1937–8), a towering account of mind and brain, and their interactions with their environment. From the images as vivid as Eddington's, and twice as numerous, all redolent with the great man's sense of wonder at the architecture of the world, let me recall his picture of the fore-brain as it awakes from sleep, points of electrical activity being conceived as flashing lights:

> The great topmost sheet of the mass, that where hardly a light had twinkled or moved, becomes now a sparkling field of rhythmic flashing points... The brain is waking and with it the mind is returning. It is as if the Milky Way entered upon some cosmic dance. Swiftly the head-mass becomes an enchanted loom where millions of flashing shuttles weave a dissolving pattern, always a meaningful pattern though never an abiding one...[11]

Yet the brain activity we can observe by neurophysiological methods does not have the character of mind.

> Mind, for anything perception can compass, goes therefore in our spatial world more ghostly than a ghost. Invisible, intangible, it is not a thing even of outline; it is not a 'thing'. It remains without sensual confirmation, and remains without it for ever.

The underlying philosophical concern of these lectures is that of the mind-brain problem, 'the "how" of mind's leverage upon matter'.

Sherrington states this problem repeatedly but does not pretend to solve it. His pupil, Eccles, in the same city 40 years later (Edinburgh, 1977–9) was to offer a solution in terms of unhesitating dualism. By contrast, of the modern brain scientists who, like Eccles, had deep religious conviction, the one to whom I personally would accredit the subtlest philosophical perception was Donald MacKay[12]. For him the 'I-story' and the 'brain-story' were different *accounts*, yet accounts of a single system.

Two more biologists demand mention, being both far removed from the mainstream but on opposite sides of it. Sir Alister Hardy (Aberdeen, 1963–5) researched religious-mystical experiences as objectively as he had previously researched marine organisms, but thereafter interpreted them in terms which most biologists find mystagogic. Hardy's main philosophical source was Henri Bergson, who had himself delivered Gifford Lectures 50 years before (Edinburgh, 1913–14) but had not published them. At the other extreme from Hardy, Sydney Brenner (Glasgow, 1979–80) who foreshadowed Sagan in his verbal brilliance, gave a dynamic overview of cell biochemistry in terms which brooked no other level of account than the molecular. Regrettably, these splendid though anti-theological lectures are unlikely to be published.

I am not equipped to write about historian-lecturers in similar judgemental terms, but they have continued to contribute their scholarship and wisdom throughout the century, their subject-matter having been broadened markedly from the early emphasis on the classical world. Etienne Gilson's perceptive history of medieval philosophy (Aberdeen, 1930–2) remains a landmark work; perhaps even more so does his fellow-Catholic's, Christopher Dawson's, 'Religion and the Rise of Western Culture' (Edinburgh, 1947–9). Close on his heels, in the same city, came Arnold Toynbee (1952–3) on 'An Historian's Approach to Religion'. Still in Edinburgh, Owen Chadwick (1973–4) examined a theme extremely pertinent to the origin of the Gifford Lectures themselves – the secularization of nineteenth century thought. Several other eminent historians, including Raymond Aron and Herbert Butterfield, lectured but did not publish, perhaps preferring to be remembered by earlier books.

This seems the place to mention three historians of science, or rather the science-religion interaction. Canon Charles Raven's 'Natural Religion and Christian Theology' (the Edinburgh lectures of 1950–2) taught me much when I was young, though Jaki would contend that they are stronger on the science than the theology. Jaki himself followed in the same city a generation later (1974–6); 'The Road of Science and the Ways to God' abounds with learning and insight, but is not easy reading. Reijer Hooykaas (St Andrews, 1975–7) has only recently published, his theme being the effect of religious and other prior beliefs on the development of science.

Let us now turn to philosophy, as it has been represented since the period dominated by the great Hegelians. There is, of course, philosophical thinking of high order in much of the writing already cited: to my mind Gilson and Jaki, von Weizsäcker and MacKay stand out in this regard. Of the more strictly philosophical edifices, two were themselves constructed out of scientific thought-forms. The earlier of these was Samuel Alexander's account of a still-unfolding 'Space, Time and Deity', surely the archetypal Gifford title! (Glasgow, 1916–18). More lastingly influential, however (though in a similar direction), was Alfred North Whitehead's 'Process and Reality' (Edinburgh, 1927–8), the central text of the Process philosophers and, more recently, the Process theologians. As an 'ecological view of life', by which events in time are considered more fundamental than objects in space, interactions are paramount, and phenomena such as consciousness are treated as emergent properties of organization, such thinking seems even closer to the common scientific world-view now than it was when Whitehead lectured. The Process account of God's involvement with the world is panentheistic (a standpoint which Adam Gifford would surely have favoured). I suspect we should and shall hear more from this school, in future Gifford Lectures.

Among the philosopher-lecturers whose thinking was less emphatically science based, John Dewey (Edinburgh, 1928–9), though by then elderly, explored the relationship of knowledge and action from the standpoint of anti-theological pragmatism. In almost diametric contrast, Gabriel Marcel, the Christian existentialist, lecturing in Aberdeen (1948–50), developed his earlier thought on the wonder and mystery of being. He was followed, in the same city, by Michael Polanyi (1951–2), whose exposition of the tacit and pre-rational dimensions of all 'Personal Knowledge' must be more widely quoted (and not only in the society set up to pursue his ideas) than the writing of any other Gifford-lecturing philosopher.

I dare to suggest, nonetheless, that even finer philosophy, though it is less widely known, was to be found in John Macmurray's Glasgow lectures (1952–4). By first asserting the primacy of the 'Self as Agent' over the self as thinker, and then that of 'Persons in Relation' over persons as individuals, Macmurray achieved – and achieved, what is more, in language for the most part deceptively simple – what Pringle-Pattison and company had been striving for two generations earlier, and something also of what Whitehead had been after. To make another comparison, his two volumes could be said to constitute a philosophically-structured version of Martin Buber's 'I and Thou'. The result was arguably one of the most systematic Natural Theologies the benefaction has yet elicited.

By shifting our standpoint from the 'I think' to the 'I do', we have restored
the reference of thought to action, and in the result have found that we
are driven to conceive a personal universe in which God is the ultimate
reality.[13]

The complete edifice would have pleased Lord Gifford greatly – *and* its
author held an Edinburgh chair!

Had John Wisdom (Aberdeen, 1948–9) and Donald Mackinnon (Edinburgh, 1964–6) published, we might now have comparable edifices from
other points of view; but this was not to be. Hannah Arendt (Aberdeen,
1972–4), the first woman lecturer, harked back 80 years in producing a
somewhat Hegelian account of 'The Life of the Mind'. Simultaneously,
in St Andrews, A. J. Ayer was delineating 'The Central Questions of
Philosophy', which for him excluded the possibility of theology. In
counterpoint, Richard Swinburne (Aberdeen, 1982–4) offered a carefully
structured modern re-presentation of traditional theism. Thus, in marked
contrast to the pre-First-World-War period, the more recent history of
Gifford philosophizing has been one of wide and constructive diversity.

The last substantial category of lecturers is of those who publicly wore
the label 'Theologian'. Here, even more than among the other categories
of scholar, great names roll off the pen. Almost every notable strand of
Christian thought is represented, though not proportionately, for there
are far too few Roman Catholics. There has also been only one non-
Christian theologian – Lord Gifford would have considered this an
insufficient representation. One's other regret must be that the theologians, stamping their professional grounds, have on average over the years
achieved much less success than the scientists in being 'public and
popular'. Even the series which, among the professionals, was arguably
the most famous (or infamous) of all, Karl Barth's attack on the very
possibility of Natural (as distinct from Revealed) Theology (Aberdeen,
1937–8), appears not to have been well attended at the time and is not
easy reading now.

To begin, however, at the beginning. One of the most interesting early
speakers, in respect of his historical position, was Alexander Bruce
(Glasgow, 1896–8). Bruce was a Free Church biblical scholar who made
continuing use of contemporary criticism but, unlike Robertson Smith,
escaped censure. In the pre-First-World-War period Bruce was also
arguably the only theologian lecturer *per se* as distinct from comparative
religionists and those who, even if they held theological chairs, spoke
essentially as philosophers. Only at the end of the 1920s did the Senates
begin frequently to invite theologians to take up Gifford Lectureships.
Four were Anglican clerics: Bishops Barnes, Gore and Henson lecturing

on modern physics, classical humanism and Christian morality respectively, in Aberdeen and St Andrews, and Archbishop William Temple (Glasgow, 1932–4) making the most serious attempt at an overall Natural Theology under the splendid title, 'Nature, Man and God'. Four more theologians at this period were from overseas. Of these, the Lutheran Archbishop Soderblom (Edinburgh, 1930–1) was the most liberal, Barth the least; in between, ideologically, came Rienhold Niebuhr (Edinburgh, 1938–40), whose thought was quite close to Barth's, and the most romantically-famous figure of all – Albert Schweitzer (Edinburgh, 1934–5) – who did not publish, but was probably at that period fairly close to Soderblom. Apart from all such groups was Edwyn Bevan (Edinburgh, 1932–4); his elegant 'Symbolism and Belief' must on no account go unmentioned.

Replies to Barth came after the war, the most direct being Emil Brunner's in St Andrews (1946–8), and later (1961–2) John Baillie's in Edinburgh. Great names in the intervening years were those of Paul Tillich in Aberdeen and Rudolf Bultmann in Edinburgh. After this period, probably the most notable theological edifice was that constructed by the Anglican Thomist, E. L. Mascall (Edinburgh, 1970–1): 'The Openness of Being'.

Finally, among the 'theological' lecturers, a special form of credit must go to those who have attempted to introduce their Western audiences to non-Christian religious thought. R. C. Zaehner (St Andrews, 1967–9) treated religious mysticism on a world basis. Frederick Copleston and Ninian Smart (in Aberdeen and Edinburgh, respectively, at the start of the eighties) both lectured on aspects of comparative religion; and Seyed Nasr (Edinburgh, 1980–1), the first Muslim Gifford lecturer, spelled out the essentially sacred character of thought in earlier eras, irrespective of culture.

To conclude this account of a century of Gifford themes, it should be acknowledged that perhaps three lecturers over the period have adopted approaches which were neither those of science (physical or biological) nor history, and not essentially either philosophical or theological, but literary. Let Macneile Dixon (Glasgow, 1935–7) represent these. His 'The Human Situation' sustains no case, save that we should glory in being and in the puzzles of our being, but overflows with humane commentary upon other people's efforts to understand. The great thinkers, including several of the Gifford lecturers who preceded him and whom we, too, have named, stride across his pages, illuminated by tellingly unexpected quotations:

Larger than human, on the frozen hills.

## The Present Day, The Present Series

Though those outside the field are for the most part still unaware of the fact, the late twentieth-century intellectual climate is a substantially more fertile one for Natural Theology than that prevailing when the Gifford Lectureships were founded. Many of the themes are of like kind to those discussed in Lord Gifford's day, yet the strength of several arguments has substantially increased. We shall return to these. In the opinion of the Glasgow Gifford Lectureships Committee, however, the most widely-influential change has been in attitudes to the environment. Perhaps here, too, the paradigm shift had begun in Gifford's time but its developments have been immense and its ramifications enormous.

Until the concept of evolution took hold, the processes of civilization had increasingly detached humankind from its environment physically, intellectually and spiritually. Darwin's was the first of the intellectual critiques which shook that detachment. Following him came the psycho-analysts (both Freud and Jung), the animal behaviourists and now the sociobiologists. In parallel with their ideas, the largely twentieth-century developments of anthropology, physiology, biochemistry and pathology have displayed *homo sapiens*, with ever more persuasive force, as just one of the most complex (and also, in some respects, one of the more vulnerable) species of animals. Recently, and perhaps most directly of all, the protagonists of Planet Earth and the Green Movement have dealt the *coup de grâce* to any remaining illusion of detachment.

Most of these specific critiques are no more than flagged in the present series. Many have been dealt with before, but the ecological theme has not: there is undoubtedly scope for a separate future series on the Natural Theology of the Ecology Movement. However, the fundamental intellectual recognition of the human situation, as being both a response to Environment and an interaction with it, is the lietmotif of these Centenary lectures. The theme could not be better introduced than by Don Cupitt's lecture, 'Nature and Culture', which examines the radical blurring, during the Gifford century, of the old distinction between these two concepts.[14]

Returning now to considerations, within the traditional subject-areas of these Lectureships, which make the late twentieth century a fertile period for Natural Theology, we find that at least four such considerations arise from physical science. Most obvious is the 'Big Bang' concept – the concept that there was an identifiable moment at which the Universe (in any sense of that word which can have meaning for us) came into existence. Enthusiasts for the obvious comparison, with the accounts of creation given in all scriptures of Middle Eastern origin, would do well to note that Georges Lemaître, priest as well as cosmologist, who had been the first to state clearly the proposal that the Universe is still expanding from the rupture of an unimaginably dense 'Primaeval Atom',[15] strenuously opposed the naive equation of cosmological and scriptural accounts. It is by no means beyond question that a start to time is a more theistic concept than infinite time: that the Universe, once it does exist, should be continually sustained by God (in theological terms, Divine immanence) is a far more essential religious perception than any once-off starting of the clock. So the fate of the Big Bang model within cosmology should decide no issue of importance to Lord Gifford; but it has certainly re-opened the debate.

Second on the list is the peculiar suitability of the Universe to life. Long recognized at one level, in terms such as the remarkable properties of carbon and water, this came widely to be seen in the 1970s and 1980s as dependent on the exact values of some of the most fundamental physical constants; for example, the exact relations of gravitational force to mass, and electromagnetic forces to electric charge. Analyses along such lines have shown that only a series of extraordinarily finely-tuned physical coincidences could have produced, in the Universe, intelligent life of anything like the form we represent. Thus it is possible to contend that the Universe was designed for us.

On the other hand, given the fact that we *are* here – incredible, beyond imagination, though that brute fact is – it is only a matter of the most elementary logic that the Universe should be found to possess the properties necessary for producing us. We encounter yet again the inescapable ambiguity of all evidence, in relation to Natural Theology;[16] but the Argument from Design has undeniably undergone a powerful twist.

The third consideration from physics has been widely recognized since the 1920s and discussed by Gifford lecturers from Eddington onwards. It is the extent to which the laws of the sub-atomic world are probabilistic rather than deterministic. Those so disposed may consequently argue that a God who wishes to intervene in the Universe has infinitely more opportunity to do so, without overtly breaking His own laws, than appeared to be the case during the period extending from the time of Newton to a little beyond that of Kelvin.

Fourthly, the very question of the objectivity of any physical laws, deterministic or probabilistic, though raised by Kant two centuries ago, may be considered increasingly difficult to evade as the involvement of the observer in each observation becomes ever harder to ignore, and the mathematics used to make sense of observation grows more and more remote.

In the present series, every one of these considerations is critically illuminated by John Barrow, within the framework of an overview of ancient and very modern thinking about the physical and cosmic environment. Although now recast into nine parts, Professor Barrow's contribution, 'Inner Space and Outer Space', is nevertheless based upon only three lectures. Readers wishing a fuller treatment of the match of the Universe to life than he has had room for here should, however, consult also the earlier book which he co-wrote, *The Anthropic Cosmological Principle* (referenced in his bibliography).

Turning from the physical feasibility of life to the evolutionary mechanism which cannot fail to operate upon life when it occurs, ambiguity is again inescapable. There can be few specific topics to which Alvin Plantinga's general maxim applies more clearly: 'The concept of God is logically basic' (again, see note 16). Thus, one who considers the mechanism of evolution from an atheistic or agnostic stance is unlikely to be converted by encounter with the biological facts. Conversely, those who understand the science and at the same time lean towards religion will probably react to natural selection much as Charles Kingsley did in 1859. Our times are not those of Paley, but they are not qualitatively changed from those of Darwin himself. Three problems, however, have crystallized. The first is the pathetic aberration of 'Creationism', which – in my view, and I suspect in that of most readers of this book – ought to be as unacceptable theologically as it is scientifically. The other two are much more intellectually, as distinct from just didactically, challenging: the problem of moral responsibility, in a world where behavioural dispositions are causally mappable, and the problem of epistemological limitation – how God-language can have meaning in brains which have evolved within the world. These hard nuts may perhaps be cracked by analyses in terms of hierarchies of meaning, analogous to the Whiteheadian consideration of the biological world in terms of hierarchies of organization. Alternatively (or is it really so different a reaction?), personalist philosophers such as Macmurray might question whether the problems were well posed: the language used is itself depersonalizing. Be these comments as they may, the problems of morality and epistemology are real ones for any naturalistic philosophy, and both of them plus Creationism are problems for Natural Theology.

Richard Dawkins, the biologist among our Centenary lecturers, attacked such problems only obliquely. He had already done a good deal of direct attacking, especially with regard to the mechanism of evolution itself, in his books, particularly *The Blind Watchmaker* (referenced in his bibliography). But Dr Dawkins' oblique attacks, as well as being challenging in themselves, constituted more pertinent commentaries on the main themes than direct treatments by many lesser speakers would have done. In one of two lectures, he expounded evidence from games theory that trusting cooperation ('reciprocal altruism') is, in long-term evolutionary perspectives, not the weak strategy it appears on short-term analysis, but a collectively strong one. The main part of this account was, however, about to appear elsewhere[17] and could not be republished here. What Dr Dawkins contributes to the present publication is therefore the text of just one lecture: 'Worlds in Microcosm'. In this he brings elegantly to the fore the extent to which the environment moulds the body, the behaviour and ultimately the consciousness of the living forms within it.

After the biological environment – at least where the living form being considered is humankind – comes the socio-historical environment. Perceptions here may well differ more from those prevailing when these Lectureships began than in any of the other disciplines we have represented: perceptions, that is to say, not as to the *importance* of a peoples' historical environment (though it might then have been referred to as 'position' or 'role' or 'privilege' or 'duty') but as to the principal factors constituting that environment in Britain and other developed yet now post-colonial countries. The challenges to theology presented by these changed perceptions are again considerable, though this time they are as much to Moral and Social as to Natural Theology.

It was John Roberts who accepted the task of discussing 'History as Environment'. Dr Roberts' text, printed here with only minor changes from that presented orally, ranges over a million years and at least four continents. Among his many impressive passages, one that made a particular impact upon Glasgow hearers was a critique of the concept of 'historical guilt'. Myths are inevitable, in a field infinitely too complex to be treated with total objectivity, but the contributions of the historian to a nation's 'collective autobiography' include the subjection of our myths, about ourselves and others, to moral as well as factual criticism.

By this stage in the series, it will be evident that philosophical problems abound. Anthony Kenny, the philosopher in our team, touched on many of them in his three lectures under the title, 'The Kingdom of the Mind'. The stated theme of these lectures was the spiritual environment but Dr Kenny interpreted this with his characteristic breadth, addressing not only the general philosophical problems of mind, consciousness and language, but the specific ones of using language about God. Uncaused Cause (e.g. 'Big Bang') arguments, and the difference it still makes to think of a Supernatural Designer underpinning evolution, are among the subjects from previous lectures to which Dr Kenny instructively returns. His contribution ends with a discussion of religious language in the poetry of Adam Gifford's shorter-lived contemporary, Arthur Hugh Clough. It would be hard to structure a more apposite lead into the final contribution.

For this contribution, we were privileged to welcome the Archbishop of York, Dr John Habgood, whose lecture asked the question: 'Is there reliable knowledge about God?' Stressing that 'reliable' does not mean 'certainly correct, as stated', but 'trustworthy, as a basis for action', Dr Habgood compared the characteristics of the knowledge achievable in fields ranging from physics to literature and theology, and found none entirely objective, none entirely independent of interpretation, history and personal perspective, none inappropriate as a subject for hermeneutics, yet each capable of providing reliable bases for action: action, that is, within the particular, formative environment of the individual at the time.

From such an outlook, as Dr Habgood notes, one beneficiary will be cross-fertilization between faiths, an ever more crying need in our multicultural society. Developing his theme, we might add that from such an outlook society's understanding not only of religion generally but, perhaps even more, of science can benefit. The swing against science, among the present generation of young people, is as marked as the swing against organized religion in the generations before this one. Each swing resulted in part from revulsion against arrogant over-assertion in practical affairs: dogmatic mission for religion or for science. Yet these arrogances themselves reflect inappropriate appraisals of the nature of each kind of knowledge. All knowledge is provisional, historical, myth-laden – a vital yet fallible response of persons seeking bases for action in their particular environments. The wider the appreciation of this, the more balanced will be the responses to both science and religion, as well as to the humanities which lie between.

As the Gifford Lectureships go forward into their second century, and their audience sizes reflect expanded not diminished interest, the belief expressed by an elderly judge in an Edinburgh garden in 1885, proves ever more appropriate: 'Nothing but good can result from free discussion'. In this light I hope and believe that readers will continue to find, within these pages and in the texts of Gifford Lectures yet ungiven, 'Thoughts that breathe and words that burn'.

NOTES

1 Stanley L. Jaki, *Lord Gifford and His Lectures* (Scottish Academic Press, 1986). In addition to Jaki's title essay, this volume provides chronological and bibliographical lists of Gifford Lectures, and reprints the full text of Lord Gifford's Will, together with other material from the Gifford family indicated in notes 2 and 3 below.

2  John Gifford, *Recollections of a Brother* (privately printed, 1891); reprinted in full in *Lord Gifford and His Lectures*, above. Direct quotations are from pp. 93 and 98 of this 1986 reprinting.

3  Adam Gifford, *Selections from Lectures Delivered on Various Occasions*, ed. Alice Raleigh & Herbert James Gifford (privately printed, 1889); excerpts reprinted in *Lord Gifford and His Lectures*. The list of topics in *Recollections of a Brother*, seven or eight of which are additional to the above selection, is on p. 99 of the 1986 reprinting.

4  Francis Bacon, *De Augmentis Scientiarum* (1623); Bk. iii, 2. Quoted by Sherrington in *Man on His Nature*, p. 9 (see note 11, below). This rendering from Bacon's Latin is non-standard but particularly felicitious; I suspect it is Sherrington's own.

5  John Durant, 'Darwinism and Divinity: a Century of Debate', in Durant (ed.) *Darwinism and Divinity. Essays on Evolution and Religious Belief* (Basil Blackwell, 1985), p. 21.

6  Asa Briggs, *The Age of Improvement* (Longmans, Green & Co., 1959), p. 465.

7  Friedrich Max Müller's opening lecture was delivered in the Bute Hall of the University of Glasgow, at 3.00 p.m. on Wednesday 14 November, 1888. The *Glasgow Herald* carried an extensive report next day (p. 3, between pieces on the Hutcheson's Educational Trust and the Crofters' Commission in Lewis). Müller's lectures (four series in all), from which quotations will appear later in this book, were published by Longmans, Green & Co. as follows: *Natural Religion* (1889); *Physical Religion* (1891); *Anthropological Religion* (1892) and *Theosophy, or Psychological Religion* (1893). The series was re-issued by the same publishers in a collected edition, with a new preface, in 1898.

8  Bernard E. Jones, *Earnest Enquirers after Truth* (Allen & Unwin, 1970). Note that Jones' title modernises Victorian spelling ('inquirers') to which I have in all direct quotations adhered: cf. 'chiaro-oscuro', 'extasies', 'phrensied'.

9  James Hutchison Stirling, *Philosophy and Theology* (T. & T. Clark, 1890), p. 33.

10  Arthur Stanley Eddington, *The Nature of the Physical World* (Cambridge University Press, 1928; republished J. M. Dent & Sons, 1935); the 'two tables' are described on pp. 5–8 of the latter edition.

11  Charles Scott Sherrington, *Man on His Nature* (Cambridge University Press, 1940; 2nd, somewhat shortened edn, 1951; reissued Penguin Books, 1955). The 'enchanted loom' is described on pp. 186–7, and the mind 'more ghostly than a ghost' on p. 286 of the latter edition.

12  Donald M. MacKay, *Behind the Eye* (Basil Blackwell, 1991). This was the first, and the present volume is the second, of what is intended to be a series of cooperations between Basil Blackwell and the University of Glasgow for the publication of its Gifford Lectures.

13  John Macmurray, *The Self as Agent* (Faber and Faber, 1957) and *Persons in Relation* (Faber and Faber, 1961). The quotation is from the second volume, p. 224.

14  Dr Cupitt's term-time duties prevented him from actually giving his lecture first in the public series, but this is its logical position and so the one in which it is printed here. For similar reasons, the order in which Drs Roberts

and Kenny contributed to the series has been transposed for publication. The other contributions are printed in the sequence of their delivery.

15  Georges Lemaître, *L'Hypothese de L'Atome Primitif: Essai de Cosmogonie* (Editions du Griffon, 1946). Also in lectures and papers for at least 15 years before that. The story of Lemaître's thought on this subject, and his firmly dissociating himself from Pope Pius XII's representation of the Big Bang (to the Pontifical Academy of Sciences, 1951) as one of the 'Proofs of the Existence of God in the Light of Modern Natural Science', is a key one in the history of twentieth century Natural Theology. Excellent accounts are given by Stanely L. Jaki, *Cosmos and Creator* (Scottish Academic Press, 1980), ch. 1; and Ernan McMullin, 'How Should Cosmology relate to Theology?' section III, in A.R. Peacocke (ed.), *The Sciences and Theology in the Twentieth Century* (Oriel Press, 1981), ch. 2.

16  These remarks do not imply that natural theology is unfruitful. It makes a huge difference to one's attitude to life, and hopefully also some difference to one's actions in life, whether one does or does not see the world as divine handiwork. However, the belief underlying my comments is that no theology, whether natural or revealed, will ever either prove or disprove that viewpoint. For one whose thought the viewpoint pervades, Natural Theology consists in the attempt (if we may modify a phrase from Einstein) 'to think some of God's thoughts after Him'. Expressing the same idea more modestly, it is the attempt somewhat better to understand God's self-expression in Creation. Natural Theology is pilgrimage, not apologetic.

17  Richard Dawkins, *The Selfish Gene*, 2nd edn (Oxford University Press, 1989), ch. 12.

# Max Muller on Language

## Language and Reason

*Whatever may be the date assigned... to the flint-makers, they must have been preceded by a race of root- or word-makers, unless we suppose that man was in possession of reason before he was in possession of language or of words as the exponents of general ideas, however primitive and imperfect. Language, we have learned, was impossible without Reason, and so was Reason, even that small amount of it which went towards the choosing and chipping of flints, without Language... Language and Reason... are as inseparable as the bark and stem of a living tree, as the concave and the convex, as the angle and the two lines which enclose it. They are held together by that intimate relation for which Hindu philosophers alone have invented a special term, viz. Samavaya.*

*And if a historical and comparative study of language has revealed to us the true growth of the human mind as realised in language, from its fossil period onward to the days of Shakespeare, it has taught us at the same time that this so-called growth or development of language was the work of myriads of human beings, building up the foundations of the temples and palaces in which we are living and moving, and even now building up new coral islands of words and thoughts for future generations to live on.*

Preface to *Collected Works*, pp. x-xi

## Lessons of Language

*If... we can decipher the original meaning of our words, if we can discover the purpose with which they were framed, we shall have opened archives which... are far superior to any other evidence within our reach...*

*So long as the real identity of thought and language had not been grasped, so long as people imagined that language is one thing and thought another... [and again] if the active verb were merely a grammatical, and not at the same time a psychological, nay an historical fact, it might seem absurd to identify the active meaning of our roots with the active meaning ascribed to the phenomena of nature. But let it once be perceived that language and thought are one and indivisible, and nothing will seem more natural than that what, as the grammarian tells us, happened in language, should, as the psychologist tells us, have likewise happened in thought; – that the two events, in fact, should prove to be one and the same.*

*Natural Religion*, pp. 385, 406

# 2
# Nature and Culture

## Don Cupitt

When they were planning this centenary series of Gifford Lectures the Senatus of the University of Glasgow decided that the course was to be concerned with 'various aspects of the environment – physical, spiritual and social.' In my contribution I want to draw out some of the implications of this characteristically modern conception of the environment. I shall suggest that its emergence is part of a wider philosophical shift.

In my childhood the environment as we now speak of it was not much in evidence. There was indeed Nature, a Greek rather than a biblical notion, which had in very varied guises been around since Aristotle; and there was also Man's Place in Nature, an important Victorian topic. But there was no environment in quite today's sense, and the word itself was not very often heard. However, I was familiar with two usages which were to contribute to our present concept.

The first was the phrase, 'the environs of London', an idiom that went back as far as the seventeenth century. I had an atlas with maps of the environs of the major European cities, the point being that as these towns grew rapidly in size during the later seventeenth century people began to notice the way they sucked in workers and goods from the surrounding regions. The environs of a city were not just its geographical neighbourhood or landscape setting. A complex economic relationship was involved. The environs of a city were its economic hinterland, in pre-industrial times typically the radius from which the city was fed and populated, and in industrial times typically the region from which people commuted daily to work in the city.

The point to remember is that when we speak of the environs of a city, of Greater London, the outer suburbs, the London region and so forth, we are viewing the city as being not isolated but immersed in and dependent upon a living web of local traffic and economic relations with the whole region in which it is set. Indeed, one could say that a city just *is* a local concentration of various sorts of traffic and economic activity.

The second usage with which I was familiar derived from the late nineteenth century. Darwin himself does not so far as I know speak of the environment, but Herbert Spencer did. From the 1870s it was customary to talk of the ways in which an organism must continually adapt itself to its environment in order to survive. This was a new and technically biological use of the term, and great stress was commonly laid on the power of the environment over the organism. The creature's environment was usually specific to it. By that I mean that the environment was not the totality of physical nature, the same for every species, but rather that for each species its environment was merely that selection from all the ambient physical conditions which was of direct and quasi-economic relevance to its own survival-to-reproduce. In that sense, each organism had its own specific environment. But this did not imply any mitigation of the harsh pressure of the environment upon the organism. On the contrary, that pressure was often strongly emphasized. In the protracted debates about heredity and environment an 'environmentalist' was one who would today be called an environmental determinist, as distinct from a genetic determinist. That is, until the late 1950s an environmentalist was a person who stressed the primary causal influence of the environment in shaping all details of the structure and mode of existence of the organism – including the human organism. Zola and Hardy are examples of novelists who reflect this view of Nature as an implacable Power.

Thus in the period which I am describing – around 1875–1950 – an environmentalist was a hard-nosed materialist and a kind of determinist. The environment was almost a physical God. It was a set of material conditions external to me which pressed demandingly upon me and dictated the terms on which I must live. It held the power of life and death over me, and I must adapt myself to it or perish. It was something utterly immoveable, physical necessity itself, not to be gainsaid.

In the *Supplement* to the *OED*, Volume 1 of 1972, P.S. Sears in 1956 is the earliest authority cited for the use of the word 'environment' in the modern sense. In the first place, the term is no longer technically biological, but has become colloquial and almost political. Secondly, the environment is no longer sovereign physical necessity before which we all must bow, but rather is our environs. We are in a thoroughly dialectical economic relationship with it. It is all-that-out-there which both sustains our life and also has to suffer the distorting impact of our human activities upon it. Thirdly, therefore, the environment is suddenly seen to have lost its old ineluctable coercive power and to have become a fragile and vulnerable web of relationships and activities in which we are set. We have got to look after it. It needs taking care of. So evidently a new awareness of the power of technology, of the priority and superiority of Culture over Nature and of our responsibility for maintaining the physical conditions of our own life has suddenly arrived. As a result the concept of the environment becomes much more salient, and changes somewhat. It is as if all Nature has become part of Culture. The God who lorded it over us has come to be seen instead as something more like the bread and the water of our life. From then on the rapidity with which, in Britain as in other countries, the modern range of uses of the term develops is highly remarkable: environmental safety is reported in 1957, and environmental areas in 1962. In 1967 we hear how man has contaminated his environment, and in 1970 of environmental health. In the same year, 1970, the final canonization arrives in the form of an environment minister.

Thus the environment, after taking on its modern sense in the 1950s, was by the end of the next decade the concern of a government minister and a whole department of state. Seldom can a concept have conquered so quickly.

The intellectual expression of this shift in the balance of power between Nature and Culture can be traced in the philosophy of the 1960s. Both in Anglo-Saxon philosophy of science and in French philosophy it came during that period to be recognized that all our ideas about Nature are produced within Culture and have an intra-cultural history. Sense-perception, scientific experimentation and reporting, and the formation and debating of theories all happen inside history and are historically conditioned. Science is at no point privileged. It is itself just another cultural activity. Interpretation reaches all the way down, and we have no 'pure' and extra-historical access to Nature. We have no basis for distinguishing between Nature itself and our own changing historically-produced representations of Nature. We represent Nature in a vocabulary borrowed, necessarily, from society. So the history of science is the true history of Nature itself. Nature and Culture have thus become thoroughly interwoven and we comprehend that we are now fully responsible, in every sense, for Nature – which is what the new environmentalism is insisting. We made Nature and it just *is* our descriptions of it and the way we treat it. Nature is a cultural product.

By this rather provocative remark I mean only that since we are always inside history and culture and language, and have no absolute or pure access to Nature, we have no basis for separating the way the world really is from our ways of representing it. So that we do not make fetishes of our current theories, it is a good thing to keep reminding ourselves that what at any particular time is called Nature is just the prevailing cultural construction of Nature. Scientific knowledge needs to be 'historicized'.

Since 1970 the development of the concept of the environment has continued. It becomes steadily more holistic. Where the nineteenth-century environment had consisted just of physics and chemistry, the increasing interest in ecology has nowadays woven together geology, geography and the biosphere into a single tapestry. In the 1970s Environmental Science appears as an academic subject. Planners start to speak of the built environment, and the city soon becomes as environmental as the countryside. But the most striking development of all has been the extension of the environment to include the ideal or superstructural realm. In the 1972 *Supplement* to the *OED* there is a citation from 1928 contrasting the environmental with the spiritual, the older presumption being that the environment was exclusively material or physical. Yet the Senatus in 1986 speaks of *spiritual and social aspects of the environment*, an idiom that calls for comment.

As everyone is aware, since the Second World War there has been a worldwide rediscovery and reaffirmation of the constitutive importance to the individual of mother tongue, ethnic roots and cultural and religious identity. This complex of language, nationality, religion and culture – for which we have no single name – has become a God to people. If they feel it is threatened, they will die for it without hesitation. Its defence has become the single most important political motive. No doubt the reason for this is that while decolonization has encouraged peoples to reassert their traditional ethnic identities, the continuing triumphant advance of Western scientific-industrial culture is at the same time effacing all local cultures. People are simultaneously and by the same historical forces being reminded and robbed of their cultural heritage. It is not surprising that they should dread the new anonymity that looms ahead of them, and should start to fight for their linguistic, cultural and religious identity. They evidently feel that it is as necessary to their life as air and water. Since the great period in French thought of the late 1950s and 1960s it has come to be widely accepted that we all live in a world of signs, a world, that is, of cultural meanings, beliefs and values. These signs are not only the milieu in which we swim and the medium by means of which we communicate; they also even more than the air and the water *pass right through us*, constituting us and sustaining our life.

I have to dwell on this point, because so many Anglo-Saxons still believe in non-linguistic thought. Yet there can be no doubt that they are wrong. The public world of signs, the river of publicly-established meanings, flows straight through your head from ear to ear without a break. All your inner world is made of public materials, because you are a cultural product. That is why it is said that your language and culture give you your *identity*. There is no inner citadel where the public language stops and pure private extra-linguistic and extra-historical thought takes over. There is no sense in the supposition that Adam the first man could have been a complete and perfect thinking and functioning human being all on his own before Eve, before language and before culture. On the popular traditional reading of *Genesis* Adam suddenly decided one day that it would be a good thing for him to invent language by naming the beasts. But a moment's thought will show the absurdity of our trying to represent to ourselves a pre-linguistic being's thought that it would be a good thing if he were to invent language. And this consideration shows us that language in a broad sense – that is, the world of signs; that is, culture – is environmental in the strongest sense, for it is the milieu in which we are wholly immersed, in which all our life is lived and in which we and all other things are constituted. As I earlier hinted that a city may be seen not as a substance but simply as a local concentration of regional economic activity, so we may view the self not as a substance but as a communications centre.

If during the past 30 years we have come progressively to realize how important our concept of the environment is to us, then nothing is more environmental than culture. I need my culture as I need the air I breathe: no wonder I'm ready to fight for it. And furthermore any reasons there may be for attempting to preserve a threatened biological species are probably going *a fortiori* to be reasons for attempting to preserve threatened natural languages and cultures, including ones other than our own. Looking back, I see I raised the question of whether we should strive to preserve threatened cultures in a little book published in 1976. I took the view that whereas animal species are fairly easy to preserve, tribal cultures are impossible to save because the very measures you take to preserve them must have the effect of destroying them. However sensitively the growth of tourism is controlled, it must destroy the local culture; and by the same token, however protective, unobstrusive and gently paternalistic the stronger culture is in its dealings with a weaker culture, just by being there it will destroy it. A culture cannot be quarantined or preserved artificially. It has to be free in its world. Put it in a zoo, and it dies. A neat and fascinating paradox which brings out the way in which during our own lifetime the ancient distinction between Culture and Nature has been deconstructed is this: a culture can survive only in the wild state. Open it up to tourism, *or refuse to do so* and fence it off – and it dies. At home we once tried keeping a species of lizard that turned out to be unsuited to captivity. It was too tense and wild, and we couldn't tame it. I picked the poor creature up and it died of a heart attack in my hand. A culture is like that; it is a wild thing. It cannot be tamed or incorporated into anything else, which is why people around the world are so fanatically determined to fight and to die for the independence and self-respect of their ethnic group. Thus, to our earlier suggestion that Nature can nowadays be seen to be a cultural product, we can add the rider that at the same time Culture is, of course, a natural product.

Nothing then is more environmental than culture, and the recent incorporation of everything cultural into our concept of the environment is a most significant development. It is taken furthest by the human geographers, amongst whom expressions such as cultural ecology, cultural hearth, culture area, cultural landscape and cultural geography have in recent years become well-established. Here is yet one more piece of evidence that in our lifetime Culture and Nature, the tame and the wild, which for millenia in all societies were carefully and sharply contrasted, have now become confused and impossible any longer to distinguish from each other.

I have an hypothesis to offer about the meaning of this great event. I think the world I was born into was still in a broad sense platonic and Cartesian, but that in the last generation or so – that is to say, since about 1959 – it has become thoroughly Hegelian. To explain this I shall begin from a brief but very illuminating comment in the *Dictionary of Human Geography* (1986 edn, s.v. 'environmentalism') which expressly contrasts environmentalism with existentialism. The hint we are given here is that the philosophy of Sartre was very influential in the first decade after the War, but that in the late 1950s environmentalism appeared as a sharp reaction against it.

Let us amplify that hint. In the world I was born into (and have taken so long to get out of) the essence of the human lay in consciousness and in a certain possibility of distancing oneself inwardly from Nature. A very long tradition in Western thought, deriving proximately from the 'I'-philosophies of Sartre, Husserl and Descartes and ultimately from Augustine and Plato, defined the human in terms of individual spiritual subjectivity. As human, I knew myself to be a unique, immortal, rational soul. What defined me as human was my inward stepping-back into subjectivity and away from the common natural world, together with my immateriality and my capacity for God. God himself was pure, deified, absolute subjectivity, and it was in the relation to God and *only* in that relation that my personal identity could be perfected. To constitute and perfect me I didn't need the world, nor the body, nor the passions, nor even other people. I needed only God. So I did not actually *have* to have any environment at all, as Descartes makes so clear. The self-before-God can stand quite alone. Its identity is constituted metaphysically and not socially.

As late as Husserl and Sartre – that is, until the early 1950s – this very ancient spiritual individualism lingered, albeit latterly in a secularized form. Put crudely and strongly, its three principal doctrines are that the self is a substance, that the self is spiritual or immaterial, and that the self's relations with its physical environment are merely external to it, contingent, and not constitutive of it. Consciousness is seen as the primary philosophical certainty, and the conscious self, observing and deliberating, stands back a little from the world. It is a little sub-world on its own. It is not unaffected by natural events; on the contrary, it registers them all the time. But it is not *constituted* by what it does and what happens to it, so that the familiar jibe, 'the ghost in the machine' is fair enough as an epitome of how the mind-body relation is seen. Although the early Sartre himself was anti-Freudian, it was perfectly possible for the mind-body dualist to allow that we also have a 'lower nature' of animal origin, which is indeed bound into the world. But when the Christian related herself to God in prayer, when the scientist observed, experimented and reasoned, and when the moral agent resolved, legislated and posited values, *then* you transcended both Nature and your own lower nature to become your real self. Once again, the real self is the self *that becomes itself as it distances itself* from the world, the body and the passions. As certain visitors were speedily sent down to the servants' quarters, so Darwin and Freud could be received, provided that they were promptly referred only to our lower nature. They were to be used ascetically. Yes, they had disclosed something of our lower nature. All the more reason for keeping it firmly in its place. So Darwin and Freud could be employed to reinforce rather than to undermine the traditional supernaturalism of the rational self. Their subject-matter was precisely that in us which the supernatural self conquered, escaped and transcended as it drew away from Nature.

Against this background we begin to see why environmentalism has been expressly contrasted with existentialism by some writers. When I was in my teens around 1950 the leading cultural influences of the day were Sartre's existentialism, a rather aggressive scientism, and popular neo-orthodox Christianity. I was influenced strongly by all three, even though at the time they seemed very different from each other. Now, they look like triplets. They were all in a broad sense platonic. They all taught the metaphysics of spiritual individualism. The value-gaining movement in the spiritual life was the one whereby the self recollects itself, steps back from its too-easy immersion in the passions and the flux of life, distances itself from its own lower nature and becomes spiritual, disengaged, purely rational and free. It thus takes up the correct stance for conquering the world by gaining objective knowledge, by moral legislation, by purity of heart and by relating itself to God. The age was still broadly Cartesian, and I was a follower of science and Augustinian Christianity, of Kant and Kierkegaard.

I hinted earlier that I regard the environmental movement as part of a large-scale cultural shift that has taken us in a more Hegelian direction. We now see why. Environmental thinking works against the spiritual-substance theory of the self. In fact we all of us, I believe, now detest the way in which that view of the self systematically disparaged our supposedly 'lower' nature, the body, the passions and our social and physical environs. We now find somewhat egoistic and unappealing the idea of becoming more real by stepping back into privacy and subjectivity. We do not want to spend all our lives wishing that we were in a better world, somewhere else. Increasingly nowadays we incline to a social, an historical, and an external-relations view of the self. I am not a spiritual substance from another world which is merely contingently related to its life in the here and now. My life is not the life of an outsider who finds himself temporarily trapped and reluctantly acting a part in this world. I just am my own life. I am not a substance: I simply am the aggregate of all the myriad small events, transactions, economic exchanges and symbolic communications that comprise my life. What you see and hear is all there is. I am only skin deep. I am quite *happy* to be only skin deep. The real me is all on my own skin surface, where Culture meets Nature. Beneath the surface there is only biology. The traditional metaphysics of substance was thoroughly alienating in the strict sense that it taught us to think of ourselves as being aliens, extra-terrestrials, or indeed spies, because your true identity was not your publicly-manifest identity but a second, secret identity known only to you and to your divine Control. Oh yes, *spy-fiction is theological,* and this particular theological metaphysics of a hidden inner self had originated early in the Iron Age as a consciousness-raising device. It was associated with a dualism of world-above and world-below, soul and body, reason and the passions, the necessary and the contingent and so on, with a characteristic set of religious beliefs and ascetical practices. It did a great job in its day, but it's dead now. We need a different metaphysics, immanent and trans-actional. It will enable me to say that I am not an alien but just my life, the sum of all the events involving me, and woven into my environment like any other organism by myriads of small daily dealings, much as the city is woven into its environs.

Thus environmental thinking has an affinity with the work of the semiologists, the structuralists and others who look to Durkheim, to Saussure and above all to Hegel. With one voice they all say that the individual does *not* stand alone. We are always already within language and culture and history, embodied (or rather, embedded) with others in a world. No particular piece of behaviour can be intelligible, no utterance can make sense, and I can't even think a thought intelligible to myself, without that great public matrix and thesaurus being already presupposed and in place. Human life is essentially lived in a medium of which we are part, which sustains us and which continually flows right through us. From the scientific point of view this medium may be called Nature, or the environment, and seen as consisting in a great flowing swarm of minute events. From the philosophical point of view the medium may be seen as a semantic field or as a 'Sea of Meanings', that is, a vast shifting expanse of differentiated and scaled feelings, valuations and meanings. So the whole environment in which we live and move and have our being is on the one face of it Culture, and on the other Nature; on one side Thought and on the other Being; on one side Language and on the other side the World. In relation to this unbounded whole our self-conscious individuality is not primary as Descartes and Husserl claimed, but merely secondary.

I suggested at the beginning that the emergence of our modern concept of the environment was a sign of and a part of a larger philosophical shift from Plato to Hegel, from certain traditional styles of dualism and foundationalism to a new vision of the world as a boundless immanently-evolving whole in which we are fully immersed and which has no outside. I no longer see myself as in any way *protruding* from my world. In the older way of thinking there was a supernatural world above, there was an ideal order of timeless standards governing our thought and conduct, and both God and the self were spiritual substances, the one being Infinite and the other his finite counterpart. These metaphysical beliefs were somewhat double-edged. On the one hand, it has to be said in their favour that they did hold the life-world firmly in place, anchoring it to eternity rather as the space inside a great marquee is held open by guy-lines, invisible to the crowd inside the tent, that run down to tent-pegs outside. Even people who never go to church like to see churches in the landscape because for them too an ancient church is a site away from which a guy-line runs invisibly out to eternity and holds this world steady. So the old metaphysical beliefs reassuringly and comfortingly anchored the world to a point outside it. They gave us security and they held the world upright; but, on the other hand, a price had to be paid for these comforts. The contingent natural world in which our life is set was relatively devalued. Life's centre of gravity was shifted out of life altogether. Nature became the Other, ambiguous, female, subordinate, threatening, tempting, moody, changeable, and we drew back nervously from her, fearing that she might swallow us up. Thus a good deal of the patriarchal metaphysics and symbolism of Christianity and of platonism was designed to encourage us to develop an autonomous masculine rational ego, consciously independent and self-distanced from our Mother/Matrix.

To become spiritual, free and adult you had to become a substance, and to become a substance you had to pull away from Mother Nature. That is, you had to be anti-environmental.

The curious feature of the times we live in is that all these ideas are in the melting pot at once – the founding doctrines of Western philosophy and religion, the relation of Culture to Nature, the cultural construction of gender, and all our ideas about spiritual freedom, power and authority. We dimly see that these themes are connected, and we dimly see that environmentalism, linked as it is with feminism, the peace movement and so forth, has called them all into question simultaneously. We are aware that a period of revolutionary change has begun, but we do not so clearly see where it may take us. Some people are apocalyptically pessimistic about the end of Western thought, and almost everyone thinks that Christianity is invested to the hilt in the old realistic metaphysics and cannot survive its downfall.

I disagree. In classical Christian thought the soul was oddly divided by being tugged in two different directions. One path to salvation was that of the monk: we were supposed to turn away from this world and to look only to the heavenly world above for solid joys and lasting treasures. The other path was that of St Francis: it led you sideways to your fellow-creatures and to everything that is merely contingent and lowly. Under the old dispensation the two paths were never fully synthesized. They could not be synthesized, while the motives that had originally distanced God from the world, the self from the world and the self from God remained active. Hegel's philosophy of mediation and reconciliation points to the coming of an age when the old dualisms and disjunctions, once thought essential to culture, are to be overcome by a compensatory movement of healing and synthesis. In this development he saw Christianity's fulfilment, not its abolition; and I have suggested that we should see environmentalism in the same way. There is a whole cluster of contemporary movements which are variously Green, pacific, feminist, vegetarian, small-scale, quasi-Buddhist and so forth, and which see our inherited cultural structures as having been excessively dualistic, repressive and antagonistic. Perhaps a new culture is trying to come to birth, and perhaps that new culture may one day come to be seen as renewing rather than replacing Christianity.

Let me conclude by suggesting how this might be so. Human thinking is and always was binary. It proceeds by separating this from that, the right hand from the left and the above from the below. Wherever a line was drawn, a preference was expressed. Thus culture made a house for us to live in, an ordered and hierarchized vision of the world which was sacralized, sealed and protected by religion. Yet while it is seemingly necessary to human life that the world shall be thus divided up, ranked and ordered, we appear to find it painful that our experience should be polarized in this way. I ask myself why, in order to be able to be myself and to think myself, I have got to be estranged from God, estranged from woman and estranged from wild Nature. So I find myself looking also to religion for reconciliation and the restoration of unity. But this means that religion ends up oddly two-faced. On the one hand it intransigently defends cultural distinctions, while on the other hand its rituals and myths simultaneously offer a tantalizing promise that the same disjunctions can be healed and overcome.

Now although philosophy ostensibly began as a protest against and an alternative to traditional ways of thinking, it in fact merely continued them by other means. Philosophy's chief problem is always to define itself, and how can it do so except by declaring that it is concerned with this and not that? Thus philosophy too divides and prefers, making the form/matter distinction in order to choose for itself the world of form, the reason/passions distinction in order to express its preference for the world of reason, and so on. In the most typically philosophical philosophers, Plato and Kant, it looks as if philosophical reflection just works by generating ever more variations on basically the same type of distinction. One can become weary of this obsessive elaboration, and Hegel sought out what he called 'speculative germs' in the Kantian system, hints as to how it might be possible to reverse the movement and join the world up again.

Historic Christianity was a fusion of religion and platonism, so that it conspicuously exhibits all the traits that I am describing. In it, the creation theme pictures God as standing over against us, laying down all the distinctions and establishing a structured and hierarchized cosmos for us to inhabit. By contrast, the redemption theme reverses and undoes all this, reconciling all the polarized oppositions and antagonisms and returning into us everything that formerly stood over against us – including God, who is distributed as Spirit so that he becomes one in many and we become many in one.

The patterns of thinking I have been trying to unfold have shown, I hope, that the popular association of the environmental movement with the Christian doctrine of creation is a complete mistake. The doctrine of creation that developed out of *Genesis* was concerned to defend a power-structure. The chain of command ran: God, his angels, the heavenly bodies, human souls, men's bodies, women's bodies, the beasts, plants and so on. By contrast, environmental thinking is part of a widespread reaction against the metaphysics of substance, hierarchy, power and control. It criticizes the historic doctrine of man's lordship over nature as God's viceroy, and counter-attacks with its own strange new notions of animal rights, speciesism and the like. In short, as Hegel's thought makes clear, the true affinity of the environmental movement is with the Christian doctrine of redemption, and *not* the doctrine of creation.

The redemption theme has not yet become properly developed in Christianity, but it is best seen as an attempt to separate value from power. Orthodox Christianity so far has been a religion of power. That which was higher in value lorded it over that which was lower. Every value-difference was a difference of rank and every rank-difference was a difference of power. But however subdued it was, there could always be heard, far-off and faintly, the theme of redemption. People dreamt of the possibility that God himself might cease to lord it over us, by returning into us and so no longer being objectively over against us. When that happened there would no longer be any justification for the domination of inferiors by superiors. The soul need not buffet the body, men would no longer rule over women, and human beings generally would stop exploiting the beasts and the earth. It would then become obvious that our cosmologies and the metaphysics of substance had been mere tools of power. They could be forgotten.

In this way, then, the environmental movement invites us to become critically aware of the cosmic politics which has hitherto inspired both our technology and our religion. If we can get there, this new awareness may do us and our religion a lot of good.

BIBLIOGRAPHY

Aristotle, *Metaphysics* Δ iv, 'Nature'.
*The Oxford English Dictionary*, s.vv. 'Environment', 'Environs'; and R. W. Burchfield, ed., *A Supplement to the Oxford English Dictionary*, Vol. 1 (Oxford University Press, 1972) s.v. 'Environment'.
Don Cupitt, *Life Lines* (SCM Press, 1986).
——*The Long Legged Fly* (SCM Press, 1987).
——*The New Christian Ethics* (SCM Press, 1988).
Jacques Derrida, *Speech and Phenomena* (North Western University Press, 1973).
——*Margins of Philosophy* (Harvester Press, 1982).
Mary Douglas, *Natural Symbols* (Barrie & Rockliffe, 1970).
Michel Foucault, *The Order of Things* (Tavistock Publications, 1970).
Michel Harland, *Superstructuralism: the Philosophy of Structuralism and Post-Structuralism* (Methuen, 1987).
T. H. Huxley, *Man's Place in Nature and other Essays* (J. M. Dent, 1906).
R. J. Johnston, et al. (eds.), *The Dictionary of Human Geography* 2nd edn (Basil Blackwell, 1986) s.vv. 'Environmentalism', 'environmental determinism', 'culture', 'cultural ecology', etc.

T. S. Kuhn, *The Structure of Scientific Revolutions*, (University of Chicago Press, 1962).

Jacques Lacan, *Écrits: A Selection* (Tavistock Publications, 1977).

Derek Parfit, *Reasons and Persons* (Oxford University Press, 1984).

Madam Sarup, *An Introductory Guide to Post-Structuralism and Postmodernism* (Harvester Wheatsheaf, 1988).

Kate Soper, *Humanism and Anti-Humanism* (Hutchinson, 1986).

Henry Staten, *Wittgenstein and Derrida* (Basil Blackwell, 1985).

Mark Taylor, *Erring: A Postmodern A/theology* (University of Chicago Press, 1984).

Keith Thomas, *Man and the Natural World: A History of the Modern Sensibility* (Pantheon Books, 1983).

A. N. Whitehead, *The Concept of Nature* (Cambridge University Press, 1920).

# Muller on the Infinite

## Germs of the Infinite

*When a Vedic poet, such as Vasishtha, stood on a high mountain in the land of the Seven Rivers, as he called the Punjab, and let his eye travel across land and water as far as it could reach, had he not a perception of the infinite?*

*When a Greek hero, such as Odysseus, was tossed about on the vast commotion of the waves, seeing no stars and no land anywhere, had he no perception of the infinite? And are we so different from them?*

## The Infinitely Great

*When we ourselves, – savages as we are, according to Bacon, in spite of all our syllogisms, – have learnt to look upon the boundless earth with its boundless ocean, no longer as a stupendous mass, but as a small globe or globule, moving with other globes across the infinite firmament; when wider infinitudes than the infinite firmament open before us, and the sun, which once was so near and dear to us, becomes a fiery mass, the magnitude of which defies our power of imagination; when afterwards, the magnitude of the sun and its distance from us, which is expressed in millions of miles, dwindle down again into nothing as compared with the nearest star, which, we are told, lies twenty millions of millions of miles from our earth, so that a ray of light, if travelling with the velocity of 187,000 miles in a second, would take more than three years in reaching us; – nay, even this is not yet all, – when we are assured by high astronomical authorities that there are more than one thousand millions of such stars which our telescopes have discovered, and that there may be millions of millions of suns within our sidereal system which are beyond the reach of our best telescopes; and that even that sidereal system need not be regarded as single within the universe, but that thousands of millions of sidereal systems may be recognised in the galaxy – if we listen to all this, do we not feel the overwhelming pressure of the infinite, the same infinite which had impressed the mind of Vasishtha and Odysseus, and from which no one can escape who has eyes to see or ears to hear?*

## The Infinitely Small

*But there is another infinite, the infinitely small, which is even more wonderful than the infinitely distant and great. When we turn away our eyes from the immensity which surrounds us, and look at one small drop of water taken from the boundless ocean, a new universe seems to open before us. There are in that drop of water atoms of atoms moving about, some visible, some invisible, some hardly imaginable. A high authority, Sir Henry Roscoe, has told us 'that the chemists are now able to ascertain the relative positions of atoms so minute that millions upon millions of them can stand upon a needle's point.' Is not that infinitude of atoms as wonderful as the infinitude of stars?*

## Infinite Inseparable from Finite

*I maintain then that the infinite is the necessary complement of the finite in every human mind, that it was involved in the first perceptions and became part of the silent clockwork within us, though it may have taken thousands of years before the necessity was felt to give it its final expression, as the Infinite, or the Unknown, or the Beyond.*

*Natural Religion*, pp. 137–9

# 3
# Inner Space and Outer Space: The Quest for Ultimate Explanation

## John Barrow

*It seemed to me a superlative thing – to know the explanation of everything, why it comes to be, why it perishes, why it is.*

Socrates

## Introduction

We are the cosmic bourgeoisie. Far below us lies the schizophrenic inner space of the elementary particles of matter but far beyond our farthest imaginations extend the astronomical reaches of outer space. We sit on the middle rung of the ladder of reality midway between the devil of the quantum world and the deep blue sea of the cosmos. In this in-between world we must create artificial environments in order to reveal the workings of the quantum world and we must enhance our senses with artificial sensors in order to glimpse the fading brilliance of the celestial realm. These two sciences – the study of the very smallest and the very largest components of the physical Universe – have traditionally been different as different could be: different problems, different methods, different scientists. But in the last decade there has been a convergence of thinking about the Universe that has brought the worlds of the very large and the very small into collision. This conjunction has rekindled old ambitions about the ultimate goals of physical science. For the first time there is a feeling within the mainstream of physics, rather than solely within the minds of a few maverick thinkers, that a 'Theory of Everything' can be formulated. What this statement means is the subject of these lectures. As we unfold its meaning and motivations we shall be at pains to indicate what ingredients are necessary for our understanding of the physical world, but stress that none of these *necessary* ingredients are by themselves *sufficient* to arrive at a full understanding of the structure of the physical Universe in which we live.

The concept of ultimate explanation was familiar to the cultures of the dim and distant past. Myths and legends, whether embroidered to provide explanations for the origins of things or concerned merely to rationalize the *status quo*, were all-encompassing and elaborate. Everything had to have its place within the cosmic tapestry of meaning. Yet what they possessed in breadth of vision these myths lacked in depth of explanation. *Ad hoc* explanations multiplied as new ideas and facts had to be woven into the tapestry. There was no sense in which the story was to be tested against the facts; it sought merely to offer a coherent and all-encompassing just-so story about the hostile world that humankind found itself within.

As we have become more demanding of our explanations and pictures of the Universe so we have found the scale of what we must explain to be far greater in extent than our predecessors could ever have imagined. As complexity has grown, so has physics fragmented into specializations until they in turn have found themselves partitioned into manageable pieces. Each enjoys its own successes in building up mathematical theories of the different fundamental forces of Nature and we find ourselves with effective descriptions of each of the different interactions between particles of matter and light. The most striking aspect of these theories, beyond that of their huge success, is that they are distinct in form and content, each compartmentalized from the others as though bearing witness to some curious paranoia in Nature. This goes against the grain of our belief in the unity of Nature.

Only very rarely have ambitious scientists attempted to construct a theory of physics which would unite all the disparate and successful theories of the different forces of Nature into a single coherent framework from which all things could in principle be derived. Rogerius Boscovich in the eighteenth century was the first to possess this unifying vision but the most famous modern attempts to implement it were those of Eddington and Einstein. They failed for many reasons. In retrospect, we recognize that knowledge of the elementary particle world was then so seriously incomplete that neither Eddington nor Einstein were in a position even to know what needed to be unified let alone how to do it. However, the flame they first ignited has remained glowing faintly in the background, often overshadowed by the latest detailed advances in the understanding of particular pieces of Nature, until being fanned into prominence by the most recent successes and speculations of theoretical physicists to illuminate our picture of the Universe. Whereas past unifiers were regarded as lone eccentrics by their colleagues, tolerated because of the brilliance of their other contributions to physics, the unifiers of today populate the mainstream of physics and continually add to their number the most gifted young students.

The current breed of candidates for the title of a 'Theory of Everything' hope to provide an encapsulization of all the laws of Nature into a simple and single representation. The fact that such a unification is even sought tells us something important about our expectations regarding the Universe. These we must have derived from an amalgam of our previous experience of the world and our inherited religious beliefs about its ultimate nature and significance. Our monotheistic traditions reinforce the assumption that the Universe is at root a unity, that it is not governed by different legislations in different places, neither the residue of some clash of the Titans wrestling to impose their arbitrary wills upon the nature of things, nor the compromise of some cosmic committee. Our Western religious tradition also endows us with the assumption that things are governed by a logic that exists independently of those things, that laws are externally imposed as though they were the decrees of a transcendent Divine legislator. In other respects our prejudices reflect a mixture of different traditions. Some feel the force of the Greek imperative that the structure of the Universe is a necessary and inflexible truth that could not be otherwise, while others inherit the feeling that the Universe is contingent.

Our attraction for that quality which we have come to call beauty, and which we associate with the detection of innate unity and harmony in the face of superficial diversity, has led us to expect that the unity of the Universe should be expressed in certain particular ways. If we are physicists we might often hear talk of the 'beauty' or 'elegance' of particular ideas or theories to such an extent that, like Dirac, we make aesthetic quality a guide or even a prerequisite for the formulation of correct mathematical theories of Nature. This imperative strikes the life scientist as strange, the more so when he or she discovers how ineffective physicists, for all their mathematical powers, so often are if they stray into his or her menagerie. For the physicist is used to dealing with the pristine symmetries and fundamental laws of Nature. This habit conditions the physicist to seek and expect symmetry and mathematical elegance everywhere he or she looks. But the living world is not a marble palace. It is the higgledy-piggledy outcome of natural selection and the competition between many interacting factors. The outcome is often neither elegant nor symmetrical. Idealization and approximation are difficult.

Let us now turn in earnest to our story. In the pages to follow we shall seek to introduce those factors upon which our understanding of the physical Universe necessarily rests. We shall see that it is necessary for us to have a grasp of them all in order to claim that our understanding of the Universe is complete. In particular, we shall see that the currently fashionable Theories of Everything, even if correct, are insufficient to complete our understanding of the physical world. Our discussion will be somewhat biased, although not completely so, towards the subjects of cosmology and elementary particles. As secondary and tertiary aims we have the exposition of new concepts in physics and mathematics as well as their interfaces with those questions pondered by natural theologians of the past. Few theologians have an adequate training in theoretical physics to follow these new developments in detail, and few physicists have a sufficient appreciation of the historical, conceptual and linguistic aspects of the wider questions to make a fruitful dialogue possible. The theologians think they know the questions but cannot understand the answers. The physicists think they know the answers but don't know the questions. The optimist might thus regard a dialogue as a recipe for real progress whilst the pessimist would predict the outcome to be a state in which we find ourselves knowing neither the questions nor the answers.

In our survey of the scope of Theories of Everything we shall consider in turn eight ingredients that can be seen as essential parts of any attempt at ultimate physical explanation. The first facet of our eight-fold way is the one which occupies the principal place in the minds of physicists in search of the elusive Theory of Everything – the laws of Nature.

## Laws of Nature

The reliability and lawfulness of Nature are things that we have come to take for granted. Our ancestors were first impressed by the irregularities and eccentricities of Nature – the earthquake, the eclipse or the shooting-star – but in time the successful exploitation of the periodicities and regularities of Nature for agriculture and navigation gave these recurrences a pre-eminent place in their world-view. The consistent association of particular events in regular succession leads naturally to the primitive notion of sequential causes and effects – that one sort of thing habitually follows another. Even an accompanying belief in magic and the supernatural intervention of the gods reinforces some underlying belief in the lawfulness of Nature because the sorcerous notion that the natural order of things can somehow be overthrown by an act of the will implicitly admits to the existence of a natural order which must be subverted. The conjuring of spells leads to a certain occult respect for cause and effect, however misplaced. Such magical notions are not so easy to overthrow because the tempting explanation for the failure of some incantation to produce the advertised effect is that it has been over-ridden by some more powerful magic or by a crucial imperfection in its practical execution.

It has been argued that the existence of monotheistic religions in Western cultures played an important role in germinating the idea that there exist laws of Nature imposed upon the world by the Creator. An earlier, essentially Greek, notion was of innate tendencies which induced things to move in particular ways in order to attain particular ends. Any belief in the uniformity of natural laws is hard to extrapolate from this view and it stifled the natural evolution of the atomists' ideas for thousands of years. Other social factors played an important role in determining whether a distinctive concept of natural laws arose in a culture. Those societies with strong central government and well-established bodies of statute law most naturally engendered the analogy of the Universe as a city state ordered by imposed diktat. By contrast, in early China the lack of a body of statute law, the absence of any notion that there existed an omnipotent Deity, and the influence of Confucian liberalism ensured that the cosmopolitan concept of natural laws was stillborn. Chinese society was organized by the holistic interaction of different individuals into a harmonious equilibrium rather than by external rules: order was seen to arise spontaneously after the manner of the ant colony rather than the dictatorship.

For the Greeks the most perfect laws of Nature were the static harmonies of things but modern science made its most spectacular progress by viewing laws of Nature first and foremost as laws of change. Thus, knowing the state of a system here and now we seek a device for predicting its state at other times and places. Intriguingly, it is always possible to rephrase these laws of change as statements that a certain aspect of the laws of Nature is invariant. Thus, for example, the conservation of energy is equivalent to the invariance of the laws of motion with respect to translations backwards or forwards in time (that is, the result of an experiment should not depend on the time at which it was carried out – all other factors being identical); the conservation of linear momentum is equivalent to the invariance of the laws of motion with respect to the position of your laboratory in space, and the conservation of angular momentum to an invariance with respect to the directional orientation of your laboratory in space. Other conserved quantities in physics, which arise as the constants of integration of the laws of change, turn out to be equivalent to other less intuitive invariances of the laws of Nature. It is interesting to note that the conservation of energy was not known to Newton and in the post-Newtonian discussions regarding the theological relevance of Newton's successful description of the world the existence of conservation laws appears to have played some role in the growth of atheism amongst scientists. Some, like Newton himself, felt that there was a need within the Newtonian dynamical model of the known Universe (the solar system) for the sustaining and regulating hand of the Deity, but the subsequent discovery of conservation laws indicated that Nature possessed built-in regulators and there were fewer gaps for the Deity to fill than had been believed. Laplace had to admit that in this respect 'nous n'avons pas besoin de cette hypothèse-là'. Later the pendulum would swing back and the need to violate a conservation law of Nature in order to bring the Universe into being out of nothing persuaded many of the need for supernatural intervention. Moreover, the evident success of the concept of laws of Nature led to a reformulation of the Design Argument for the existence of God. We shall refrain from elaborating upon it here, but later in our discussion we shall return to highlight its special significance.

Even today there persists a feeling that the creation of the Universe out of nothing must violate some basic conservation law that stops one getting something for nothing. Nonetheless, there is no evidence that the Universe as a whole possesses a non-zero value of any such conserved quantity. It could apparently appear without violating the conservation of mass-energy. The total rest mass energy of all the constituents of a closed finite Universe appears to be always equal in magnitude but opposite in sign to their total gravitational potential energy. Similarly, there is no evidence that the Universe possesses any overall net rotation or electric charge.

The fact that laws of change can be represented as invariances of the world under all possible changes to it that respect a particular symmetry struck a resonant chord with physicists' expectations regarding the presence of symmetry and harmony in Nature. Symmetry has become the dominant theme in fundamental physics. Elementary particle physics is singularly Platonic in this respect. Mathematicians of the past have catalogued all the distinct patterns of change that exist and encoded their essential ingredients into a branch of mathematics now known as 'group theory'. By searching though its catalogue of all possible patterns the particle physicist can extract candidate symmetries to impose upon the World. The candidates need to pass some initial screening to ensure that they can accommodate all the necessary ingredients of the elementary particle world and do not have some obvious consequence at variance with reality. The successful candidates now graduate to a more detailed mathematical outworking which results in a gamut of predictions as to how particles should interact in a world governed by the imposed symmetry. Thus, one's faith in symmetry provides an efficient methodology for generating candidate theories of elementary particle interactions. No such machinery exists to generate candidate theories to explain the workings of less basic entities like economies or weather systems.

Each of the four forces of Nature – gravity, electromagnetism, the weak and strong nuclear forces – is governed by a theory that is derived from the assumption of a particular invariance under all possible changes. The quest for unification proceeds by seeking to embed the separate patterns preserved by the several forces of Nature within a single 'Grand Unified' pattern into which the sub-patterns fit uniquely. Such schemes are not easy to find and until recently carried with them unfortunate defects which came to light when the resulting pattern of invariance was used to compute observable quantities. Infinite answers were obtained which had to be dealt with in particular ways in order to produce sensible predictions. This flaw has been found to be absent in a narrow class of unusual physical theories which have been proposed as the most complete laws of Nature. These are known as 'Superstring' theories. The prefix 'Super' alludes to a powerful symmetry that they respect. 'Supersymmetry' has been proposed as a symmetry between fermions and bosons. (Fermions are particles with half-integral units of quantum mechanical spin, bosons possess integral units of spin.) In the world of mundane elementary particles this amounts to a symmetry between matter and radiation. But it is the 'string' that contains the potent new concept. In the past, theories of elementary particles regarded the most elementary entities of Nature as point particles having no finite extent (their wave functions could be arbitrarily localized and they would offer no evidence of any finite extent when bombarded by other high-energy particles). They were described by quantum field theories in which the most basic elements are points of zero size. However, if the most elementary entities are regarded as strings (lines) rather than points, then all the unpleasant divergences in calculated quantities magically disappear for only a few of the possible universal symmetries. In effect, a certain collection of possible laws of Nature, and these only, are self-consistent. The fundamental strings possess a tension that varies inversely with the energy of the environment in which they reside and this tension becomes large enough to shrink the loops of string to approximate points at the low energies we witness in the Universe today. But in the extremities of the Big Bang the essential stringiness of things should be apparent. It is theories of this sort that have aroused talk of a 'Theory of Everything'. If we had the correct version it should in principle contain all the laws of radioactivity, gravity, electromagnetism and nuclear physics.

Our attitude towards the laws of Nature and some ultimate codification of them into a possibly unique and self-consistently specified 'Theory of Everything' is a search for an ultimate symmetry of the World from whose strait-jacket there follow all the allowed causal laws of change governing the forces and particles of Nature. Our approach to such an apparent panacea must be tempered by an appreciation of how the laws of Nature – the 'Theory of Everything' – could be related to the Universe. Let us label the material Universe by U and the laws of Nature by L, then we can immediately conceive of three possibilities with regard to their inter-relationship. The one that we choose has some bearing upon the type of explanation for the Universe that we seek.

The first option is $U \subset L$; that is, the Universe is smaller than the laws of Nature. This transcendent view of the laws of Nature is a traditional assumption that has become implicit in most cosmological studies. It amounts to regarding the laws of Nature as pre-existent to the beginning of the Universe (if indeed it had a beginning). The unusual status of mathematics gives some support to this picture, but this amounts to a type of neo-Platonism in which the position of God has been replaced by mathematics. The most interesting feature of this assumption for our discussion is that it clearly shows that even if a correct Theory of Everything were found (and that may be a big 'if') then we would be using the term 'Everything' in a somewhat cavalier fashion because we would still be left with explaining the existence of very particular laws of Nature, space, time and logic. Any cosmological investigation that assumes there to exist mathematical equations which govern the behaviour of entire universes is implicitly acknowledging the idea that the laws of Nature are larger in some sense than the Universe they govern. This is the assumption of all those who believe in the existence and attainability of some all-encompassing Theory of Everything or attempts to provide mathematical descriptions of 'creation out of nothing' in which the Universe appears at some moment of past time.

A second stance is that U is identical in scope to L; that is, $U = L$. This is analogous to St Augustine's famous dictum that the Universe was not created in time but rather that time was created with the Universe. In recent cosmology this idea has been embodied in the view that the Universe began at an initial singularity or 'Big Bang'. The singularity theorems proved by Hawking and Penrose in the late 1960s established this concept, but it is currently a less compelling picture of

the beginning of the Universe because these theorems merely give sufficient conditions upon the properties of matter for there to be a beginning
to time in the past, and these conditions are no longer believed to be
obeyed by matter at high density. Such theorems give conditions under
which space-time has an edge. The edge marks the initial singularity; no
space-time exists before this moment, indeed there is no concept of
'before'. This situation cannot occur in Newtonian physics where space
and time are absolutely fixed and the laws of Nature describe how
motions are played out upon them. Irrespective of how great the density
of matter at any point in space becomes (even were it to become infinite)
the nature of space and time is, for Newton, unaffected. By contrast, in
Einstein's general relativity, and related theories of gravitation of a
geometrical sort, the structure of space-time is determined by the motion
and presence of mass-energy upon it. If material densities become infinite
then this coupling generally destroys the space-time as well.

The final option open to us is to regard the laws of Nature as a subset
of the Universe, that is $L \subset U$. Thus, there might exist islands of
rationality in an infinite chaotic universe. We would necessarily find ourselves living in one of the ordered suburbs of the Universe where coherent
structures are possible. Implicit in this view is the expectation that
spatial variations might exist in the values of the so-called constants of
Nature. This picture has been assumed as a possible cosmological initial
condition by some supporters of a 'chaotic inflationary Universe'. They
envisage a period of very rapidly accelerating expansion in the early
Universe which has the effect of expanding a very small coherent region
into one that exceeds the size of the visible part of the Universe (about
fifteen billion light years) by the present. A more extreme version of this
stance is the proposal that there may not be any exact laws of Nature
in the traditional sense. If we associate laws of Nature with invariances
or symmetries, as we discussed above, then we might imagine that in the
very high energy state of the Big Bang a vast number of symmetries held
sway; so many that the situation was effectively lawless. As the temperature fell so some symmetries would come to dominate the others and
eventually come to endow our low-energy world with a small number of
over-riding symmetries. These 'chaotic gauge theories', as they have
become known, assume the opposite to the standard approach to high-
energy physics which has the world becoming simpler and more symmetrical as temperatures and energies rise. Chaotic gauge theory envisages
symmetry being progressively lost at high energies. In some variants there
is no exact symmetry at any temperature, merely an asymptotic approach
to symmetry as the Universe cools, leaving us inhabiting a world of
'almost symmetries' which give us the impression of exact laws. All these

theories which flow from an assumption that L ⊂ U significantly downgrade the status of laws of Nature. They are neither universal nor unchanging. They become increasingly identified with human approximations which look for symmetry and exactness where they do not quite exist.

We can also extend our U–L game to include the traditional notion of God, G. With regard to laws of Nature we have the three options, L = G, L ⊂ G and L ⊃ G. For pantheists, like Einstein, the first option is merely one of terminology. For others, like Newton, the traditional picture of the laws of Nature as the thoughts or decrees of the Deity is enshrined in the second option. The third case includes the atheistic view that the notion of a God or gods is an inevitable or accidental outcome of the evolutionary process in the minds of complex biochemical computers called human beings. It would also include a picture in which God was bound by certain constraints; for example, the laws of logic or mathematics. This raises an interesting question. Historically, there has been vast attention paid to the question of whether the Deity does or could suspend the laws of Nature. But the deeper question of whether He can suspend logic or mathematics has not attracted quite the same attention.

Although we require laws of change to understand the Universe we must be aware of one awkward feature of our existing laws of Nature which creates ambiguities for any metaphysical deductions that might be drawn from them. It is possible for there to exist different mathematical representations of a particular law, which despite having the same physical and observational content, possess totally different metaphysical implications. Consider, for example, classical mechanics. We can use the differential equations provided by Newton, Lagrange or Hamilton to determine the paths followed by particles acted upon by particular forces. These representations all yield a causal description in which the present uniquely and completely determines the future. Alternatively, it is possible to determine the paths taken by the particles using the Principle of Least Action. This dictates that the path actually taken between two points is the one which possesses the minimum value of a particular quantity, called the 'action', which was first introduced by Maupertuis in 1748.

The metaphysical implication of this formulation of the problem of motion is quite different from the causal one. It is essentially teleological since both the initial and the final state determine the actual path taken. In fact, Maupertuis used his discovery of the Principle of Least Action to make precise Leibniz's notion of 'the best of all possible worlds'. From this example we learn to be cautious when drawing metaphysical conclusions from our edition of the laws of Nature. They can possess representations with identical physical content but different metaphysical implications.

## Initial Conditions

One of the reasons why differential equations are so useful in physics is that they neatly separate our knowledge from our ignorance. Our knowledge can be coded into the algorithmic component of the equation which governs how things change in space and time. Our ignorance can be parcelled up into those things we call 'initial conditions' and 'physical constants'. The initial conditions give the starting state for the deterministic evolution. Differential equations allow us to use the algorithmic content without knowing either the initial conditions or the physical constants. In general, the qualitative form of an algorithm's predictions will not be sensitive to the precise values of the physical constants of proportionality that appear in it. However, it is possible that the traditional distinction between laws, initial conditions and physical constants is an artefact of this particular way of representing the world in mathematical form. In reality we may not possess freedom to consider changes in each of these ingredients independently of the others.

An awkward feature of the division between evolution equations and initial conditions is that often the form of the evolution can be very sensitive to the precise initial conditions. Systems which exhibit this extreme sensitivity to their starting state – the weather for instance – are for all practical purposes unpredictable in detail and we shall have more to say about them later.

One further curiosity about initial conditions is that they can sometimes exert an influence that creates the impression that a law of Nature exists where none exists. A familiar example is the 'Second Law' of thermodynamics, which stipulates that the entropy, or disorder, of a closed system cannot decrease with time. Thus we see coffee cups breaking into pieces but never pieces of china coming together to form cups. Our desks naturally evolve from a state of tidiness into one of untidiness but never vice versa. The laws of mechanics which govern such changes do not contain any in-built favouritism for entropy-increasing behaviour. For every solution of Newton's equations of motion which describes a cup breaking into pieces there is another solution with the time direction reversed describing pieces convening into a cup. The laws of physics do not forbid entropy-decreasing behaviour. The reason we never see such behaviour is because the initial conditions required to realize it are so fantastically improbable. We require appropriately shaped pieces of china, all moving at precisely the right speeds in just the right directions to come together to make a cup. By contrast, the conditions required to realize the breaking cup are very easy to realize, and often are.

One situation in which the question of initial conditions is of special significance is cosmology. Even if we have been successful in discerning the Theory of Everything and know the unified laws of change of all the forces and particles in Nature, we still need to know either the initial state of the Universe or its exact state at some time early in its history in order to understand its present structure. Traditionally, there have been three 'religions' amongst cosmologists with regard to initial conditions:

(1) *Remove initial conditions to the infinite past by showing (or assuming) that the Universe did not possess a beginning in time.* The steady-state Universe of Bondi, Gold and Hoyle, proposed in 1948, was a scenario of this sort. However, it should be recognized that conditions still have to be placed upon the state of the Universe at past temporal infinity in order to deduce its present state from the law of gravitation. In the steady-state Universe the rate of continuous creation of matter, which in turn fixed the rate of expansion of the Universe, was not fixed by the laws of change. It was simply taken to be equal to the observed expansion rate. One cannot avoid the requirement of knowing something about 'initial' conditions by having a Universe without a beginning in time. An added subtlety for any attempt to place the 'beginning' of the Universe at past infinity is that we do not know if there exists a fundamental cosmic time and, if so, what it is. One can carry out arbitrary mathematical transformations of the time coordinate one is using to clock the age of the Universe, so that what exists at a finite time in the past when clocked by one time coordinate is relegated to the infinite past on transforming to another (for example by the transformation of the time $t$ to the logarithm of $t$).

(2) *Show that the present state of the Universe is largely or completely independent of its initial conditions.* This is methodologically rather appealing. If we could show that the present structure of the Universe does not depend in any significant way upon the initial conditions then we would not require knowledge of those (possibly unknowable) initial conditions in order to predict what the present structure of the Universe should be.

In the early 1970s considerable effort was expended in trying to show that the regularity of the Universe today, observed over its largest scales, could be explained in this way. Attempts were made to show that no matter how chaotic or irregular the starting state of the Universe there would subsequently arise frictional processes able to damp down this irregularity to the present low level so long as the Universe is old enough. If we stir a bucket of oil in a vigorous fashion then soon the oil will relax into a uniform stationary state irrespective of how it was first stirred. Unfortunately, this idea did not work. By virtue of the Second 'Law' of thermodynamics, this frictional dissipation of irregularity has to be paid for by the production of heat and the heat density in the Universe today is exceedingly low. This consideration reveals that only a minute amount of irregularity could have been smoothed out by frictional processes in the past.

Only since 1980 has this approach to initial conditions found a successful implementation without the need for the frictional dissipation of irregularity and the consequent heat production problem. The inflationary Universe theory of Alan Guth, proposed in 1980, does not dissipate non-uniformities, but instead sweeps them beyond the farthest distance that we can see.

In this 'inflationary' picture we can imagine that the Universe began in almost any state we choose. If there is a short period of *accelerated* expansion during the first moments of the Universe's history then that part of the (possibly infinite) Universe that we now see will be the expanded image of a tiny region – small enough to be initially kept near uniformity by quantum fluctuations. By contrast, in the traditional Big Bang model the expansion never accelerates, and that part of the whole Universe which we see today arises from the expansion of a large region at very early times – a region too large to be kept uniform by quantum fluctuations. Thus, in the inflationary theory, the present observed regularity is a manifestation of conditions within a tiny initial region. If there existed chaos outside this region in the very early history of the Universe then it may still exist but it is present beyond our visible horizon.

This picture attempts to make the present largely independent of the past by making it a magnification of conditions on microscopically small dimensions of space where quantum fluctuations maintain smoothness. There will still exist some very small deviations from the average, of course. But these turn out to possess a very special statistical form and may well lead to the existence of galaxies today, and thereby allow the entire inflationary Universe picture to be tested against observations.

(3) *Find a law of initial conditions or link the laws of evolution to initial conditions.* Some differential equations possess particular solutions which do not permit the initial conditions to be specified freely. They are uniquely fixed by the solution. These are special solutions. They do not contain the arbitrary constants of integration that the general solution would, for it is these arbitrary constants that allow the freedom to choose different

starting conditions. In the same vein it has been proposed that the correct theory of quantum cosmology may pick out the allowed initial conditions for the Universe in a unique way. Alternatively, initial conditions may not be freely specifiable. There might be meta-laws governing initial conditions.

Suggestions of possible constraints upon initial conditions have been made in recent years. It has been mooted that there may exist some counterpart of entropy in thermodynamics which monitors the total level of disorder in the gravitational field of the Universe. If this were so then it would imply an initial state of low, or even zero, entropy for the Universe. This idea has not yet been worked out in a useful way but it illustrates how a physical principle might render certain initial conditions preferred. A more detailed proposal for a natural initial condition is that proposed by Hartle and Hawking in 1983 for quantum cosmological models. Quantum cosmology is a new subject that is exploring certain avenues of investigation. One such avenue is to study a version of Schrödinger's equation (familiar from quantum mechanics) which has been adapted to the presence of gravitation and curved space. Its solutions provide wavefunctions for the whole Universe. In order to extract and interpret one of these solutions as the description of our Universe we require some boundary conditions.

The initial condition that Hawking and Hartle prefer is not the only possible one, and others have been proposed because they appear to have nicer consequences for the subsequent evolution, but in many respects the Hawking-Hartle proposal is the most aesthetically appealing. It minimizes the information content required to specify the beginning of the Universe. Paradoxically, it amounts to the proposal that there is no boundary for freely specifying initial conditions. There is undoubtedly metaphysical motivation for this. Some scientists regard the prescription of initial conditions in addition to laws of Nature as tantamount to the incorporation of the whim of God into their description of the Universe. Einstein regarded the presence of arbitrary constants of Nature, not fixed by the self-consistency of the laws of Nature, in this way. Similarly, Hawking regards the presence of freely specifiable initial conditions in cosmology as an admission that there are arbitrary elements in the make-up of the Universe and these he identifies with God.

The general trend of these recent discussions of cosmological initial conditions is rather striking. The traditional attitude in cosmology has been that physics cannot tell us about initial conditions. At present, cosmologists appear determined to make initial conditions part of the scientific discussion and to show that there are ways of determining which are possible or probable and to link them to the form of the laws of Nature themselves. The other recent change has been in attitude towards the likely initial state of the Universe. Before the serious study of quantum cosmology, those cosmological models which had a beginning were always envisaged to begin at a singularity of infinite density. Quantum cosmologies do not naturally begin at such singularities. They can have beginnings that correspond to the Universe having quantum mechanically tunnelled from a state of absolutely nothing into a small finite expanding state. These 'tunnelling' evolutions have no classical, Newtonian counterpart. This small Universe can only grow to the vast size of our observed Universe if a process like inflation can arise to accelerate its expansion during its early stages. Any ideas of this sort concerning the beginnings of the Universe can at present be only conjectural. But for the first time there exist mathematical theories of physics which can address such issues. This is a new speculative chapter in the theoretical investigation of the Universe.

In order to use a Theory of Everything to understand the structure of the Universe we require knowledge of initial conditions. These initial conditions may be arbitrary. They may be fixed by some undiscovered principle. Whether we can discern if such principles do exist depends upon which of the three attitudes towards cosmological initial conditions (if any) is the correct one to take. If the laws which govern the evolution of the Universe do lead to a loss of memory of its initial conditions, for example because 'inflation' occurs, then our present observations will not tell us anything very specific about the initial conditions. Our knowledge will always be fundamentally incomplete. Moreover, schemes like inflation in which our visible Universe evolves from a minute portion of the entire initial conditions of space, only allow us to gather observational data about an infinitesimal portion of the initial conditions. Both these warnings lead us to expect that we may well be condemned to ignorance about cosmic initial conditions irrespective of whether or not we are in possession of a Theory of Everything.

## Forces and Particles

A knowledge of the laws of Nature is of little use unless one knows what it is that those laws govern. In this respect the contrast between classical physics and elementary particle physics is striking. Newton's laws of motion are universal in a dramatic sense that Newton highlighted in his statement of them ('all bodies...'). They claim to govern the motion of all bodies irrespective of their many idiosyncratic features. Yet, it is because of their very universality that Newton's laws do not tell us anything about the types of particle that can exist. The laws of elementary particle behaviour are different. Elementary particles like electrons differ from rocks and cricket balls in one important respect. Every electron is the *same*. Once you've seen one electron, you've seen them all. This makes it possible for the laws governing the behaviour of electrons to be strongly linked to the nature of electrons.

The importance of the identical nature of elementary particles was first appreciated by Maxwell in the nineteenth century. He laid great stress upon the presence of a family of identical microscopic building blocks in Nature (we now call them atoms but Maxwell called them 'molecules') as evidence that there was a limit to the domain of influence of Darwinian natural selection in shaping the structure of the physical world:

> No theory of evolution can be formed to account for the similarity of molecules, for evolution necessarily implies continuous change, and the molecule is incapable of growth or decay, of generation or destruction... None of the processes of Nature, since the time when Nature began, have produced the slightest difference in the properties of any molecule... They continue this day as they were created... (*Address to the British Association*, 1873)

A central dogma concerning the Galilean and Newtonian revolutions in the description of Nature is that scientists ceased asking 'why' questions of Nature and started asking 'how'. Curiously, modern particle physicists are quite different. They are not content to possess theories that are perfectly accurate in their description of *how* particles move and interact. They want to know 'why' those particles exist and 'why' they interact in the manner seen.

The most successful fundamental theories of physics – general relativity (the theory of gravity), quantum chromodynamics (the theory of the strong sub-nuclear forces between quarks and gluons) and the Weinberg-Salam theory (the unified theory of the electromagnetic and weak interactions) – are all theories of a particular type known as *local gauge theories*.

We have already mentioned how certain geometrical invariances of the laws of Nature are equivalent to the imposition of physical invariances: for each symmetry there exists an associated conserved quantity. This correspondence is maintained even when the symmetries involved are more esoteric than simple rotations or translation in space. These additional invariances are called internal symmetries and correspond to invariances under various relabellings of the particles involved – for example, swopping the identities of all protons and neutrons.

Gauge symmetries are different again. They do not lead to conserved quantities in Nature, rather they impose powerful requirements upon the form and scope of the laws of Nature. In particular, they dictate what forces of Nature exist and the properties of the elementary particles which they govern. The simplest example is that of a *global gauge symmetry*. It demands that the world be invariant if we move every point in the same way. Imagine such an operation performed upon an object like your hand. It would be transported in space but would look the same. But it is unnatural to suppose that the changes be the same everywhere. If a particle changes at this moment on the other side of the Universe then a particle here and now cannot know this at least until a light signal has had time to pass between them. It would require instantaneous signalling to keep in step. This leads us to demand the more stringent requirement that things be invariant under *local gauge symmetry* wherein every point can change in a different way. Invariance in this case seems impossible. Every part of your hand, in our example, would move off in different directions. The only way in which things can be kept invariant under such general changes is if certain forces exist which constrain the allowed motions – imagine some elastic bands taut around your hand. In this way the imposition of invariance under local gauge symmetry actually dictates what forces of Nature exist between the particles involved. They reveal why there is electromagnetism as well as how it operates. Einstein's general theory of relativity is a local gauge theory of this sort. Einstein wished to generalize his principle of special relativity, which maintained that the laws of physics be the same for all observers moving at constant relative velocities, to the situation where accelerated observers are considered. The only way in which this is possible for all observers in arbitrary accelerated motions is for there to exist a gravitational field.

The Platonic faith in symmetry and the implementation of those symmetries as the bases for gauge theories is the foundation of our knowledge of elementary particle interactions. Yet it does not tell us everything. It fails to tell us how many particles of a similar type there must be: why there are three types of neutrino rather than just one. Moreover, we have many different gauge theories which must be unified into a single description by embedding the different symmetries associated with individual theories into a bigger over-riding pattern, or *grand unified theory*. Grand unification removes the problems of different disjoint theories but it still does not solve the problem of what limits the number of types of similar particles.

What is interesting about these Platonic investigations of the consequences of symmetry in the elementary particle world is that they are not motivated primarily by observations, because there are very few relevant observations: they are often far too difficult and expensive to make at present. Occasionally, a theory will be formulated and seen immediately to be at variance with observation in one particular, perhaps minor, respect. Yet it will not be discarded. Investigation and development of its properties will often continue because of a belief that a 'cure' for its particular 'disease' will eventually be found which leaves its other attractive features unchanged.

The most topical aspect of the identification of the forces and particles of Nature is to know the identity of the most elementary entities in Nature. Until only a few years ago they were invariably imagined to be idealized 'points' of zero size. Quarks and leptons were assumed to be particles of this sort, exhibiting no evidence of internal structure in any particle-scattering experiment. However, theories in which the most basic entities are points – quantum field theories – possess unpleasant mathematical properties. They lead to mathematical infinities that must be ignored in the process of calculating observable quantities. This can usually be done by following a systematic recipe but the procedure is aesthetically rather unappealing. As has already been remarked briefly in these lectures, it has now been recognized that theories in which the most elementary objects are lines or loops ('superstrings'), rather than points, can avoid these defects. Moreover, whereas the point particle schemes require a separate point to be specified for each elementary particle, a single string possesses an infinite number of normal modes of vibration – just like a violin string – and the energy of each different mode will correspond to a different elementary particle mass (via the mass-energy equivalence $E = mc^2$). Most of this collection of particle masses will be concentrated around unobservably high energies but the others will include the masses of the known elementary particles. As we mentioned earlier, superstrings also possess a tension that varies with their energy so that at low energies the tension shrinks the strings into points and we recover the favourable features of a world of point-like elementary particles. At high energies their essential stringiness becomes evident and their properties differ from those of point theories. Superstring theories have the potential to predict the masses of all elementary particles. Unfortunately, at present the mathematical expertise required to unravel those properties is beyond us. For the first time modern physicists have found that off-the-shelf mathematics is insufficient to extract the physical content of their theories. But, in time, suitable techniques will no doubt emerge or perhaps a better way to look at the theory will be found: one that is conceptually and technically simpler.

In summary, we have seen that we need to know the identity of the forces and particles of Nature. At present we believe, perhaps mistakenly, that we have identified all the fundamental forces. We have working gauge theories, based upon particular group symmetries which determine the structure of these forces and indeed tell us why they must exist. Schemes exist which unify these different gauge theories together but they fail to limit the number of types of particle that can exist. Ultimately, the demand for self-consistency alone may narrow the range of options for the single over-arching symmetry of Nature from which everything else follows. However, we may then be faced with the question of whether this entire scheme may itself be embedded within some larger symmetry whose other ingredients govern feeble forces of Nature we have yet to witness directly. In the march towards such a self-consistent single description of the forces of Nature the post-war viewpoint that the most basic theories of physics must be quantum field theories has been undermined by the theoretical attractions of superstring theories and their promise to explain the properties of all the elementary particles of Nature.

## Constants of Nature

In our mathematical equations that purport to describe the workings of Nature there arise certain quantities to which we ascribe a special status and which we have come to call the 'constants of Nature'. They arise naturally in our equations as constants of proportionality between different variable physical quantities. As such, they can be determined only by measurement. Although the form of the relationship between the physical variables will be dictated by some symmetry principle or invariance, the principle will tell us only that, for example, energy is proportional to mass. It cannot give the numerical value of the constant of proportionality. The first such universal quantity to be discovered was the gravitational constant of Newton. It arose implicitly from his deduction that the force of gravity between any two masses is proportional to the product of those masses and inversely proportional to the square of their separations. This constant of proportionality is called the Newtonian gravitational constant. Although the existence of such a parameter is inevitable in Newton's scheme, and also in Einstein's theory of gravitation that superseded it, its numerical value cannot be determined by the theory. It can be ascertained only by observation of the actual strength of the gravitational force.

The fact that these constants arise as proportionality constants in equations describing natural phenomena might ultimately turn out to be misleading. They may be artefacts of our particular mode of description. Nevertheless, this possible bias is a small price to pay for the convenience of a way of describing the world which is able to separate automatically those parts which must be measured from those parts which are dictated by symmetry considerations.

A constant of proportionality in a physical equation will only be given the epithet 'constant of Nature' if it appears in a law of Nature which is believed to be universally true. Newton believed that his law of gravitation applied to everything, whether it be on the Earth or in the heavens, and so the constant of gravitation which it implies lays claim to the status of a universal constant of Nature. The elasticity of your bicycle tyre is also a proportionality constant in an equation describing the stretching of the tyre under pressure, but it is hardly a universal constant because it is associated with a particular piece of rubber which differs from every other piece in some way. We would, however, be interested in attributes of individual objects all of which were identical throughout the known Universe; for example, the amount of electric charge on an individual electron, since we believe all electrons to be identical in every respect.

Real advances in our understanding of the physical world always seem to involve either:

1 The discovery of a new fundamental constant of Nature;
2 A formula showing how the value of one constant of Nature is determined only by the numerical values of others, or;
3 The discovery that a quantity believed to be a constant of Nature is not constant.

For example, the introduction of the quantum theory of radiation by Planck, Einstein, Bohr and others, brought with it the new fundamental quantity known as Planck's constant, which dictates the smallest packets of energy that take part in physical interactions. Einstein's theory of special relativity gave universal status to the velocity of light in vacuum and Einstein showed that it also provides the link between the concepts of mass and energy. Towards the end of the nineteenth century Maxwell's combination of the theories of electricity and magnetism into the unified picture of electromagnetism was also mediated by the fundamental status of the velocity of light. The grand unified theories of particle physics allow some of the constants of Nature defining the strengths of different forces of Nature to be related and predict that certain quantities, previously thought to be conserved in physical interactions, can be altered. The price of unification is that everything must be able to interact with everything. There must be no enclaves of the elementary world where small collections of elementary particles keep themselves to themselves. Unification of known laws of Nature creates fewer laws, fewer conserved quantities and fewer independent constants of Nature.

To most physicists the ultimate goal of their subject is nothing less than a determination of the numerical values of all the universal constants: the demonstration that they can possess only one possible set of self-consistent values and that this requirement of self-consistency, together with a minimum of symmetry principles, is sufficient to determine the structure of the world uniquely. This desideratum requires the development of theories in which the role of constants is deeper than that of mere proportionality constants. The existence of the proportionalities themselves must be contingent upon the value of the proportionality constants. This view has been continually echoed by different scientists in slightly more specific ways.

Einstein remarked with regard to the constants of Nature that

> I would like to state a theorem which at present cannot be based upon anything more than upon a faith in simplicity, that is, in the intelligibility of nature: there are no arbitrary constants of this kind; that is to say, Nature is so constituted that it is possible logically to lay down such strongly determined laws that within these laws only rationally completely determined constants appear (not constants therefore, whose value could be changed without destroying the theory). (Letter to I. Rosenthal-Schneider)

And

> I cannot imagine a unified and reasonable theory which explicitly contains a number which the whim of the Creator might just as well have chosen differently, whereby a qualitatively different lawfulness of the world would have resulted... A theory which in its fundamental equations explicitly contains a non-basic constant would have to be somehow constructed from bits and pieces which are logically independent of each other; but I am confident that this world is not such that so ugly a construction is needed for its theoretical comprehension. (Ibid.)

Here, we see a statement of a general belief concerning the existence of a unified theory of all aspects of Nature as well as a belief in the rational determination of all constants of Nature through the stipulation of self-consistency. This view has always been in opposition to the belief that the structure of the world, being an expression of the Creator's will, could have been different. Such a view, which was held by Newton with considerable passion, was the source of much of his long-running disagreement with Leibniz over the matter of God's interaction with the world.

Today, we have a more difficult job choosing between these two opposing expectations. On the one hand there may be some constants of

Nature which are built into the bedrock of reality, whilst others may be the result of sequences of quasi-random or random events. Even if we hold that members of the former class could not have been different, we must accept that the latter could well have been – and may in fact actually be different elsewhere in the Universe.

The quest to explain these pure numbers is horribly complicated by the expectations aroused by the latest attempts to find a Theory of Everything. Superstrings offer the possibility of calculating the constants of physics in terms of the mathematical symmetry dictated by self-consistency alone. However, the small collection of self-consistent theories do not have three dimensions of space like the world we live in. Two of the favourite theories have nine and 25 dimensions of space. These are to be reconciled with our present observation of three dimensions in some as yet undiscovered way. A process must be found which keeps all but three of the dimensions of space imperceptibly small. This expectation that there might well exist unseen dimensions of space opens the door to a wealth of new possibilities regarding the constants of Nature.

Suppose that our Universe possessed four space dimensions but that the fourth dimension was imperceptibly small. The real laws and constants would be those governing the full four-dimensional world. As a result our three-dimensional 'slice' of it will not reflect the true constants of Nature. In fact, our three-dimensional 'constants' (like Newton's constant of gravitation, for example) will be found to vary in time at a rate dictated by the rate at which the extra dimensions of space are changing in size. There is no understanding yet as to why three (and not some other number of) dimensions have grown to fifteen billion light years in size and are still expanding whilst any others remain small and evidently static.

The lesson we draw from these possible future directions of physics is that we may be living in a small slice through a Universe of more than three dimensions. The true laws and constants of Nature and their associated symmetries can thus be understood only when we have an appreciation of the whole Universe and not just our low-dimensional slice of it. The constants of Nature that we are seeing may be but the shadow of the true constants defining the fabric of the full multi-dimensional reality. Moreover, these strictures about the influence of extra dimensions are not baseless speculations. The superstring theories upon which the principal expectations of a Theory of Everything are based may require the presence of these extra dimensions of space. If, by mathematical consistency, they determine the numerical values of the constants of Nature then those constants will have to be projected in some way into the three dimensions we experience before being compared with the results of our experiments.

Superstring theories do not have the field to themselves when it comes to making predictions about the values of the constants of Nature. They have recently been joined by a rival idea of Sidney Coleman's. This proposal has been motivated by the attempts to derive a quantum description – a wavefunction – for the entire Universe which we mentioned earlier. From this wavefunction the probability of the Universe manifesting certain attributes can be deduced. It is deduced from a formulation of quantum theory analogous to Maupertuis' Principle of Least Action which we have already discussed. When quantum mechanics is formulated in this fashion it considers a particle to take all the possible paths from the initial to the final state. All these paths are then weighted together to give the probability that a particular path will be observed to be followed. By an extension of this principle to the cosmological problem one considers all the possible paths from some initial to a future state in the evolution of the Universe. Coleman proposed that certain very unusual paths should be incorporated into the collection of weighted paths – those involving 'wormholes'. These concepts, familiar in science fiction, are tubes joining widely separated parts of space-time. These are allowed but not required by the theory of gravitation. Remarkably, it appears that the interaction between these wormholes and the rest of the Universe can under certain circumstances determine the observed constants of Nature. However, these theories would not predict the values of the constants exactly. By reason of their quantum character they would provide only a probability distribution for their different possible values. It is hoped that these probabilities would be overwhelmingly concentrated around one particular value so that this could be taken to be the most likely *observed* value. Even so, we see here a downgrading of the status of fundamental constants of Nature into contingent quantities.

Coleman's idea has recently produced a deluge of interest in this problem. It appears that even if a superstring theory were to determine the basic values of the constants of Nature, the values would still be altered in some way by the influence of wormholes (if they exist). The net result would be the observed values of the constants. These may be calculable by including the wormhole effects, but they may turn out to be quite unpredictable because of the intrinsic information lost down the wormholes. They add an extra element of uncertainty into physics beyond that of traditional quantum theory. They also relate constants of Nature to some more basic topological and geometrical elements in the structure of space-time.

We have seen that a Theory of Everything need not tell us all the constants of Nature; but even if it does, we may find them altered by unusual space-time perturbations. The particular numerical values taken by the constants of Nature give our Universe its particular properties. They determine the density of matter around us, the sizes of planets and stars, and the large scale structure of the Universe. Any complete explanation of the physical Universe must tell us why these constants have the values they do.

## Broken Symmetries

The most awkward complication about the structure of the Universe is the propensity it possesses for broken symmetries. Even if we subscribe to a belief in the existence of laws of Nature based upon invariant symmetries we must recognize that we do not observe the laws of Nature directly. We observe the *outcomes* of those laws. From the standpoint of a mathematical formulation we would say that we observe the solutions of equations not the equations themselves. This is a vital distinction to draw because the outcomes of the laws of Nature need not possess the same symmetries as the laws themselves. We admit this implicitly when we set out to explain all the complicated states we see around us in the world in terms of simple laws.

This is one reason why astronomy and physics is so difficult. We observe the asymmetrical outcomes of symmetrical laws and are faced with the task of reconstructing the hidden symmetries from the lopsided evidence.

Before we delve a little further into the consequences of this dichotomy, it is enlightening to discuss how the history of some natural theology can be most effectively understood by focussing upon this distinction between laws and outcomes.

Since the Newtonian revolution there have been two strands to the traditional Design Argument for the existence of God. There have been those like Bentley who have focused upon the universality and mathematical precision of the laws of Nature themselves to argue for an Author of those laws. Our hymnbooks bear eloquent witness to the persuasiveness of those 'Laws which never shall be broken / For their guidance hath He made'.

This form of the Design Argument, from the laws of Nature (sometimes called the eutaxiological design argument), appealed most powerfully to physical scientists and astronomers. By contrast, there co-existed another form of teleological Design Argument which drew its examples from the marvellous adaptations evident in the natural world. Its staple consisted of apparent contrivances like the human eye and hand, or the way in which the natural environment was tailor-made for the creatures found in it. This is an argument which focuses upon the outworkings of the laws of Nature rather than upon the laws themselves. When the Darwinian hypothesis of natural selection was proposed it provided a general and simple explanation for the contrivances of the natural world – which we shall see, below, to be the broken symmetries – but it had no consequences at all for the form of the Design Argument based upon the laws of Nature themselves. If we study a classic like William Paley's *Natural Theology* then we find both strains of the Design Argument being presented by a writer who had graduated in mathematics but was also a keen naturalist. Yet, whenever one reads instant criticism of Paley, it cites his book as a paradigm of the (now) naive Design Argument from biological adaptation. There is no mention of the second half of his study which deals with the properties of the Newtonian laws of motion and gravitation. Interestingly, however, Paley himself favoured the biological examples because they are more firmly rooted in observation, and disliked the astronomical examples because there he was divorced from his favourite rhetorical device – analogy.

Let us consider some particular examples of symmetry breaking. Similar problems caught the eye of some ancient philosophers like Aristotle who considered the dilemma of a man, equally hungry and thirsty, caught midway between offerings of food and drink. And in medieval writings there is the famous story of Buridan's ass who starved to death unable to choose between two bales of hay equidistant from it.

If we balance a pencil vertically on its point, then the law of gravity which governs how it will fall when released does not favour any particular direction in space. Yet when the pencil is released it will always fall in some particular direction and the underlying symmetry is then broken. If dinner guests stand around a circular table each with napkins symmetrically placed on their right and left then the symmetry of the gathering will be broken by the first diner to take a napkin. If she reaches to the left then all the other guests will follow suit and the proceedings will have become left-handed.

Sometimes symmetry is broken spontaneously in this way but at others it may be violated in a particular realization of the laws of Nature by the starting conditions for the evolution. When a symmetry is broken the ensuing behaviour is complicated and there are no general rules known which tell us what will happen. It was once suspected that the situation tries to retain as much symmetry as possible but it is now known that this is not always the case. When a gauge symmetry is broken in a particular realization something unusual occurs. The carrier particle of the force of Nature that is required to implement the local gauge invariance will take on a mass. This is called the Higgs mechanism. It is based upon the presence of an energy field (the Higgs field) at every point in space and this field induces a mass for the carrier particle if symmetry breaking occurs. Some gauge symmetries, for example those giving rise to the forces of electromagnetism and gravitation, are not broken, and hence their respective carrier particles, the photon and the graviton, remain massless. But the gauge symmetry giving rise to the weak force is broken and the carrier particles, the W and Z bosons, thereby aquire masses. These W and Z bosons have been found to possess the masses predicted but the Higgs particle itself (a manifestation of the Higgs field) has yet to be discovered.

The phenomenon of symmetry-breaking introduces an essentially random element into the evolution of the Universe. Certain qualities of the Universe, for example the balance between matter and antimatter, may be determined from place to place by the particular way in which things fell out there. In the laboratory situation it is usually clear to us which aspects of a physical situation can be attributed to random symmetry breakings and so complete explanations are not sought for them in terms of the fundamental laws of Nature. This situation is characteristic of our understanding of the in-between world of condensed forms of matter that is of neither sub-molecular nor astronomical scale. By contrast, in a subject like cosmology we do not yet know which aspects of the large-scale structure of the Universe should be attributed to the laws of Nature and which to the random outworkings of those laws wherein the underlying symmetries are broken. This is a vital distinction to be able to make because if a feature of the Universe is a consequence of laws, or even of initial conditions, then there is a case for regarding it as a necessary feature of the Universe that could not have been otherwise. If, on the other hand, the feature is a consequence of symmetry breaking then it could have been otherwise and should not be regarded as a key indicator of the structure of Nature.

Thus, even if we are in possession of information about the laws of Nature, the initial conditions and the forces, particles and constants of Nature, but do not have an understanding of the way in which the symmetries of the laws of Nature and the initial conditions have been disguised by the hierarchy of random symmetry breakings that occur during the history of the Universe, our understanding will remain incomplete.

There is a form of symmetry breaking with a vengeance that has become of considerable topical interest. It is known as 'chaos'. Chaotic phenomena are those whose evolution exhibits extreme sensitivity to the starting state. Most complicated, messy phenomena – like turbulence or the weather – have this property. The significance of such behaviour was first recognized by Clerk Maxwell in the second half of the nineteenth century. When asked to lead a conversazione on the problem of freewill he drew his colleagues' attention to systems in which a minute uncertainty in their current state prevents us from accurately predicting their future state. Only if the initial state were known with perfect accuracy (which it cannot be) would the deterministic equations be of use. The neglect of such systems, which are the rule rather than the exception in Nature, led to a bias in favour of determinism in natural philosophy. He suggests rather that,

> Much light may be thrown on some of these questions by the consideration of stability and instability. When the state of things is such that an infinitely small variation of the present state will alter only by an infinitely small quantity the state at some future time, the condition of the system, whether at rest or in motion, is said to be stable; but when an infinitely small variation in the present state may bring about a finite difference in the state of the system in a finite time, the condition of the system is said to be unstable.
>
> It is manifest that the existence of unstable conditions renders impossible the prediction of future events, if our knowledge of the present state is only approximate, and not accurate... It is a metaphysical doctrine that from the same antecedents follow the same consequents. No one can gainsay this. But it is not of much use in a world like this, in which the same antecedents never again occur, and nothing ever happens twice... The physical axiom which has a somewhat similar aspect is 'That from like antecedents follow like consequences'. But here we have passed from sameness to likeness, from absolute accuracy to a more or less rough approximation. There are certain classes of phenomena, as I have said, in which a small error in the data only introduces a small error in the result... The course of events in these cases is stable.
>
> There are other classes of phenomena which are more complicated, and in which cases of instability may occur. (Campbell & Garnett, 1882, pp. 440-2)

The study of chaotic phenomena has proceeded with a methodology that differs significantly from that employed in traditional applications of mathematics to the physical world. In the past a complicated physical phenomenon like fluid turbulence would have been modelled by attempting to produce as accurate an equation as possible to describe its motions. However, the extreme sensitivity of this type of phenomenon to its initial state also means that it will be extremely sensitive to the form of this equation. If it contains even an infinitesimal inaccuracy or omission then very soon the modelled behaviour will deviate dramatically from that which would occur in the real world. As a result of this sensitivity, interest has turned to elucidating the general features of all possible equations.

Strictly speaking there can be no common properties of *all* possible equations because any property one cares to list will be manifested by some equation. However, if one refines expectations to the properties of *almost every* equation – that is, excluding only a set of very special cases that are highly unrealistic or improbable – then there do exist general properties common to all the remaining equations.

These studies of equations in general rather than equations in particular have revealed to us that chaotic behaviour is the rule rather than the exception. We have come to think of linear, predictable and simple phenomena as being prevalent in Nature because we are biased towards picking them out for study. They are the easiest to understand. But now we must swing around and regard it as a mystery that there are such a reasonable number of linear and simple phenomena in Nature. At root this is why the world is intelligible to us. Simple linear phenomena can be analysed in pieces. The whole is nothing more than the sum of its parts. Thus we can understand something about a system without understanding everything about it. Non-linear chaotic systems are different. They require a knowledge of the whole in order to understand the parts because the whole amounts to more than the mere sum of its parts.

Cosmological studies have found that the most general known models that could describe the very first moments of the Universe's expansion exhibit this chaotic sensitivity to the starting conditions. If the Universe undergoes some transition in which a number of its spatial dimensions are confined to an infinitesimally small extent then the number that escape this fate may be determined in a chaotically sensitive fashion by the conditions that exist in the very early Universe. How much of the Universe we are able to deduce from physical or logical principles may hinge precariously upon how delicate is the sensitivity to any initial conditions there may have been.

## Organizing Principles

So far we have been talking primarily about the situation that confronts the student of the very smallest or the very largest scales in Nature. However, there exist fundamental problems characteristic of the intermediate range of sizes and masses that we experience in between the realms of astronomy and elementary particles. In this in-between world there are structures which result from a balance between many competing forces far from thermal equilibrium. Things are complicated and sensitive to environment. They amount to more than the sum of their elementary constituents and display the subtleties characteristic of many bodies in mutual interaction.

If we want to understand the structure and evolution of complex systems then it is not sufficient to know the laws governing the basic intersections of Nature. It is necessary to possess additional information about the organization of the system and its complexity. Thus, for example, the laws of electromagnetism are necessary but not sufficient to explain the operation of a desk-top computer. Additional information is required to understand how the circuits are wired together and how the software is organized by its own logical rules. In particle physics and cosmology we have not encountered highly organized systems of this sort. It is only in the life sciences, in thermodynamics and in the study of condensed forms of matter that these new features come forcefully into play. Nonetheless, they raise important questions about what type of science is most basic. This issue has received considerable publicity during the last few years through the arguments concerning the level of funding required for the SSC (Superconducting Super Collider) in the United States. A powerful lobby of non-particle physicists argued strongly against the notion that particle physics was in any sense more fundamental than condensed state physics. Particle physicists argued that each discovery in physics pointed towards unanswered problems at smaller scales and to investigate such scales we require higher energies to be attained and hence bigger and better accelerators. At root this is a debate about the truth and nature of *reductionism.*

There are various common forms of reductionism. A useful classification and set of rough definitions is as follows:

1 *Ontological reductionism* claims there is no élan vital. The material content of the world can be reduced to the forces and elementary particles studied by physicists.
2 *Methodological reductionism* claims that all basic explanations must be deterministic, and cast in the language of mathematical physics. All explanation of complexity should be sought at lower levels, and ultimately at the level of elementary particles where the most basic laws of Nature apply.
3 *Epistemological reductionism* claims that 'laws' formulated in one area of science can always be reduced to special cases of those in other areas of science – for example, all psychology to biology, all biology to chemistry, all chemistry to physics.

There is no reason at present to disbelieve (1), no reason to believe (2), but every reason to maintain that (3) is false.

A classic phenomenon to which such notions are applicable is that of 'life'. Life and consciousness are recognized as phenomena that emerge when a particular level of complexity is attained. This complexity level is beyond our present ability to visualize or simulate. The most powerful computer that exists has information storage and processing capacity between ten and one thousand times less than that of the human brain. A high level of complexity is necessary but by no means sufficient to produce such intricate effects as 'thought' because we know that even at the chemical level very special environments and catalysts must be present in order to perform such complex functions.

Life can be viewed as a form of 'software' that runs on certain complex biomolecules. As such it cannot be 'explained' or reduced to the laws of physics that govern the forces of Nature any more than can the operation of a computer game like *Pac-Man*. A structure like the human brain is more complex than the underlying laws governing the chemical and atomic forces of Nature. It operates because of the way in which components are organized, just as a computer operates because of the way it is hard-wired together. Hence a knowledge of the individual operation of each of the brain's myriad of nerves and cells will not tell us how it works collectively any more than the subject of human anatomy could be used as a basis for predictive sociology. A knowledge of the alphabet is necessary but far from sufficient to produce the collective effects that Shakespeare achieved. There can be no laws of thought and action which are described by equations containing fundamental constants of Nature.

We should stress that we are not suggesting any form of vitalism – the discredited notion that living matter differs from all other matter by possessing some peculiar ingredient or *élan vital*. The manifest difference between living and non-living systems is not in basic atomic components but in the attainment of particular thresholds of complexity where new self-organizing principles can come spontaneously into play.

The *aficionados* of artificial intelligence in its strongest form take an operationalist view of the mind and define it to be nothing but the algorithmic content of its information-processing – that is, a piece of 'software' that produces particular outputs for each input. As such it can be mimicked or simulated by a computer, which can in turn be defined as intelligent if no operational procedure can distinguish a human's responses from its own. Alan Turing enabled the discussion to be carried forward in a rigorous fashion by isolating the basic attributes of all conceivable computation devices. They amount simply to an ability to read a finite string of numbers and then transform them into another finite string, over and over again. Such devices are now called 'Turing machines'.

We should first remark that even this goal could not be completely attained if the human mind carries out procedures which are *non-computable* mathematical functions and hence not within the scope of the action of a Turing machine. This could conceivably be true if quantum processes play some role on the scale of the human brain but there is as yet no positive evidence for such a view. If we lay to one side this tantalizing possibility, we might question the operationalist view that intelligence is nothing but an algorithm. Such a simple view seems to fail to distinguish between the processing of information which our brain carries out subconsciously, or when we dream, and *understanding* which we associate with conscious information processing. Whether this is a distinction without a difference is the question that the pursuit of artificial intelligence may one day answer. Moreover, it seems clear that the mind is not just one algorithm if only because (unlike systems of formal logic) we find it possible to hold the occasional pair of contradictory views without believing every possible statement to be true. But perhaps the prospects of unravelling the problem are not as promising as many naively think because even if the artificial intelligentsia are successful in their quest they will face curious new problems of understanding. If a complex mind were to be fabricated then the amount of information necessary to specify and understand it would be prohibitively high. Moreover, it would exhibit disconcerting properties like those that we call irrationality, free-will, subjectivity and probably the occasional statement of disbelief in artificial intelligence. A full understanding of such a machine would be impossible – and it would be a job for the psychologists and psychiatrist as much as for the computer scientist.

The attribute of self-reference plays some role in complex systems both at a 'hardware' and a 'software' level. This need not be very subtle. We could devise an 'expert' system capable of upgrading computer hardware and R(ead)O(nly)M(emory) circuits which is attached to a robotic motor system able to perform mechanical and electrical manipulations of the expert system itself. In this way it might appear to act with some purpose.

Biological systems possess teleological aspects, not in the form of some grand plan or final cause to which the whole course of the evolutionary process is heading and which determines their ultimate form, but by virtue of the fact that organisms surpassing a critical level of complexity exhibit intricate behaviour which can alter the way in which they subsequently evolve. Human beings are no longer entirely at the mercy of environmental forces and natural selection because we can imagine and simulate the effects of these pressures. We do not have to learn only by experiencing them. Our minds allow us to imagine many plausible futures and act accordingly.

From our discussion it should be clear that, whilst we are happy to believe in the reasonableness of ontological reductionism, there is no convincing reason to believe in methodological reductionism and every reason to maintain that epistemological reductionism is false. Large, complicated systems which exhibit chaotic behaviour and possess stable statistical properties argue against the methodological reductionist. The existence of laws of organization which are independent of the under-lying physical laws, the existence of teleonomic behaviour in living sys-tems, the requirement that anthropomorphic considerations be intro-duced in order to understand our observation of the Second Law of thermodynamics and the observed outworkings of cosmological models of the inflationary variety: all witness to the error of the epistemological reductionist and the shifting sands upon which the methodological reductionist is erecting his or her house. There are no fundamental laws of human history, no theorems about human behaviour, no laws of thought. We recall Werner Heisenberg's remarks in his Gifford Lectures of 1955:

> The concepts 'soul' or 'life' do not occur in atomic physics, and they could not, even indirectly, be derived as complicated consequences of some natural law. Their existence certainly does not indicate the presence of any fundamental substance other than energy, but it shows only the action of other kinds of forms which we cannot match with the mathematical forms of modern atomic physics... If we want to describe living or mental processes, we shall have to broaden these structures. It may be that we shall have to introduce yet other concepts.

Chaotic non-linear systems of the sort we discussed in the last section display remarkable propensities to generate ordered structures spontan-eously despite their superficial chaotic behaviour. Typically, such systems describe physical situations where there exists some connection of a local system with the outside environment, either in the form of a continuous throughput of energy, a consistent small perturbation, or disruption of the main system. As the outside influence is slowly altered a series of sudden changes occurs during which the behaviour of the local system changes in dramatic fashion. For example, if the speed of a flow of water from a tap is increased steadily there is a sudden transition to turbulent behaviour which displays new types of order. This common phenomenon of 'bifurcation' into qualitatively new types of behaviour when laws of Nature have non-linear aspects teaches us important lessons. First, it shows how sudden changes are to be expected rather than slow and gradual evolution to new equilibrium states. Second, it reveals how transitions can occur which move a complex non-linear system into a regime where qualitatively new types of law dictate what occurs. These laws of organization are not inconsistent with the basic laws of physics which govern the gross aspects of the physical phenomenon under study, but in no sense are they reducible to the fundamental laws governing the basic forces and elementary particles of Nature. The new structures which appear at the bifurcation points are associated with the appearance of new principles of complex-ordering which emerge when a particular threshold of complexity is crossed. The third lesson we draw from these spontaneously ordered phenomena is the importance of understanding 'chance' correctly. The intuitive view of random behaviour would persuade us that it is improbable that ordered behaviour arises spontaneously in Nature. But this assumption is based upon our intuitive feeling for the Gaussian 'law of large numbers' which is predicated upon the assumption that many *independent* events constitute the realm of possibilities. In particular, this is the situation when thermal equilibrium holds. However, when physical systems approach bifurcation points such an assumption is no longer valid. The long-range correlations within the system and the coupling to the outside world drive the system far from the equilibrium state which it would inhabit in the absence of external influences, and this makes the appearance of ordered structures probable. Flames are a familiar example of this out-of-equilibrium order. This is in complete contrast to the situation when the system is close to thermal equilibrium where the 'law of large numbers' applies.

This departure from the conventional reductionist story has many interesting parallels and extensions. In general, we see that there can exist strata of laws which govern physical situations not all of which are hierarchically reducible to one law. For example, the word-processor on which I am writing this page combines several complementary levels of law. There are the laws of quantum electrodynamics which control the basic atomic and sub-atomic structure of all the components of my personal computer's electronics. Then there is a set of software programming 'laws' which have been imposed upon that circuitry to produce the operating system of the computer. Then there are the rules of grammar, or in the case of a computer game, the rules of play which have been coded into the program disc. In no sense are the latter two sets of laws, which dictate the rules by which information can be processed, reducible to the quantum laws of Nature which govern the electromagnetic interactions of Nature. Such reductionism is logically impossible. Highly ordered systems possess propensities for organization that is novel. Laws of physics are necessary but not sufficient for their explanation.

At present there is a burgeoning interest in the study of complexity in order to find comprehensive ways of describing it and to discover whether there exist unknown general rules regarding its evolution in time. It is well known that Claude Shannon first invented the discipline now known as information theory, which describes certain aspects of the transfer of information and the influence of noise. However, his concept of information does not give a measure of the organizational *quality* of that information. Attempts to assess the quality of information in the abstract have focused upon the logical depth of the information or the amount of effort that must be expended to attain the organized state from a random beginning. It is hoped that some deep principles will emerge which will govern the evolution of a suitable measure of complexity. An earlier related idea is one which Frank Tipler and I have called the 'Final Anthropic Principle'. This is a conjecture about the possibility of indefinite information-processing in the Universe and might be more accurately termed the 'Final Anthropic Conjecture'.

The Final Anthropic Conjecture is that information processing can continue indefinitely to the future in our Universe and the total amount of information processed and stored can be infinite. Surprisingly, one cannot disprove this using known laws of physics. It is a subtle question because we face the problem of assessing how information can be stored (in quantum spin states of elementary particles for example), the ambient conditions in the future Universe and whether they allow signals to be discriminated above noise, whether free energy is available for processing, the presence of non-equilibrium behaviour, and finally, the nature of time. The latter is a delicate issue because there need be no correspondence between the duration of various measures of physical time such as the 'proper time' of special relativity and the number of bits processed in that time interval. It is possible for the Universe to have only a finite future in proper time and yet process an infinite number of bits of information. We have displayed cosmological models consistent with our known Universe in which an infinite number of bits are processed by some suitably defined computer throughout the future of the Universe. Surprisingly, it appears that no barrier to indefinite information processing is presented by the known laws of physics or the actual structure of the Universe. Since one can define a sufficient condition for the definition of 'life' based upon such computer architecture so long as some form of hardware exists, the hypothesis of indefinite information processing can be interpreted as one of whether 'life' (appropriately defined) can continue indefinitely once it has evolved spontaneously. If some deep unfound rules exist which govern information processing and organization in its most abstract form, irrespective of what hardware is being employed, then it will impinge in an important way upon this conjecture. The problems raised by the Final Anthropic Conjecture will be strongly entwined with any theory that develops about the growth of complexity in physical systems or the Universe as a whole.

In summary, we have stressed that many of the complex structures around us require us to know more than a Theory of Everything in order to understand them. They owe their complex, non-linear structures to the way complicated systems are organized. A Theory of Everything will shed no light upon the structure of the human brain and consciousness. It remains to be seen whether there exist unfound 'laws' governing information or complexity in general. Principles governing the make-up of complex states will be required to reconcile our understanding of the complicated observed states of the world with its simple laws.

## Selection Effects

No science can be founded upon observation alone. We would know neither what we were observing nor how our observations are biased by a propensity to gather some types of evidence more readily than others. As any good cross-examiner knows, certain types of evidence are more readily obtained than others. Consequently, the mark of a good experimentalist is the ability to understand and foresee these biases as completely as possible.

Scientists are familiar with two types of experimental 'error'; neither has anything necessarily to do with the everyday sense of the word 'error'. The first is the limiting accuracy with which a measurement can be made. This form of error always exists at some level and the aim of the scientist is to minimize it. The second variety of error – 'systematic error' – is more subtle and not necessarily avoidable. It requires some explanation. In laboratory experiments there is the possibility of repeating experiments with certain of the underlying conditions changed to investigate whether the results depend upon some of those conditions. However, in astronomy we are less fortunate. We can observe the Universe but we cannot alter its configuration so as to carry out controlled sequences of experiments upon it. We are faced with a confinitive system (where we are not at liberty to gather all the information we would like) rather than an infinitive system (where all conceivable observations can in principle be made), and we must therefore be aware of all the possible biases that may make certain observations inevitable. Thus, if we were to commission a survey of all the visible galaxies with a view to determining their relative brightnesses, we would have to deal with the in-built bias towards finding the brighter galaxies more easily than the fainter ones.

In cosmology this type of selection bias is all pervading and a recognition of the fact is enshrined in what has become known as the Weak Anthropic Principle. This is most usefully viewed as the recognition that our own existence requires certain necessary conditions to be met regarding the past and present structure of the visible universe. Our observations must not be viewed as having been taken from some unconstrained ensemble of possibilities but from some subset conditioned by the necessary conditions for carbon-based observers like ourselves to have evolved before the stars die. Cosmologists view the Weak Anthropic Principle as a qualification of the famous stricture of Copernicus that Humanity does not occupy a special position in the Universe. For although we rightly disregard the prejudice that our position in the Universe is special in *every* way, we should not conclude from this that our position cannot be special in *any* way. We could not exist within a star; we could not exist when the Universe was less than a million years old and temperatures were high enough to dissociate any atom or molecule. If the Universe did happen to possess a centre (there is no evidence that it does) and conditions were only conducive to the evolution and continued existence of life near that centre, then we should not be surprised to find ourselves living there. One of the most important features of the Weak Anthropic Principle – which is not a falsifiable scientific theory of any sort, simply a methodological principle – is that its disregard will lead to erroneous conclusions being drawn about the structure of the Universe. The most notable example is that of Dirac, who was misled into proposing a very radical change to the law of gravitation in order to explain a numerical coincidence between constants of Nature and the age of the Universe because it was not recognized that this coincidence was a necessary condition for the existence of observers.

The Universe, it was once assumed, existed within the framework of some vast unchanging background of space upon which all the observed motions of the heavenly bodies are played out. We have discovered that there is no such static cosmic stage. Everything that is – the entire visible Universe of stars and galaxies – is in a state of perpetual motion. The Universe is expanding: its clusters of galaxies are flying away from each other at a speed that increases in proportion to their separations. This cosmic recession is revealed to us by the systematic redshifting of the light from distant sources.

If we retrace the course of this expansion backward in time, we can visualize an apparent beginning to the current state of expansion, about fifteen billion years ago, when all separations extrapolate back to zero. Current cosmological research focuses upon events during the first fraction of a second after the apparent beginning. In these moments, the

Universe resembled a cosmic experiment in high-energy physics, the fall-out from which enables us to partially reconstruct its structure.

The problem of fitting human life into the impersonal tapestry of cosmic space and time has been pondered by mystics, philosophers, theologians and scientists of all ages. Their views straddle the entire range of options. At one extreme is painted the depressing materialistic picture of human life as a local accident, totally disconnected and irrelevant to the inexorable march of the Universe from the 'Big Bang' into a future 'Big Crunch' of devastating heat, or the eternal oblivion of the 'Heat Death'. At the other is preached the traditional teleological view that the Universe has some deep meaning, and part of that meaning is ourselves. On this optimistic view, we might not be surprised to find our local environment tailor-made for our needs. This latter view remained that of many biologists until, in the middle of the nineteenth century, Charles Darwin and Alfred Russel Wallace made their crucial observations and deductions of the evolutionary adaption of organisms to their environment. Since that time biologists have rejected any notion that evolution is goal-directed in any way. If the environment were to change in some unusual way so as to render intelligence a liability, then we would find ourselves following in the distinguished footsteps of the Dodo and the dinosaurs.

Cosmology does not have anything interesting to say about the detailed functioning and evolution of terrestrial life but it does have some surprising things to say about the necessary prerequisites for it. Let us take a simple but striking example. The visible universe is about fifteen billion light years across. It contains at least one hundred billion galaxies, each of which contains about one hundred billion stars like the Sun. Why is the Universe so big?

Living systems on Earth are based upon the subtle chemical properties of carbon and their interplay with hydrogen, nitrogen, phosphorus and oxygen. These biological elements, and all much-vaunted alternatives like silicon, do not emerge as fossils from the inferno of the Big Bang. They are the results of nuclear reactions in the interiors of the stars. There, primordial hydrogen and helium nuclei are burnt into heavier elements by the process of nuclear fusion. When these stars reach the ends of their lives they explode and disperse these biologically essential elements into space where they become incorporated into grains, planets and eventually people. Almost all the carbon atoms in our bodies share this dramatic astral history.

This process whereby Nature produces the biological building blocks of life from the inert relics of the Big Bang is long and slow by terrestrial standards. It takes more than ten billion years. More than ten billion years of stellar alchemy are necessary to provide the necessary precursors to life. Since the Universe is expanding we now discern why it is necessary for it to be at least ten billion light years in size. A Universe as big as our Galaxy has room for a hundred billion stars but it would be little more than a month old. There is a niche in the history of the Universe when life could and did evolve spontaneously. That niche is bounded on one side by the requirement that the Big Bang cool off sufficiently to allow stars, atoms and biomolecules to exist, and on the other by the fact that all the stars will have burned out after a hundred billion years.

The simple lesson to be drawn from this example is that the large scale structure of the Universe is unexpectedly bound up with those conditions necessary for the existence of living observers within it. When cosmologists are confronted with some extraordinary property of the Universe, they must temper their surprise by considering whether we would be here to be surprised if the Universe were significantly different. This type of 'weak anthropic' consideration is not a falsifiable conjecture or a theory. It is an example of a methodological principle which, if ignored, will lead one to draw incorrect conclusions from the data at hand.

The impact of ignoring this principle will depend upon the basic structure of the Universe. If there exists some intrinsically random element in the make-up of the Universe then it becomes crucial to our programme of understanding the physical world. If the Universe has one necessary and unique possible structure because there is only one possible logically consistent Universe then our Weak Anthropic selection effect allows us to conclude little more than our good fortune that 'the' Universe happens to allow life to evolve. However, we appreciate from our discussion of the role of symmetry breaking in Nature, that the Universe does not seem to be like this. There exist aspects of the Universe which could have been otherwise, and indeed may actually be otherwise in different parts of the cosmos. Earlier, we pointed out that in controlled terrestrial experiments we can repeat the experiment with various conditions altered. Hence, it is often straightforward to elucidate which phenomena display features intrinsic to the laws of Nature as opposed to those which are merely the consequence of some symmetry having broken one way rather than another. When we move to the astronomical realm things are not so clearcut. We do not know whether the sizes of galaxies and galaxy clusters are fundamental consequences of physical laws, of special initial conditions, or of some symmetry-breaking process having fallen out in one particular way.

Until only a few years ago this last option would have been regarded as a mere speculation with no basis in the favoured picture of the evolution of the very early Universe. This has now changed. The gradual maturing of the 'inflationary Universe' hypothesis, first proposed by Alan

Guth in 1980, has made the idea of a quasi-random beginning to the Universe appear a natural scenario. The inflationary Universe theory differs from the standard picture of the expanding Universe in one vital respect. Whereas the standard Big Bang expansion of the Universe decelerates at all times after the start (whether or not the expansion continues forever), an inflationary Universe has a brief period of accelerated expansion during its very early stages. This acceleration is created by the gravitational effect of a certain class of quantum matter fields whose existence is the key assumption upon which the whole theory rests. The effect of the accelerated expansion is to enable our entire visible Universe today (about fifteen billion light years across) to have expanded from a region small enough to be causally coherent at $10^{-35}$ seconds after the expansion begins (which is roughly when the acceleration would begin). In the standard decelerating Big Bang model the present-day visible Universe would have been $10^{25}$ times larger at that key time and must therefore arise from the expansion of billions of causally disjoint regions. This makes its present uniformity and coherence very difficult to understand. The inflationary hypothesis has a number of other appealing features: it leads naturally to a present-day Universe, like our own, which expands close to that critical divide separating indefinite future expansion from future recollapse and, moreover, it offers an explanation of where the fluctuations that lead to galaxies come from.

Now, suppose the Universe begins expanding from a state in which conditions vary from place to place, say in a random fashion. Then different microscopic regions will inflate by different amounts; that is, they will each undergo accelerated periods of varying length. Only those regions which grow large enough for stars, and hence life, to evolve will be sites for subsequent cosmological speculation. When we come to compare the predictions of this theory with observation and to understand the structure of the observed Universe in terms of this chaotic inflationary Universe theory we need to take into account the bias that is present in our observations of the Universe. Observations can only have been made in particular types of Universe. We would not be justified in excluding this theory from consideration on the grounds that the majority of the inflated regions are tiny. We would have to be living in one of the large ones regardless of how low was its *a priori* probability. Moreover, if the Universe is spatially infinite then our observations of a particular habitable backwater make the extrapolation to grandiose conclusions about the nature of the Universe as a whole precariously dependent upon untestable assumptions about the nature of the Universe beyond our visible horizon.

There is a further refinement of this chaotic inflationary picture of the early Universe in which the process of inflation is self-perpetuating. Each microscopic region that inflates creates the conditions for its own microscopic sub-regions subsequently to inflate and the process need never end. By the same token the region which you imagined as being the starting point for this sequence could form part of a past infinite sequence. Only in those members of the infinite sequence where the necessary conditions for the evolution of observers are met will cosmological deductions be drawn.

The influence of the Weak Anthropic Principle has grown as cosmologists have probed closer and closer to the initial state in their attempts to reconstruct the past history of the Universe. The closer one approaches to the apparent beginning so do the effects of symmetry breaking and quantum randomness proliferate to supply the intrinsically random elements that the Weak Anthropic Principle requires in order to play a significant role in the interpretation of the Universe. A nice topical example, which we introduced earlier, is the attempt to show that the values of the constants of Nature are determined by a certain type of interaction between regions of space-time through connecting tubes of space-time called 'wormholes'. This picture may allow us to predict the numerical values of the constants of Nature. In the examples studied, the quantum gravitational effects ensure that these values cannot be predicted exactly. Rather, we will find some probability distributions which will tell us the most probable values of the constants today. The simplest case to predict is that of the cosmological constant which appears (for no good reason in the standard picture of the Universe) to be zero – or at least to be so close to zero that it is as good as zero. When there is a cosmological constant the presence of wormholes creates stresses that mimic the presence of a cosmological constant of similar magnitude but of opposite arithmetical sign, so that a net cancellation occurs with high probability. This prediction looks like a success for this speculative theory but its likely predictions for other non-zero quantities – like the mass of the electron – do not look so promising. At present (and it is very early days for these speculative possibilities) the probability distributions for the values of physical constants other than the cosmological constant do not look as if they will peak around the observed non-zero values. However, one must be careful to take the Weak Anthropic Principle into account here. We should not be interested in the most probable values of the constants but the most probable values in a Universe which satisfies the conditions necessary for the evolution of observers. This can be quite different because those necessary conditions are connected to values of the fundamental constants of Nature in very intricate and sensitive ways. Amazingly, tiny changes in many of the fundamental constants of Nature prevent the existence of atom-based life of any sort.

We have seen that a complete understanding of our observations of the physical Universe requires an understanding of those elements which bias our observations and interpretations of data. If the Universe possesses intrinsically random elements in its make-up, inherited from its quantum origins or from random symmetry breakings during its early evolution, then we must take our own existence into account when evaluating the correspondence between reality and the predictions of our Theory of Everything. Moreover, if these random cosmological elements lead to a Universe which differs significantly from place to place over very large distances, then our local observations of a possibly infinite Universe will inevitably leave our knowledge of its global structure seriously incomplete.

## Categories of Thought

It has been widely recognized, at least since the time of Kant's critical writings, that there exists a barrier between reality and our perception of it that is erected by the modes of human thinking. For some scientists, like Eddington, this barrier looms large and they regard our successful theories of Nature as mere pieces of mental scaffolding erected to organize the edifice of sense data that we amass about reality. Because of Kant's early influence it has been traditional to suspect the influence of human categories of thought to be both significant and irreducible. However, there are interesting biological arguments that can be presented in support of the realist case for a negligible distortion of reality by human observation.

Kant's categories of thought need not place a significant barrier between our understanding of the world and the bedrock of reality. For our minds and their categories of thinking are the products of the evolutionary process. Like our other bodily features they are the products of a natural selective process in which reality (rather than perceived reality) dictates what survives. Accordingly, our eyes have evolved as effective light detectors in tune with the real properties of light and they carry information about the real nature of light; our ears, likewise, encode information about the reality of sound. By the same token, our minds should be clear recorders of those aspects of reality that are crucial for the evolution of sentience. If our mental categories were distorting reality then we would not have survived. Certain basic mathematical notions like symmetry and geometry and counting could thus have emerged in the human mind as reflections of external reality.

Nonetheless, one might be wary of taking this argument too far. Whilst, if correct, it promotes confidence in our images of those parts of Nature that play a crucial role in the evolution of life and consciousness, it gives us no grounds for confidence in their faithfulness when we move into the esoteric realms of quantum physics and cosmology. For the concepts unique to these disciplines appear to play no role in human evolution.

The most all-consuming category of thought that dominates our deepest images of the physical Universe is mathematics. Mathematics is the 'language' that allows us to talk most effectively, efficiently and logically about the nature of things. But this mathematical language differs from other languages. It is not like English or Spanish. It is more like a computer language because it possesses a built-in logic. When we write a grammatically correct English sentence like 'All dogs have four legs and my table has four legs therefore my table is a dog', there is no guarantee that the sentence either be logically correct or have a correspondence with events in the world. Conversely, the grammatical incorrectness of a sentence like 'To boldly go where no man has gone before' does not render its realization impossible. The rules of English grammar can be broken without sacrificing meaning. But break a rule of mathematics and disaster ensues. If any false mathematical statement is allowed it can be used to prove the truth of *any* mathematical statement. When Bertrand Russell once made this claim during a lecture he was challenged by a sceptical heckler to prove that the questioner was the Pope if twice 2 were 5. Russell at once replied that 'If twice 2 is 5, then 4 is 5, subtract 3; then 1 = 2. But you and the Pope are 2; therefore you and the Pope are one'.

So mathematics is a language with a built-in logic. But what is so striking about this language is that it seems to describe how the world works: not just sometimes, not just approximately, but invariably and with unfailing accuracy. All the fundamental sciences – physics, chemistry and astronomy – are mathematical sciences. No phenomenon has ever been discovered in these subjects for which a mathematical description is not only possible but often beautifully appropriate. 'A rose by any other name would smell as sweet' but not a rose by any other number. Yet one could still fail to be impressed. After the fact, we can force any hand into some glove and maybe we have chosen to pick the mathematical glove because it is the only one available. Yet, it is striking that physicists so often find some esoteric pattern, invented by mathematicians in the dim and distant past only for the sake of its elegance and curiosity value, to be precisely what is required to make sense of new observations of the world. In fact, confidence in mathematics has grown to such an extent that one expects (and finds) interesting mathematical structures to be deployed in Nature. Scientists look no further after they have found a mathematical Explanation.

Mathematics is no longer treated as a category of explanation, it has become the definition of explanation.

There are many striking examples of the unexpected and unreasonable effectiveness of mathematics. In 1914, when Einstein was struggling to create a new description of gravity to supersede that of Newton, he wished to endow the Universe of space and time with a curved geometry and write the laws of Nature in a form that would be found the same by any observers no matter what their state of motion. His old student friend, the mathematician Marcel Grossman, introduced him to a little-known branch of nineteenth-century mathematics that was tailor-made for his purposes. In modern times particle physicists have discovered that symmetry dictates the way elementary particles behave. Collections of related particles can behave in any way they choose so long as a particular abstract pattern is preserved. The laws of Nature are treated as the catalogue of habitual things that can occur in the world and yet preserve these patterns – in effect they define all those things that you can do to the world without changing its essence. To every such catalogue of changes we can ascribe an unchanging pattern although the pattern is often subtle and rather abstract. In the last century mathematicians set about investigating all the possible patterns that one could invent. These patterns are represented most basically by a branch of mathematics called 'group theory'. The catalogue of mathematical patterns that the early group theorists established have become the guiding force in the study of elementary particles. So successful were the simple patterns of the group theorists in describing the way the forces and particles of Nature behave, that physicists have taken to exploring all the possible patterns on a trial and error basis to discover those that give the most interesting consequences if used in the construction of the Universe.

In this way the expectation that elegant mathematical ideas will be found in Nature allows detailed predictions to be made about the behaviour of elementary particles. Experiments at particle accelerators enable these aesthetic fancies to be tested against the facts. The theory of superstrings has become a focal point of interest and has also created a new phenomenon. For the first time fundamental physicists have run into concepts that require the extension of known mathematical structures to cope with them. For the first time 'off the shelf' mathematics has proved insufficient to unravel all the patterns. Elsewhere, the beautiful subject of fractals has revealed itself to underwrite the whole spectrum of natural phenomena – from the clustering of galaxies to the crystalization structure of snowflakes. Again, fractals were once no more than an idiosyncratic branch of mathematics investigated for its own sake. Fractal pictures offer striking images that resonate with our aesthetic sense of beauty. Presumably the reason again has roots in our evolutionary history. For we have discovered that many aspects of the Earth's natural scenery – mountain ranges, snowflakes, trees and plants – that we find so visually appealing owe their structure, like fractals, to the process of self-similarity; that is, to the reproduction of a basic pattern over and over again on many different size scales.

Science seems to believe so deeply in the mathematical structure of Nature that it is an unquestioned article of faith that mathematics is both necessary and sufficient to describe everything from the inner space of elementary particles to the outer space of distant stars and galaxies – even the Universe itself. What are we to make of the ubiquity of mathematics in the constitution of the Universe? Is it evidence of a deep logic within the Universe: if so, where does that logic come from? Is it just a creation of our own minds or is God a mathematician after all?

We are confronted by a mystery. Why does the symbolic language of mathematics have everything to do with the falling apples, splitting atoms, exploding stars or fluctuating stock markets? Why does reality follow a mathematical lead? The sort of answers we can offer to such puzzling questions depend crucially upon what we think mathematics actually is. There are four clear options – *formalism, inventionism, realism* and *constructivism*

At the beginning of this century mathematicians faced several bewildering problems which rocked their confidence. Logical paradoxes like that of the barber ('A barber shaves all those individuals who do not shave themselves. Who shaves the barber?') or the dilemma of the set of all sets that are not members of themselves threatened to undermine the entire edifice. And who could foresee where the next paradox might surface? In the face of such dilemmas David Hilbert, the foremost mathematician of the day, proposed that we cease worrying about the *meaning* of mathematics altogether. Instead, *define* mathematics to be no more and no less than the tapestry of formulae that can be created from any set of initial axioms by manipulating the symbols involved according to specified rules. This procedure, it was believed, could not create paradoxes. The vast embroidery of interwoven logical connections that results from the manipulation of all the possible starting axioms according to all the possible non-contradictory collections of rules is what mathematics 'is'. This is *formalism.*

Clearly, for Hilbert and his disciples the miraculous applicability of mathematics to Nature is something about which they neither care nor seek to offer any explanation. Mathematics does not have any *meaning.* The axioms and rules for the manipulation of symbols are not connected with observed reality in any necessary way. Formulae exist on pieces of paper but mathematical entities have no other claim to existence whatsoever. The formalist would no more offer an explanation for the mathematical character of physics than seek to explain why physical phenomena do not obey the rules of poker or black-jack.

Hilbert thought that this strategy would rid mathematics of all its problematic areas – by definition. Given any mathematical statement it would be possible in principle to determine whether it was a true or false conclusion from any particular set of starting assumptions by working through the logical network of connections. Hilbert and his disciples set to work confident that they could trammel up all known mathematics within this strait-jacket. Unfortunately, and totally unexpectedly, the enterprise collapsed overnight. In 1931, Kurt Gödel, an unknown young mathematician at the University of Vienna, showed Hilbert's goal to be unattainable. Whatever set of consistent starting axioms one chooses; whatever set of consistent rules one adopts for manipulating the mathematical symbols involved; there must always exist some statement framed in the language of those symbols whose truth or falsity cannot be decided using those axioms and rules. Mathematical truth is something larger than axioms and rules. Try solving the problem by adding a new rule or a new axiom and you just create new undecidable statements. Checkmate – Hilbert's programme cannot work. If you want to understand mathematics fully you have to go outside of mathematics. If a 'religion' is defined to be a system of ideas that contains unprovable statements then Gödel has taught us that, not only is mathematics a religion, it is the only religion that can prove itself to be one.

*Inventionism* is the belief that mathematics is simply what mathematicians do. Mathematical entities like sets or triangles would not exist if there were no mathematicians. We invent mathematics: we do not discover it. The inventionist is not very impressed by the effectiveness of describing the world by mathematics. The reason that we find mathematics so useful is perhaps merely an indication of how little we know of the physical world. It is only the properties well-suited to mathematical description that we have been able to uncover.

This view of mathematics is more commonly held by 'consumers' of mathematics – social scientists or economists for example – than by mathematicians themselves. It is closely associated with a non-realist philosophical viewpoint. Although there may exist some ultimate reality we cannot apprehend this except by filtering our observations and experience of it through certain mental categories which order it for our understanding. So, although we see the Universe to be mathematical, this does not mean that it really *is* mathematical any more than the sky is pink because it looks that way when we wear rose-coloured spectacles.

If mathematics were entirely a human invention and used by scientists simply because it is useful and available then we might expect significant cultural differences within the subject. However, whereas there are discernable styles in the presentation of mathematics and in the type of mathematics investigated in different cultures, this is just a veneer. The independent discovery of the same mathematical theorems by different mathematicians from totally different economic, cultural and political backgrounds at different times throughout history argues against such a simple view. Moreover, this unusual phenomenon of the independent multiple invention of the same mathematical truth sets creative mathematics apart from music or the arts. Pythagoras' theorem was independently discovered many times by different thinkers. It is inconceivable that Shakespeare's 'Hamlet' or Beethoven's fifth symphony could be independently duplicated. This contrast argues that the foundation of mathematics lies outside of the human mind and is not totally fashioned by our human way of thinking.

The most straightforward view of mathematics is to maintain that the world *is* mathematical in some deep sense. Mathematical concepts exist and they are discovered by mathematicians, not invented. Mathematics exists whether or not there are mathematicians. It is a universal language that could be used to communicate with beings on other planets who had developed independently of ourselves. For the realist, the number seven exists as an immaterial idea which we see realized in specific cases like seven dwarfs, seven brides or seven brothers. It is sometimes called *mathematical Platonism* because it assumes that there exists some other world of perfect mathematical forms which are the blueprints from which our imperfect experience is derived. Moreover, our mental processing of sense data is assumed to have a harmless effect upon the mathematical nature of reality. Realism of this sort seems tantamount to the view that God is a mathematician. And indeed, if the entire material Universe is described by mathematics (as modern cosmology assumes) then there must exist some immaterial logic that is larger than the material Universe.

The introduction of a Platonic interpretation of mathematics produces a striking parallel between mathematics and philosophical theology. The entire panoply of properties and attributes of God developed by early neo-Platonic religious philosophers can be taken over almost word for word to describe mathematics if we replace the word 'God' by 'mathematics'. The mathematics of the Platonist transcends the world and is viewed as existing both before and after the creation of the material world. When ancient philosophers tried to integrate concepts like the laws of Nature into a theological picture of the Universe they succeeded without great difficulty. Moreover, they were able to incorporate suspensions of the laws of Nature, or miracles, in suitable ways. But the omnipotence of God rides awkwardly with mathematics. We can imagine a suspension or breach of a law of Nature (especially since we observe the outcomes of laws and not the laws themselves) but what about a breach of a law of logic or mathematics? Opinion was deeply divided over whether the omnipotence of God could run to creating a world where mathematical impossibilities exist. Spinoza believed that this freedom existed but ranged against him was the view that God did not have any such freedom of manoeuvre because it did not exist. This appears to make the Deity subservient to the laws of mathematics and logic. Platonic mathematical reality was a rival to an omnipotent, omnipresent Deity. One can pursue this argument further and discover analogues of dilemmas like the problem of evil and even the issue of revelation versus reason in mathematical discovery. But this would take us too far afield.

Realism regards the unreasonable effectiveness of mathematics in the description of Nature as crucial evidence in its support. Most scientists and mathematicians carry out their day-to-day work as if realism were true even though they might be loath to defend it too strongly at the weekend. But realism of this sort has a most extraordinary consequence. If we can conceive of any mathematical scheme for the evolution of the Universe in which observers like ourselves can exist (and clearly we can conceive of such a scenario) then this scenario 'exists' in every sense of the word. Intelligent observers must exist.

*Constructivism* was another response to the foment of uncertainty about logical paradoxes that spawned formalism in the early years of this century. Its starting point, according to Kronecker, one of its creators, was the recognition that 'God made the integers, all else is the work of man'. What he meant by this was that we should accept only the simplest possible mathematical notions – that of the whole numbers 1, 2, 3, 4,... and counting – as a starting point and then derive everything else from these intuitively obvious notions step by step. By taking this conservative stance the constructivist wished to avoid encountering or manipulating entities like infinite sets about which we could have no concrete experience and which have counter-intuitive properties (infinity minus infinity = infinity, for instance). Mathematics now consists of the collection of statements that can be constructed in a finite number of deductive steps from the starting point of the whole numbers. The 'meaning' of a mathematical formula is simply the finite chain of computations that have been used to construct it. This view may sound harmless enough but it has dire consequences. It creates a new category of mathematical statement. Its status can now be true or false or *undecided*. A statement whose truth cannot be decided in a *finite* number of constructive steps is given this latter limbo status. The most important consequence of this policy is that a statement is no longer either true or false. This trichotomy is reminiscent of Scottish courts of law, where a verdict of guilty, not guilty or 'not proven' may be returned (the latter permits a retrial of the defendant on the same charge), whereas English or American courts require a verdict of either guilty or not guilty.

Pre-constructivist mathematicians had developed all manner of ways of proving formulae to be true that do not correspond to a finite number of constructive steps. One famous method beloved of the ancient Greeks is the *reductio ad absurdum*. To show something to be true we assume it to be false and from that assumption deduce something contradictory (like $2 = 1$). From this we conclude our original something to have been true. This argument is based upon the presumption that a statement which is not false is true. Therefore it is an invalid move according to the constructivists' rules. The whole body of mathematical theorems which prove that something exists but do not construct an example of it explicitly are outlawed.

This philosophy of mathematics would have interesting but largely unexplored consequences if adopted in physics because many important physical theories, like Einstein's general relativity or Niels Bohr's quantum mechanics, make important use of non-constructive reasoning in deducing properties of the Universe. To most mathematicians such a strategy seems rather depressing, tantamount to fighting with one arm tied behind your back. There are a number of theorems in cosmology and black-hole physics with non-constructive proofs which establish something to be true by deriving a contradiction from the assumption that it is false. One example is a proof that black holes cannot split into pieces. Also, a number of formulations of the famous 'cosmic censorship hypothesis' have forms which would require non-constructive proofs.

In general all physicists use non-constructive mathematical arguments without a second thought. The only area of physics where the restriction to constructive methods and its accompanying three-valued logic has been investigated closely is in the quantum measurement problem where it has been proposed as a way of accommodating the issues raised by the Einstein-Podolsky-Rosen paradox. Yet if a constructivist view is at root the correct one it radically affects our attempts to deduce a Theory of Everything. How such a view might be forced upon us by adopting a computational paradigm for the Universe, we shall discuss shortly.

There have always been passionate advocates of the constructivist interpretation of mathematics. One particularly dogmatic supporter was the leading Dutch mathematician Luitzen Brouwer who, whilst an editor of the German journal *Mathematische Annalen* (the foremost mathematical journal of the day) declared war on non-constructivist mathematicians by rejecting any papers submitted for publication which used non-constructive methods, infinities or the *reductio ad absurdum*. This created a considerable rumpus amongst mathematicians. The other members of the editorial board resolved the crisis by resigning *en bloc* and then recreating a new editorial board – excluding Brouwer. The Dutch government viewed this as an insult to their distinguished countryman and responded by creating a rival journal with Brouwer as editor.

Now what has constructivism to say about the mathematical character of Nature? We can see that it inherits something of what remained of Hilbert's formalist programme following its devastation by Gödel's discovery. We learn that there must always be some statements whose truth we can neither prove nor disprove, but what about all those statements whose truth we can decide by the traditional methods of mathematics. How many of them could the constructivists prove? Can we build, at least in principle, a computer which reads input, displays the current state of the machine and possesses a processor for determining a new state from its present one, and use it to decide whether a given statement is true or false after a finite time? Is there a specification for a machine that will decide for us whether all the decidable statements of mathematics are either true or false? Contrary to the expectations of many mathematicians the answer was again *no*. Alan Turing in Cambridge, and Emil Post and Alonzo Church in Princeton, showed that there were statements whose truth would require an infinite time to decide. They are, in effect, infinitely deeper than the logic of step-by-step computation. The idealized computer is simply the Turing Machine we introduced earlier; it is the essence of every computer. No real existing computer is believed to possess greater problem solving ability.

The mathematical operations that a Turing machine cannot perform in finite time are called *non-computable*. Many examples are known and could have many interesting physical consequences. We do not know whether Nature incorporates non-computable things into its fabric. If, for example, the action of the human mind or the phenomenon of human consciousness involve non-computable operations then the quest for artificial intelligence cannot succeed in producing computer hardware able to mimic the complexity of human consciousness completely. Whether such a restriction would be of any practical interest depends of course upon how crucial the non-computable aspects are to brain function. At present it seems unlikely that this is the case.

If we return to the puzzle of the applicability of mathematics to Nature we can cast it into an interesting statement about computability. If an operation is computable it means that we can fabricate a device from matter whose behaviour mimics that operation. Typical devices might be swinging pendulums or electrical impulses. By the same token, physical devices like these can be well described by computable mathematical operations. The fact that Nature is well described by mathematics is equivalent to the fact that the simplest mathematical operations, like addition and multiplication, along with the more complicated operations used so effectively in science, are computable functions. If they were not then they could not be equivalent to any natural process and we would not be terribly impressed by the practical usefulness of mathematics.

It is a fascinating question to ask whether or not the laws of Nature contain non-computable elements. Already the quest to create a quantum theory of the whole Universe has created this possibility. There exist potentially observable attributes of the Universe defined by infinite sums of terms which possess no computable listing. They cannot be listed by any systematic calculation which just applies the same principles over and over again. Each entry requires qualitatively different and novel principles to be used for its itemization.

Our categories of thought are often biased by certain cultural trends. Our images of the Universe have a tendency to make use of fashionable concepts which have proven useful in more mundane circumstances. Thus we find in ancient times the image of the Universe as an organism or as the expression of static geometrical harmony. For Newton and the users of the newly invented pendulum clock it was the image of the clockwork Universe that held sway. For the Victorians of the Industrial Revolution it was the machine or the heat engine that was the dominant paradigm. Today, it is the computer and the microchip that govern our everyday life. It is too much to expect the paradigm of the computer to be ignored in the quest to understand the Universe.

The computer invites us to abstract its essence. Stripped of its accoutrements of hardware and task-specific software, it is a Turing machine – a processor of information, a mapping of one finite string of integers into another. We might take this image with a Kuhnian pinch of salt as the latest in a never-ending sequence of fashions of explanation to be discarded when the next technological revolution occurs. Aware of this possibility, let us nonetheless assume computation to have non-ephemeral significance. We can ask ourselves whether it is more basic to view the evolution and structure of the Universe as a computation or as the consequences of laws of Nature. Or, merging the two concepts, whether we should treat the laws of Nature as though they are a form of software that happens to be running upon the material content of our Universe. Whereas the picture of laws of Nature as symmetries and invariances so beloved by the physicist blends naturally with the Platonic view of mathematical reality, the computational picture seems to point more naturally to the more limited constructivist view.

The most fruitful outcome from a computational image of Nature is that it reveals the bare bones of why Nature is intelligible to us, why science is possible, and why mathematics is so effective in the description of the physical world.

If we are presented with a sequence of numbers or symbols then it may be possible to replace the list by an abbreviated statement which has identical information content. Thus the infinite sequence of numbers 2, 4, 6, 8, 10,... could be replaced by the formula for generating the even numbers. We say that our sequence is *algorithmically compressible*. A random sequence is characterized by the fact that there is no formula shorter than itself that encapsulates it (it is an interesting consequence of Gödel's undecidability theorem that one cannot prove a sequence to be random in this sense). Truly random sequences cannot be compressed into simplifying formulae. They are algorithmically incompressible: defined by nothing less than their own listing. Science exists because the natural world appears to be algorithmically compressible. The mathematical formulae that we call laws of Nature are economical compressions of huge sequences of data about how the states of the world change. This is what it means for the world to be intelligible. We can conceive of a world in which most phenomena were chaotically random (just as some of them are seen to be). Its properties could only be described by listing innumerable time sequences of observed phenomena. Science would become more like train-spotting. Observed phenomena would have that uniqueness which we find in the world of creative art. If the Universe is a unique and necessary entity then we might not be surprised to find the Universe as a whole to be an algorithmically incompressible entity: ultimately irreducible to any abbreviated formula: defined most simply by nothing less than its complete unfolding sequence of events. The search for a Theory of Everything is the ultimate expression of our faith in the algorithmic compressibility of Nature.

Mathematics is useful in the description of the physical world because the world is algorithmically compressible. It is the language of sequence abbreviation. The human mind allows us to make contact with that world because the brain possesses the ability to compress complex sequences of sense data into abbreviated form. These abbreviations permit the existence of thought and memory. The natural limits of sensitivity that Nature imposes upon our sensory organs prevent us from being overloaded with information about the world. These limits act as a safety valve for the mind. Yet we still owe everything to the brain's remarkable ability to exploit the algorithmic compressibility of the world. And most remarkable of all, the brain is an evolved complex state of the very world whose complexity it seeks to compress, albeit one that has yet to fathom its own complexity.

## SELECT BIBLIOGRAPHY

The following bibliography is designed to allow the interested reader to delve further into the topics covered in this chapter. The works cited are at a variety of different levels; some are designed for the general reader whilst others are suitable only for those who possess some background in mathematics and physics. It includes works published in the years after the series of lectures from which this chapter is drawn were delivered. More detailed discussions of many of the topics included in this chapter are to be found in the author's four books *The Anthropic Cosmological Principle* (1986), *The World Within the World* (1988), *Theories of Everything* (1991) and *Pi in the Sky* (1992), referenced under 'Introduction', 'Laws of Nature', 'Selection Effects' and 'Categories of Thought', below.

*Introduction*
Barrow, J. D., *Theories of Everything* (Oxford University Press, 1991).
Bettelheim, B., 'The Uses of Enchantment'. In C. Blacker and M. Loewe (eds), Ancient Cosmologies, (Allen & Unwin, 1975).
Chaitin, G., *Algorithmic Information Theory* (Cambridge University Press, 1987).
Lewis, C. S. *The Discarded Image* (Cambridge University Press, 1964).
Lloyd, S. and Pagels, H., Complexity as Thermodynamic Depth. *Annals of Physics* (US), 188, 186 (1988).
Pagels, H., *The Cosmic Code* (Schuster, 1982).
Rescher, N., Some Issues Regarding the Completeness of Science and the Limits of Scientific Knowledge. In G. Radnitzky & G. Anderson (eds), *The Structure and Development of Science*, (Reidel, 1979, pp. 15–40).
von Weizsäcker, C. F., *The Relevance of Science* (Collins, 1964).
Smith, J. W., *Essays on Ultimate Questions* (Avebury, 1988).
Yates, F. A., *Giordano Bruno and the Hermetic Tradition*, (Routledge & Kegan Paul, 1964).

*Laws of Nature*
Barrow, J. D., *The World Within The World* (Oxford University Press, 1988).
Boscovich, R. J., *A Theory of Natural Philosophy*, English translation of Venice edition of 1763, (MIT Press, 1966).
Chaitin, G., Randomness in Arithmetic. *Scientific American* (July 1988) p. 80.
Cobb, J. B. and Griffin, D. R., *Process Theology: an Introductory Exposition* (Westminister Press, 1976).
Feynman, R., *The Character of Physical Law* (MIT Press, 1965).
Funkenstein, A., *Theology and the Scientific Imagination from the Middle Ages to the Seventeenth Century* (Princeton University Press, 1986).

Jaki, S., *The Relevance of Physics* (University of Chicago Press, 1966).
Needham, J., *The Grand Titration: Science and Society in East and West*, (Allen & Unwin, 1969).


*Initial Conditions*
Barrow, J. D. and Silk, J., *The Left-hand of Creation* (Basic Books, 1983).
Bondi, H., *Cosmology* (Cambridge University Press, 1953).
Bondi, H., The Steady-State Theory of the Universe. In H. Bondi, W. B. Bonnor, R. A. Lyttleton and G. J. Whitrow (eds), *Rival Theories of Cosmology* (Oxford University Press, 1960).
Craig, W. L., *The Cosmological Argument from Plato to Leibniz* (Macmillan, 1980).
Davidson, H. A., *Proofs for Eternity, Creation and the Existence of God in Medieval Islamic and Jewish Philosophy* (Oxford University Press, 1987).
Drees, W., *Beyond the Big Bang: Quantum Cosmologies and God* (Open Court, 1990).
Grunbaum, A., The Pseudo-Problem of Creation in Cosmology. *Philosophy of Science* 56, 373 (1989).
Guth, A., The Inflationary Universe: A Possible Solution to the Horizon and Flatness Problems. *Physical Review* D 23, 347 (1981).
Guth, A. and Steinhardt, P., The Inflationary Universe. *Scientific American* (May 1984) p. 116.
Hartle, J. B. and Hawking, S. W., Wave Function of the Universe. *Physical Review* D 28, 2960 (1983).
Hawking, S. W., *A Brief History of Time* (Bantam, 1988).
Nasr, S., *Introduction to Islamic Cosmological Doctrines* (Harvard University Press, 1964).
Russell, R. J., Stoeger, W. R., and Coyne, G. V., *Physics, Philosophy and Theology* (University of Notre Dame Press, 1988).
Sorabji, R., *Time, Creation and the Continuum* (Duckworth, 1983).
Vilenkin, A., Creation of Universes from Nothing. *Physics Letters* 117B, 25 (1982).
Whitehead, A. N., *Adventures of Ideas* (Cambridge University Press, 1933).
Whitehead, A. N., *Science and the Modern World* (Cambridge University Press, 1953)  .


*Forces and Particles*
Bailin, D., Why Superstrings. *Contemporary Physics* 30, 237 (1989).
Green, M., Superstrings. *Scientific American* (Sept. 1986) p. 48.
Jammer, M., *Concepts of Force* (Harvard University Press, 1957).
Pagels, H., *Perfect Symmetry* (Joseph, 1985).
Peat, F. D., *Superstrings and the Search for the Theory of Everything* (Contemporary Books, 1988).
Schwarz, J. H., Superstring Unification. In S. W. Hawking and W. Israel (eds), *300 Years of Gravitation* (Cambridge University Press, 1987) p. 652.
Wilczek, F. and Devine, B., *Longing For The Harmonies* (Norton, 1988).
Wilczek, F., Gauge Theories of Swimming. *Physics World* 2, 36 (1989).
Zee, A., *Fearful Symmetry: The Search for Beauty in Modern Physics* (Macmillan, 1986).

*Constants of Nature*

Barrow, J. D., Observational Limits on the Time-evolution of Extra Spatial Dimensions. *Physical Review* D 35, 1805 (1987).

Barrow, J. D., Constants of Physics and the Structure of the Universe. In M. Batato, R. Behn, J-F. Loude and H. Weisen (eds), *Saas Fee Lectures on Unites de Mesure et Constantes Physique* (Lausanne, Assoc Vaudoise des Chercheurs en Physique, 1988 ), ch.5.

Barrow, J. D., The Mysterious Lore of Large Numbers. In S. Bergia and B. Bertotti, (eds), *Modern Cosmology in Retrospect* (Cambridge University Press, 1990).

Carr, B. J., and Rees, M. J., The Anthropic Principle and the Structure of the Physical World. *Nature* 278, 605 (1979).

Coleman, S., Why There is Nothing Rather Than Something: A Theory of the Cosmological Constant. *Nuclear Physics* B 310, 643 (1988).

Hawking, S. W., Wormholes in Space-time. *Physical Review* 37, 904 (1988).

Hawking, S. W., Baby Universes. *Modern Physics Letters* A 5, 453 (1990).

Jungnickel, C. and McCormmach, R., *Intellectual Mastery of Nature: Theoretical Physics from Ohm to Einstein* (University of Chicago Press, 1986).

Levy-Leblond, J. M., Constants of Physics. *Rivista Nuovo Cimento* 7, 187 (1977).

McCrea, W. H., and Rees, M. J., (eds) *The Constants of Physics* (The Royal Society, 1983).

Pais, A., *Subtle is the Lord: The Science and Life of Albert Einstein* (Oxford University Press, 1982).

Rosenthal-Schneider, I., *Reality and Scientific Truth: Discussions with Einstein, Von Laue and Planck* (Wayne State, 1980).


*Broken Symmetries*

Bartholemew, D. J., *God of Chance* (SCM, 1984).

Bartholemew, D. J., Probability, Statistics and Theology. *Journal of the Royal Statistical Society* A 151, 137 (1988).

Campbell, L. and Garnett, W., *The Life of James Clerk Maxwell* (Macmillan, 1882; reprinted by the Johnson Reprographic Corporation, New York, 1969).

Ford, J., How Random is a Coin Toss? *Physics Today* April 1983, p. 40.

Gleick, J., *Chaos: Making A New Science* (Viking, 1987).

Linde, A., *Particle Physics and Inflationary Cosmology* (Gordon & Breach, 1989).

Stewart, I., *Does God Play Dice? The Mathematics of Chaos* (Basil Blackwell, 1989).


*Organizing Principles*

Ayala, F. J. and Dobzhansky, T., (eds) *Studies in the Philosophy of Biology* (Macmillan, 1974).

Bohm, D., *Wholeness and the Implicate Order* (Routledge & Kegan Paul, 1980).

Davies, P. C. W., *The Cosmic Blueprint* (Heinemann, 1987).

Delbrück, M., *Mind From Matter: An Essay on Evolutionary Epistemology* (Blackwell Scientific, 1986).

Eigen, M. and Winkler, R., *Laws of the Game: How the Principles of Nature Govern Chance* (Penguin, 1983).

Langton, C. G., (ed) *Artificial Life* (Addison Wesley, 1989).
Leggett, A. J., *The Problems of Physics* (Oxford University Press, 1987).
Moravec, H., *Mind Children* (Harvard University Press, 1988).

*Selection Effects*
Barrow, J. D., Life, the Universe, and the Anthropic Principle. *World and I Magazine* (August 1987) p. 179.
Barrow, J. D., Patterns of Explanation in Cosmology. In F. Bertola and U. Curi (eds), *The Anthropic Principle* (Cambridge University Press, 1989).
Barrow, J. D. and Tipler, F. J., *The Anthropic Cosmological Principle* (Oxford University Press, 1986).
Carter, B., Large Number Coincidences and the Anthropic Principle in Cosmology. In M. Longair (ed.), *Confrontation of Cosmological Theories with Observational Data* (Reidel, 1974).
Carter, B., The Anthropic Principle: Self-selection as an adjunct to Natural Selection. In C. V. Vishveshwara (ed.) *Cosmic Perspectives* (Cambridge University Press, 1989).
Carter, B., Anthropic Selection Principle and the Ultra-Darwinian Synthesis. In F. Bertola and U. Curi (eds), *The Anthropic Principle* (Cambridge University Press, 1989).
Leslie, J., Observership in Cosmology: the Anthropic Principle. *Mind* 92, 573.
Leslie, J., *Universes* (Macmillan, 1989).
Linde, A., The Universe: Inflation Out of Chaos. *New Scientist* (March 1985) p. 14.
Nicolis, G. and Prigogine, I., *Self-organization in Non-equilibrium Systems*, (Wiley, 1977).
Page, D. N., The Importance of the Anthropic Principle. *World and I Magazine* (August 1987) p. 392.
Polanyi, M., Life's Irreducible Structure. *Science* (June 1968) p. 1308.
Prigogine, I., *From Being to Becoming: Time and Complexity in the Physical Sciences* (Freeman, 1980).
Prigogine, I., and Stengers, I., *Order Out of Chaos* (Heinemann, 1984).
Weinberg, S. W., Newtonianism, reductionism and the art of Congressional testimony. *Nature* 330, 433 (1987).

*Categories of Thought*
Barrow, J. D., The Mathematical Universe. *World and I Magazine* (May 1989) p. 306.
Barrow, J. D., *Pi in the Sky: Counting, Thinking and Being* (Oxford University Press, 1992).
Birkhoff, G., The Mathematical Nature of Physical Theories. *American Scientist* 31, 281 (1943).
Deutsch, D., Quantum Theory, the Church-Turing Principle, and the Universal Quantum Computer. *Proceedings of the Royal Society*, London A 400, 97 (1985).
Dyson, F., Mathematics in the Physical Sciences. *Scientific American* (Sept. 1964) p. 129.
Field, H., *Realism, Mathematics and Modality* (Basil Blackwell, 1989).

Hadamard, J., *The Psychology of Invention in the Mathematical Field* (Princeton University Press, 1945).

Kitcher, P., *The Nature of Mathematical Knowledge* (Oxford University Press, 1983).

Kline, M., *Mathematics and the Search for Knowledge*. (Oxford University Press, 1985).

Lehman, H., *Introduction to the Philosophy of Mathematics* (Basil Blackwell, 1975).

Wigner, E., The Unreasonable Effectiveness of Mathematics in the Natural Sciences. *Communications in Pure and Applied Mathematics* 13, 1 (1960).

Wolfson, H. A., *Religious Philosophy* (Harvard University Press, 1961).

# Muller on Evolution

## Religions Without a Creator

*Unless it were known that the Negroes of Africa, for instance, and the Buddhists of Ceylon, either ignored or rejected the idea of creation altogether, and yet possessed religions of great efficacy and extreme subtlety, we should doubt whether religion was even possible without a belief in a Creator. But it is a fact that the very denial of a creating God arose in some cases from too exalted a conception of the deity, whether on moral or philosophical grounds. From a moral point of view it has been asserted again and again that so imperfect a world as this ought not to be looked upon as the work of a perfect Being; while from a philosophical point of view it has been urged that a belief in a Creator would involve belief in a time when there was a divine cause, but no effect.*

*The denial of a Creator, therefore, so far from being necessarily anti-religious, may be traced back to religion itself, that is, to a feeling that shrinks away from assigning to a Supreme Being anything unworthy of it, or contradicting its essential attributes.*

## The Theory of Evolution

*If this had been clearly seen, and if our modern philosophers had learnt from history that a man who does not admit a creator is not ipso facto an atheist, a controversy which in England at least has excited the most passionate heat, might have been carried on with the most perfect scientific composure – I allude, of course, to the theory of evolution, as revived by Darwin. It was disheartening to hear the followers of Darwin stigmatised as atheists, because they rejected the theory of a Creator in the ordinary acceptation of that word. It was equally painful to see the opponents of Darwin's theories treated as mere bigots because, if they did not accept the theory of evolution, they must believe in the account of creation as given in Genesis...*

*It was owing to a want of what I should like to call 'historical preparedness' that all this unseemly squabbling about evolution was stirred up. In Germany the idea of evolution had so completely pervaded the popular literature and become so familiar to every thinking man that I was as much surprised at the excitement caused by the 'Origin of Species', as by the ferment stirred up by 'Essays and Reviews'. Darwin's book ushered in a new intellectual spring, but it produced no cataclysm in the world of science...*

*Darwin's real merit consisted, not in discovering evolution, but in suggesting new explanations of evolution, such as natural selection, survival of the fittest, influence of environment, sexual selection, etc. These explanations, whether they are still adequate or not, give to Darwin his commanding place in the history of natural philosophy.*

*Natural Religion*, pp. 256–8, 273

# 4
# Worlds in Microcosm

## *Richard Dawkins*

A living organism is a model of the world in which it lives. That may seem a strange statement. My justification will come later.

The sense in which I am using the word 'model', however, is not strange. It is the ordinary scientific usage: a model resembles the real thing in some important respects, whether or not it looks, to the human eye, like a replica of the real thing. A child's train set is a model, but so also is a railway timetable. I first learned about models in the scientific sense from my grandfather. In the pioneering days of radio, his job was to lecture to young engineers joining Marconi's company. To illustrate the fact, important in both radio and acoustics, that any complex waveform can be broken down into summed simple waves of different frequencies, he took wheels of different diameters and attached them with pistons to a clothes-line. When the wheels went round, the clothes-line was jerked up and down, so that waves of movement snaked along it. The wriggling clothes-line was a *model* of a radio wave, giving the students a more vivid picture of wave-summation than the mathematical equations could ever have done.

Today, my grandfather would have used a computer screen rather than a clothes-line. Well, on second thoughts, perhaps he wouldn't. Though he lived on into the age of computers, he was never able to appreciate their beauty and he died in the mistaken belief that they were nothing but crutches for lazy calculators. I should have explained to him that they are really just like his clothes-line. It is, indeed, a significant fact that the clothes-line model, like many other models in mathematics and engineering, is a model of many things simultaneously: not only radio waves and waves in an analogue or digital computer, but sound waves and tidal waves too. This is because the mathematical equations describing the behaviour of all these waves are fundamentally similar. Any of these physical systems can be seen as a 'model' of any other, and mathematicians would use the word 'model' for the set of equations, too.

Grandfather's clothes-line was a teaching aid, but engineers can put models to more practical purposes, to solve problems that defy calculation. Long before a new aeroplane is actually built, models that replicate only its outer shape are exhaustively tested in wind tunnels. Although mathematicians could in theory calculate the turbulence patterns whipped up by any particular shape, these patterns are so intricate and their mathematics so difficult that it is almost infinitely (for once, this is no exaggeration) quicker to put a model of the plane through ordeal by wind tunnel. Once again, by the way, a computer model can stand in for what happens in the wind tunnel – but it must be a very powerful computer.

More complicated turbulence patterns by far come from the winds and ocean currents that eddy about the spinning earth and bring us our weather. In a perfect world a mathematician, given the present wind directions, wind speeds, temperatures, and rates of change of these and similar measured quantities all round the world, might hope to calculate an infallible forecast of next week's weather – indeed, next century's weather. In practice the very idea of anyone performing such a vast calculation is a joke, and even moderately accurate forecasting is possible for only a few days ahead. The problem is even worse if, as is increasingly believed, weather patterns are 'chaotically' deterministic.[1] Modern weather forecasters in fact make use of a greatly simplified, though still very elaborate, computer *model* of the earth's weather. This model is not a visible replica like a model train (although it could have a visible 'readout' on the screen – perhaps a simulated picture of what a satellite might 'see', looking down from a great height on the model world). It is a dynamic model, continually updated as new information flows in from weather stations, ships, planes, balloons and satellites all round the world, and calculations are continually being performed on the updated information. To make predictions, forecasters allow the model to free-run into the 'future'.

As a biologist I am endlessly fascinated by the arcade games of this computer age. In one game the player sits in what appears to be the driving seat of a racing car, holding a steering wheel in one hand and a gear lever in the other. On the screen ahead of him (observation suggests that it is seldom her) is a moving coloured image that simulates the road ahead. Trees and other objects appear small in the distance, then rapidly grow as the car approaches and flashes past them. Rival cars loom up on the road ahead and can be overtaken, or crashed into, depending on the skill of the player. Engine noise from a loudspeaker changes in tune with the manoeuvres of the driver. Though the resemblance to the real thing is in truth quite crude, the impact on the senses is surprisingly life-like. Yet all that is 'really' happening is that cells in the memory of the computer behind the screen are changing their state from 3 volts to 0 volts and back again at high speed.

The programmer – the original creator of the game – has had to create a make-believe world that embodies a good dose of reality. He has had to decide where, in his world, to place each tree and hill. In a sense, there is a sort of racing circuit in the computer, with its own geography and landmarks that bear a fixed 'spatial' relationship to one another. The model car, in a mathematical sense, 'moves' through the landscape, all the time obeying the programmed-in laws of 'reality'. If the programmer wanted to he could, of course, make his imaginary cars violate the normal laws of reality – a car might suddenly split into two cars, or turn into a horse – but this would make the game less commercially appealing.

Remember the racing car in the arcade, for we shall see that it has something to tell us about how our own brains perceive reality. But I began by saying, not that an animal's brain contains a simulated model of its world (though it does, and this is a point I shall return to), but that an animal *is* a model of its world. What is the sense of such a statement? One way to approach it is to realize that a good zoologist, presented with an animal and allowed to examine and dissect its body in sufficient detail, should be able to reconstruct almost everything about the world in which the animal lived. To be more precise, she would be reconstructing the worlds in which the animal's *ancestors* lived. That claim, of course, rests upon the Darwinian assumption that animal bodies are largely shaped by natural selection. If Darwin's theory is correct, the animal is the inheritor of the attributes that enabled its ancestors to be ancestors. If they hadn't had those successful attributes they would have been not ancestors but the childless rivals of ancestors.

So, what *are* the attributes that make for success as an ancestor, the attributes that we should expect to find in the body of our animal when we inspect it? The answer is anything that helps the individual animal to survive and reproduce *in its own environment*. If the species happens to live in a desert, individuals will have inherited whatever it takes to survive in arid heat. If the species happens to live in a rain forest, they will have inherited whatever it takes to survive in cloistered humidity. Not just one or two attributes in each case, but hundreds, thousands of them. This is why, if you present an animal's body, even a new species previously unknown to science, to a knowledgeable zoologist, she should be able to 'read' its body and tell you what kind of environment it inhabited: desert, rain forest, arctic tundra, temperate woodland or coral reef. She should be able to tell you, by reading its teeth and its guts, what it fed on. Flat, millstone teeth indicate that it was a herbivore; sharp, shearing teeth that it was a carnivore. Long intestines with complicated blind alleys indicate that it was a herbivore; short, simple guts suggest a carnivore. By reading the animal's feet, and its eyes and other sense organs, the zoologist should be able to tell how it found its food. By reading its stripes or flashes, its horns, antlers or crests, she should be able to tell something about its social and sex life.

But zoological science has a long way to go. By 'reading' the body of a newly discovered species, we could at present come up with only a rough verdict about its probable habitat and way of life. 'Rough' in the same way as a pre-computer weather forecast was rough. The zoology of the future will put into the computer many more measurements of the anatomy and chemistry of the animal being 'read'. More importantly, it will not take the teeth, guts and chemistry of the stomach separately. It will perfect techniques of combining sources of information and analysing their interactions, resulting in inferences of enormous power. The computer, incorporating everything that is known about the body of the strange animal, will construct a model of the animal's world, to rival any model of the earth's weather. This, it seems to me, is tantamount to saying that the animal, any animal, *is* a model of its own world, or the world of its ancestors. Hence my opening sentence.

In a few cases, an animal's body is a model of its world in the literal sense of a doll or a toy train. A stick insect lives in a world of twigs, and its body is a precise replica of a twig. A fawn's pelage is a model of the dappled pattern of sunlight filtered through trees onto the woodland floor. A peppered moth is a model of lichen on the tree bark that is its world when at rest. But models, as we have seen, do not stop at replicas, and if an animal's skin or plumage literally resembles features in its world, this is just the tip of the iceberg. Any animal is a detailed model of its world, whether camouflaged to mimic its background or not.

For the next stage in the argument, we need to make use of the distinction between static and dynamic models. A railway timetable is a static model, while the weather model in the computer is dynamic: it is continually – in advanced systems continuously – being updated by new readings from around the world. Some aspects of an animal's body are a static model of its world – that millstone slab of a horse's tooth, for instance. Other aspects are dynamic; they change. Sometimes the change is slow. A Dartmoor pony grows a shaggy coat in winter and sheds it in summer. The zoologist presented with a pony's pelt can 'read', not only the kind of place it inhabited, but also the season of the year in which it was caught. Many animals of high northern latitudes, like Arctic foxes, snowshoe hares and ptarmigans, are white in winter and brownish in summer.

In these cases, then, the model of the world that is an animal is dynamic on a slow timescale, a timescale of weeks or months. But animals are dynamic on a much faster timescale as well, a timescale of seconds and fractions of seconds. This is the timescale of behaviour. Behaviour can be seen as high-speed dynamic modelling of the environment. Think of a herring gull adroitly riding a sea cliff's upcurrents. It may not be flapping its wings, but this doesn't mean that its wing muscles are idle. They and the tail muscles are constantly making tiny adjustments, sensitively fine-tuning the bird's flight surfaces to every nuance, every eddy of the air around it. If we fed information about the state of all these muscles into a computer, from moment to moment, the computer could in principle reconstruct every detail of the air currents through which the bird is gliding. It would assume that the bird was well-designed to glide, and on that assumption construct a model of the air around the bird. Again, it would be a model in the same sense as the weather forecaster's. Both are continuously revised by new data. Both can be extrapolated to predict the future. The weather model predicts tomorrow's weather; the gull model could 'advise' the bird on the anticipatory adjustments that it should make to its wing and tail muscles, in order to glide on into the next second.

The point we are working towards, of course, is that although no human programmer has yet constructed a computer model to advise gulls on how to adjust their wing and tail muscles, just such a 'computer' model is almost certainly being run continuously in the brain of my gull and of every other bird in flight. Similar models, pre-programmed in outline by genes and past experience, and continuously updated by new sense data from millisecond to millisecond, are running inside the skull of every swimming fish, every galloping horse, every echo-ranging bat.

The Cambridge physiologist Horace Barlow long ago developed an intriguing view of sensory physiology which fits very well with the point I am making.[2] We shall need a digression in order to understand his idea, and its relevance to my theme. Barlow began by pointing out what a formidable problem sensory recognition systems face. They have to respond to a subset of all possible stimulus patterns; while at the same time not responding to the rest. Think of the problem of recognizing a particular person's face: by convention it is assumed to be the face of the distinguished neurophysiologist J. Lettvin's grandmother. Lettvin's recognition mechanism must respond when the image of her face, but not any other image, falls on his retina. It would be easy if we could assume that the face would always fall exactly on a particular part of the retina. There could be a keyhole arrangement, with a grandmother-shaped region of cells on the retina wired up to a grandmother-detecting cell in the central nervous system. Other cells – members of the 'anti-keyhole' – would have to be wired up in inhibitory fashion, otherwise the central nervous cell would respond to a white sheet just as strongly as to Lettvin's grandmother.

But the keyhole arrangement is not feasible. Even if Lettvin needed to recognize nothing but his grandmother, how could he cope with her image falling on different parts of the retina, changing size and shape as she approaches or recedes, as she turns sideways, and so on? If we add up all possible combinations of keyholes and anti-keyholes, the number enters the astronomical range. When you realize that Lettvin can recognize not only his grandmother's face but hundreds of other faces, all the other bits of his grandmother and of other people, all the letters of the alphabet, all the thousands of objects to which a normal person can instantly give a name, the combinatorial explosion gets completely out of control. The psychologist F. Attneave, who independently arrived at the same general idea as Barlow,[3] dramatized the point by the following calculation. If there was just one central nervous cell to cope with each keyhole combination, the volume of the brain would have to be measured in cubic light years.

How, then, with a brain capacity measured only in hundreds of cubic centimetres, do we do it? Barlow's answer is that we exploit the massive redundancy in all sensory information, reducing it with redundancy-detecting circuits (arranged in a hierarchical cascade). These detectors are not scanning for particular objects like Lettvin's grandmother. Instead, they are scanning for statistical redundancy.

Redundancy is information-theory jargon. It refers to messages or parts of messages that are not informative because the receiver already knows the information. Newspapers do not carry headlines saying, 'The sun rose this morning'. But if a morning suddenly came when the sun did not rise, headline writers, if any survived, would note the incident. Technically, a message contains redundancy to the extent that, out of the repertoire of possible signals, some of them occur more frequently than others.

Sensory information is full of redundancy. The easiest kind to understand is temporal redundancy. The state of the world at time $t$ is usually not greatly different from the state of the world at time $t-1$. The temperature, for instance, changes, but it usually changes slowly. A sense organ that signalled 'It is hot' in any one second would be wasting its time if it gave exactly the same signal in the next second. The central nervous system can usually assume that if it is hot in any one second it will be hot until further notice.

'Further notice' gives the clue to what a well designed sensory system should do. It should not signal 'It is hot, it is hot, it is hot, it is hot...'. It should signal only when there is a change in temperature. The central nervous system can then assume that the *status quo* is maintained until the next change is signalled. It has long been-known to physiologists that most sense organs do exactly that. The phenomenon is called sensory adaptation.

Figure 4.1 shows a particular example, the dying away of nerve impulses from a single sensory hair of a fly in response to beer. When it first detects the beer the nerve fires rapidly. The beer remains but the rate of firing decreases back to a steady, low, 'no news' value.[4]

*Figure 4.1*

There is analogous redundancy in the spatial domain. The top picture in figure 4.2 is the scene we are actually looking at. If we represent spots on the retina where light falls with '+', and spots where there is darkness with '−', the middle picture shows that there is massive redundancy: most pluses are next to other pluses, minuses next to minuses. In the bottom picture the redundancy has been eliminated, leaving pluses and minuses only round the edges. It is only the edges that need to be signalled. The redundant interiors can be filled in by the central nervous system. This can be done by the mechanism known as lateral inhibition. If every cell in a bank of photocells inhibits its immediate neighbours, maximal firing comes from cells that lie along edges, for they are inhibited from one side only. Lateral inhibition of this kind is common in both vertebrate and invertebrate eyes.

The straightness of many lines constitutes another kind of redundancy. If the ends of the line are specified, the middle can be filled in. Among the most important neurones that have been discovered in the visual cortex of mammals are the so-called line-detectors, neurones that pick out lines or edges orientated in particular directions. Each cortical line-detector cell has its own preferred direction.[5] From Barlow's point of view, what is going on here is this. If it were not for the line-detector, all the cells along a straight edge would fire. The nervous system economises by using a single cell to signal that edge.

Movement over the spatial field is information-rich, in the same kind of way as change over time is information-rich. Just as in the temperature

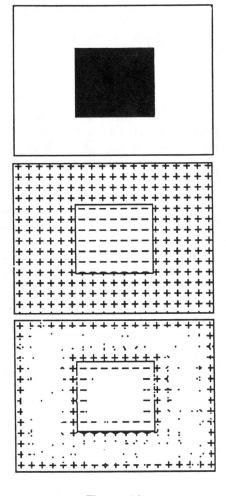

*Figure    4.2*

example, a static visual field does not need continuous reporting. But if a part of the visual field suddenly detaches itself from the rest and starts to crawl over the background as a small, black fly, it is news, and should be signalled. Visual physiologists have indeed discovered, again and again, neurones that are silent until something moves in their visual field. They don't respond when the entire field moves – that would correspond to the sort of movement the animal would see when it, itself, moved. They only respond when something moves relative to the rest of the visual field. The most famous of these relative movement detectors are the so-called 'bug-detectors' of Lettvin and Maturana in the retina of the frog.

As for the apparent movements of the world that result when an animal walks around or swivels its eyes, these are of low information content – high redundancy – and should therefore be filtered out before they reach the brain. And indeed, as you walk around, although your retinal image moves your perception is of a steady world. Poke yourself in the eye, however, and you'll see a minor earthquake. Yet the retinal image is moving in the same kind of way in both cases. The difference, according to the well known reafference theory of von Holst and Mittelstaedt, is this.[6] Whenever the brain sends a message to the eye muscles, telling them to move the eye, it sends a copy of the message to the sensory part of the brain, telling it to expect the apparent position of the world to move accordingly, and to compensate by exactly the right amount. The brain perceives movement only if there is a discrepancy between the expected movement and the observed movement. This is beautifully demonstrated by the following fact. It has long been known that people who have had their eye muscles paralysed see the earth move when they try to move their own eyes (and in the same direction as the intended eye movement). The brain is told to anticipate movement and allows for it. But the movement never comes, so the model of the world is seen to move.

Returning to information-rich movement relative to the rest of the world, Lettvin and his colleagues found fascinating variations on the basic bug-detector theme in the optic tectum in the brain of frogs. The most interesting from our present point of view are the so-called 'Sameness' neurones. I quote:

> Let us begin with an empty gray hemisphere for the visual field. There is usually no response of the cell to turning on and off the illumination. It is silent. We bring in a small dark object, say 1 to 2 degrees in diameter, and at a certain point in its travel, almost anywhere in the field, the cell suddenly "notices" it. Thereafter, wherever that object is moved it is tracked by the cell. Every time it moves, with even the faintest jerk, there is a burst of impulses that dies down to a mutter that continues as long as the object is visible. If the object is kept moving, the bursts signal discontinuities in the movement, such as the turning of corners, reversals, and so forth, and these bursts occur against a continuous background mutter that tells us the object is visible to the cell...[7]

It is as if the nervous system is tuned, at successive hierarchical levels, to respond strongly to the unexpected, weakly or not at all to the expected. Switching back to Barlow's language derived from the theory of codes, we could say that the nervous system uses short, economical words for messages that occur frequently and are expected, long, less economical words for messages that occur rarely and are not expected. Another way of putting it – and this brings us back to my main theme – is to say that a well-tuned nervous system embodies, in its dictionary of code symbols, a statistical model of the world in which the animal lives. Barlow puts it like this:

> The effect of coding to reduce redundancy is not just the elimination of wasteful neural activity. It constitutes a way of organizing the sensory information so that, on the one hand, an internal model of the environment causing the past sensory inputs is built up, while on the other hand the current sensory situation is represented in a concise way which simplifies the task of the parts of the nervous system responsible for learning and conditioning...[8]

When I look at any object, say a wooden box on the table, I have the strong impression that the thing I am looking at really is the box itself, and that it is outside myself. Ancient Greeks thought that the eyes spout invisible rays that feel the object we are looking at, and this idea has the ring of truth to my subjective consciousness. Although I know that in fact rays of light from the sun are being reflected from the box, and refracted through my lens and humours so that a tiny, upside-down image of the box appears on each of my two retinas, I cannot help feeling that my percept of the box is really 'out there' waiting to be felt by my eyes. The box, after all, looks solid; it has depth. The solid percept of it corresponds to neither of the two flat images on my two retinas. It is a compound, and it looks solid because the brain has made some sophisticated calculations based on the disparity between the images on the two retinas. The box that I actually perceive is neither 'out there' nor on either of the two retinas. If it is anywhere, it is in the brain, a computer model of a box. If somebody now rotates the box, the two-dimensional images on my two retinas change in complicated ways, but the solid, three-dimensional model in my brain remains intact. I seem to see a different face of the box as it turns, and the box may appear larger or smaller if it is moved closer or farther from me. But the overwhelming subjective experience is that it is the same box. Even though it rotates, swells or recedes, it has a stream of sameness. This is because what I am seeing is indeed the same 'thing'; it is the same computer model in the brain that I am 'looking at' as the box rotates, and as the images on my retinas change.

The distinguished psychologist Richard Gregory has shown how visual illusions can easily be understood once we realize that there is a sense

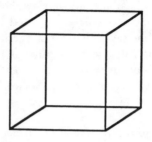

*Figure   4.3*

in which we are looking, not at reality itself, but at a model of reality in the brain.[9] One of the best known visual illusions is the Necker Cube. (figure 4.3). This is not a cube. It is a two-dimensional pattern of ink on paper. Yet a normal human sees it as a solid cube, with one of the two end faces nearer than the other. The brain has made a three-dimensional model based upon the two-dimensional pattern on the paper. This is, indeed, the kind of thing the brain does almost every time we look at a picture. What is revealing about the Necker Cube is that the flat pattern of ink on paper is equally compatible with two alternative three-dimensional brain models. Stare at the Necker Cube for some seconds, and you will see it apparently flip over. The face that had previously seemed nearest to you will now appear farthest. Carry on looking, and it will flip back to the original cube. The model in the brain, like the weather model, is constructed by the computer, but it is not entirely free-running: it makes use of information fed in from the outside world. The brain might have been designed to stick, abitrarily, to one of the two cube models, say the first of the two that it hit upon, even though another model would have been equally compatible with the information from the retinas. But in fact the brain takes the other option of running each model alternately for a few seconds at a time.

When we are looking at an actual wooden box, the brain is provided with additional information that enables it to arrive at a clear preference for one of the two cube models. We therefore see the box in one way only, and there is no alternation. But this does not diminish the truth of the general lesson that the Necker Cube teaches us about how the brain works. Whenever we look at anything, there is a sense in which what we are actually looking at is a model of that thing in the brain.

The following anecdote will, I am sure, strike a chord in your memory. As an undergraduate, I was once in the cinema and a man needed to push past me to get to a vacant seat. In the dim light I saw him as a weasel-faced man in early middle age. Then, with the abruptness of a Necker Cube, his features flipped. The face became younger and rounder as I realized that he was, in fact, a friend aged about twenty. The flip had occurred, of course, not in his visage but in my brain. At first, my brain had constructed a rough computer model to accommodate the vague and ill-defined image that the dim light of the cinema afforded my retinas. Suddenly, as another part of my brain recognized him as a fellow undergraduate, the weasely brain-model was destroyed and the more attractive – and presumably more accurate – model of my friend was, as it were, taken out of the tape cupboard and loaded into the computer.

This 'model in the head' analysis helps us to think our way into minds that move through alien worlds. Bats don't see the world, they hear it, often in pitch darkness. But I have suggested[10] that the subjective sensations of a bat may be very like those of a visual animal such as a bird flying by day. The reason is that both bat and bird 'see' a model that they construct in the brain. The type of model constructed – by natural selection – will be the type of model needed for navigating at high speed in three dimensions through the air. The fact that the external information being used to update the model comes from light rays in the case of the bird, and from sound echoes in the case of the bat, is irrelevant to the functional properties of the internal model itself. I even conjectured that bats may perceive colour. Our subjective experience of colours has no necessary connection with particular wavelengths of light. Hues are parts of our internally constructed model, used as arbitrary labels for wavelength. There is no reason why bats should not use the same arbitrary labels to stand for some aspect of the echo-reflectance of textures. A male bat may, to a female's ears, appear as gorgeously coloured as a peacock's train does to our eyes.

We have seen that, in one sense, an animal's body *is* a model of its world. We have also seen that, at least in animals with advanced nervous systems, like birds and bats, the brain can contain dynamically updated models – computer simulations – of the animal's world. Unlike the animal's body, which is on the whole a static model, these computer simulations in the brain are capable of changing rapidly in time. The aspect of this fluctuation that I have so far stressed is the continuous updating of the model as nerve impulses flood in from the sense organs, like weather data from distant recording stations. But the weather analogy also reminds us that computer models can run on into the future – forecasting. Can an animal's brain model, too, run on into the future, providing the animal with useful forecasts? The answer is yes. But before we discuss this we need to consider what 'forecasting' means in general, what it might mean to an animal and why it might be useful to it.

The first thing to say is that we are talking about statistical forecasting, prediction that is not guaranteed to be right. Weather forecasting is, of course, statistical. Certain American radio stations announce the probability of rain (or 'precipitation' as it is pompously called) as, say, 80 per cent. English weather forecasts do not state numerical probabilities, perhaps because the probability of even the most probable weather would be embarrassingly low. Life insurance companies make a living by statistically predicting the longevity of their clients. A racing tip is a statistical prediction that a particular horse is likely to win. Statistical predictions, imperfect though they must be, are well worth making, nevertheless. It is statistical predictions that animals can be said to make.

The second general thing I want to say is that all sensible prediction of the future (this excludes astrology and other techniques used by charlatans to exploit the gullible) is based upon extrapolation from the past. We assume that the laws that govern the future are the same as the laws that govern the past, and so whatever has happened in the past will probably happen in the future. If a day's weather was random with respect to previous days, forecasting would be impossible. If all human deaths were due to the purest accident and bore no relation to age, health or habits, actuaries would be out of a job and we'd all pay the same life-insurance premium. There'd be no betting on favourites if horses capriciously flouted past form.

The past, then, can be used for forecasting the future only because the world behaves lawfully rather than randomly. Scientists are sometimes successful in investigating the underlying reasons why the future is related non-randomly to the past. But a statistical prophecy does not require such understanding: we may observe, statistically, that red berries in autumn presage a hard winter, without having any understanding of the mediating causes. The working rule of thumb, 'Assume that whatever has happened in the past will continue to happen in the future', is a successful rule. It is the one that every animal and plant uses to ensure that it survives in its own little future.

Any forecasting system has at least the theoretical possibility of exploiting natural cycles. The rule of thumb here is: 'Whatever has happened at regular intervals in the past will probably go on happening at the same regular intervals in the future.' But simple rhythms constitute only one kind of patterning in the world. Patterning of any kind is the same thing as non-randomness, and any kind of non-randomness can potentially be used to predict the future. If, in your world, the booming of a gong is reliably followed by a good meal, you will probably find after a while that, whenever you hear the gong and are hungry, your mouth will start to water. As is well known, this is what Pavlov found with his dogs.

What is less well known is that it is the reliability with which the 'gong' and 'food' – the conditional and unconditional stimulus – are paired that matters. This has been shown in ingenious experiments by R. A. Rescorla and others.[11] If you present two conditional stimuli, say a bell then a light, before food, which will be most effective at eliciting mouthwatering? The answer is not necessarily the first of the two, nor necessarily the second. Neither is it that bells are inherently more effective than lights, or vice versa. What really matters seems to be reliability. The stimulus that counts is whichever of the two can more reliably be used to predict the arrival time of food. If the time interval between bell and food is long but *constant*, while the interval between light and food is short but *variable*, the bell is the more reliable predictor of when the food will come, and the bell is the one that makes the animal's mouth water. Conversely, if the time interval between bell and food is long and variable, while the interval between light and food is short and constant, the light is the most reliable and the most mouthwatering. Pavlovian conditioning is a device used by the brain to predict future events from events that have already happened. It exploits the fact that particular events reliably follow others in the animal's world.

We can see all learning, not just Pavlovian conditioning, as a device whereby brains make use of past events in an individual animal's life, to make that animal better at predicting the future and therefore at surviving in that future. There is no need to think of the animal as making conscious predictions, of having any kind of mental picture of the future – though of course it might. Learning can achieve its predictions by mechanical means, every bit as mechanical, indeed, as natural selection itself. It is a consequence of learning that the animal's brain model becomes an ever more accurate model of its world. Many animals behave as if they have a detailed mental picture of the world around their home, in the same kind of way as the arcade computer has a 'mental' picture of its model racetrack's geography; or in the same kind of way as a chess computer has a picture of the chess board inside it. This is true even of animals that some would like to think of as 'humble' or 'lowly'.

Female digger wasps are solitary predators that dig burrows and bring prey back to their underground chambers. The males don't seem to do anything much. The prey that the female brings back to her burrow are for her larvae, who need the protein to grow. She herself, by the way, eats nothing but flower nectar – pure aviation fuel. Each female has one burrow on the go at any one time (in some species two or three), into which she drags the stung carcases (caterpillars, grasshoppers, flies, depending upon her species), paralysed but – macabre touch – in some species still alive so that they stay fresh. She has to hunt far and wide for each victim, and it is imperative that she remembers the way home. We now know that the wasp carries, in her brain, a kind of map of the principal landmarks in the area. The map is especially detailed with respect to the vicinity of her burrow (the entrance of the burrow itself is inconspicuous, as it has to be because of the constant danger of flies and other parasites exploiting the hard-earned cache of frozen meat). It was one of the very first achievements of my own revered teacher, the late Niko Tinbergen, to demonstrate this by characteristically ingenious but simple experiments. The wasp he worked on is called *Philanthus*, and it hunts bees. When a wasp leaves her burrow, instead of flying straight off on the hunt, she flies several circuits round the burrow first. Could it be, Tinbergen wondered, that she was making a map in her head of the landmarks around her nest? If so, could he demonstrate this by fooling her?

Yes, he could. While a wasp was about her business down in the burrow, Tinbergen planted his own chosen landmarks. In one experiment he placed three pine cones and a forked twig in a particular arrangement around the wasp's burrow. The wasp emerged, flew round and round as usual, then set off on her long hunting trip. While she was away, Tinbergen moved the pine cones and the twig so that they still formed the same pattern, but the constellation was a yard or so away from the burrow entrance. When the wasp returned, she dived straight to the place where her burrow *should* have been in relation to the constellation of landmarks. The experiment was repeated many times, of course, and again and again the results confirmed that the wasps use their circling flight to, in effect, take a mental photograph of the vicinity of the nest. Each new aerial photography mission wiped out any earlier memories. Follow-up experiments by Tinbergen and his colleagues showed that the wasps seemed to be using the whole constellation as their beacon, not singling out just one pine cone or twig.

The digger wasp certainly has some kind of mental picture or model of her home area, but does this mean a conscious picture such as you or I might have? We don't know. The facts do not compel a yes answer, although they don't rule it out either. But whether or not a wasp's mental picture is conscious, I am convinced that the arcade computer's mental picture of its racetrack is not. Don't get me wrong. I am not one of those smug philosophers who argue by hectoring assertion that consciousness is the prerogative of human minds alone, and that computers, or 'animals' (by which they snobbishly mean non-human animals), by definition or *ex cathedra*, can't have it. I have an open mind here, and a private suspicion that one day computers will be at least as conscious as we are, and that many non-human animals already are. All I am saying is that I know enough about how computer programs are written to be confident that the present state-of-the-art arcade computer is not conscious of its race-track. We know too little about how wasp brain programs are 'written' to be sure that they are not conscious. Whether wasps are conscious of their mental models of the world or not, they *have* mental models of the world, and so do arcade computers.

I should not wish, by using the metaphor of the computer, to imply that brains work like modern digital electronic computers. They probably don't. It is the principle of getting about the real world by simulating it internally that I want to emphasize, and it happens that the digital electronic computer is a familiar and powerful tool for simulation. But there are other conceivable tools that are not digital and not electronic, and the brain might well resemble them more. Before digital computers became readily available, engineers used a variety of devices to simulate reality. My grandfather's clothes-line was a simple example. Other such 'analogue' devices were, and sometimes still are, used to solve serious mathematical problems. A mathematical function can be represented as a curve of a particular shape. If you carve a piece of wood to that shape, the wood is an analogue of anything in the world that follows that mathematical function. Carve two bits of wood to represent two mathematical functions, and the two bits of wood can then be brought together to represent anything in the world that behaves as the sum of the two functions.

Nowadays wooden curves have been superseded by electronic analogue computers. But, as recently as the Second World War, differential equations were solved by elaborate mechanical analogue computers, consisting of concatenations of mathematically curved cams and rods sliding over each other. Even today, the simplest way of solving that mathematician's chestnut, the 'travelling salesman' problem, is by knotting bits of string together. The same is true of some other optimization problems. The brain obviously doesn't tie knots in string, but it has been conjectured, for example by the psychologist and philosopher Kenneth Craik[12] and the biologist John Maynard Smith[13] that brain models have more in common with knotted string than with digital computers. For our purposes here it doesn't matter. It is sufficient that the brain makes simulation models of the outside world. I think in terms of digital electronic computers because I am familiar with them, but it is not their digitalness nor their electronicness that is important to the analogy.

Leaving aside what *kind* of computer a brain is, I want to return to the question: Can an animal's mental model of its world free-run into the future and so simulate future events, like the computer model of the world's weather? Suppose we set up the following experiment. Find a steep cliff in a mountainous area of Ethiopia inhabited by Hamadryas baboons, and place a plank so that it sticks out over the edge of the precipice, with a banana on its far tip. The centre of gravity of the plank is just on the safe side of the edge, so that it does not topple into the gorge below, but if a monkey were to venture out to the end of the plank it would be enough to tip the balance. Now we hide and watch what the monkeys do. They are clearly interested in the banana, but they do not venture out along the plank to get it. Why not?

We can imagine three stories, any of which might be true, to account for the baboons' prudence. In all three stories the prudent behaviour results from a kind of trial and error, but of three different kinds. According to the first story, the baboons have an 'instinctive' fear of precipitous heights. This fear has been built into their brains directly by natural selection. Contemporaries of their ancestors that did *not* possess a genetic tendency to fear cliffs failed to become ancestors because they got killed. Consequently, since modern baboons are all descended, by definition, from successful ancestors, they have inherited the genetic predisposition to fear cliffs. There is indeed some evidence that the newly born young of a variety of species have an innate fear of heights.[14] The first story, then, involves trial and error of the crudest and most drastic kind: Darwinian natural selection, dicing with ancestral life and death. We can call this the 'Ancestral Fear' story.

The second story talks about the past experience of the individual baboons. Each young baboon, as it grows up, has experience of falling. If it fell down a huge cliff, of course, the experience would be its last. But it has enough encounters with small cliffs to learn that falls can be painful. Pain, in trial and error learning, is the analogue of death in natural selection. Natural selection has built brains with the capacity to experience as pain those very sensations that, in a stronger dose, would lead to the animal's death. Pain is not only the analogue of death; it is a kind of symbolic substitute for death if we think in terms of an analogy between learning and natural selection. Baboons build up in their brains, through experience of the pain of falling down small cliffs, perhaps through experience that the bigger the cliff the worse the pain, a tendency to avoid cliffs. This is the second story, the 'Painful Experience' story, of how it has come about that the baboons resist their natural tendency to rush out along the plank to seize the banana.

The third story is the one this is all leading up to. According to this story, each baboon has a model of the situation in its head, a computer simulation of the cliff, the plank and the banana, and it can run the simulation program on into the future. A baboon's brain simulates his body walking along the plank. Just as the arcade computer simulates the racing car passing a tree, the baboon's computer simulates his body advancing towards the banana, the model plank teetering, then toppling and crashing into the simulated abyss. The brain simulates it all, and evaluates the results of the computer run. And that, according to our 'Simulated Experience' story, is why the baboon doesn't venture out in actuality. It is a trial and error story, just like the Ancestral Fear and Painful Experience stories, but this time it is trial and error in the head, not in reality. Obviously, trial and error in the head, if you have a powerful enough computer there to do it, is preferable to trial and error in real earnest.

Now, as you read these stories, I have little doubt that you had an imaginary picture of the scene. You 'saw' the cliff, you saw the plank and you saw the baboons. If you have a vivid imagination you may have seen everything in great detail. Your imagined banana may have been bright yellow, perhaps with a precise pattern of black spots on the skin. Or you may have imagined it peeled. You may have seen the chasm in every detail of its rocks and crannies, with stunted bushes clinging to the scarp, whereas I, not having a vivid imagination, saw a rather abstract precipice like a sketch in a mathematics textbook. The details of all of our imaginary pictures are, no doubt, very different. But we all set up a simulation of the scene, which was adequate to the task of predicting a baboon's future. We all know, from the inside, what it is like to run a computer simulation of the world in our heads. We call it imagination, and we use it all the time to steer our decisions in wise and prudent directions.

The experiment with the baboons and the banana has not been done. If it were, could the results tell us which of our three stories was true, or whether the truth were some combination? If the Painful Experience story were true, we should be able to find out by looking at the behaviour of young or inexperienced baboons. One who had been sheltered all his life from falls should prove fearless when eventually confronted with an edge. If such a naive baboon turned out in fact to be fearful, this would still leave both the other two stories open. He might have inherited ancestral fear, or he might have a vivid imagination. We could try to decide the issue by a further experiment. Say we place a heavy rock on the near end of the plank. Now we humans, at least, can see from our own mental simulation that it is safe to venture along the plank: the rock is obviously a secure counterbalance. What would the baboons do? I don't know, and I'm not sure that it would be a very informative experiment in any case. I know that, however certain I was from my mental model that the rock would be a staunch counterweight, I wouldn't go out along the plank, not for a crock of gold. I just can't take heights. The Ancestral

Fear story sounds pretty plausible to me. What is more, so powerful is this fear that it enters into my Simulated Experience! When I simulate the scene in imagination, I literally feel a frisson of fear up my spine, however vividly I simulate a ten ton rock firmly clamped down on the plank. Since I know that all three stories are true for me, I could easily believe the same of baboons. Incidentally, what I am now simulating in my mind is an enterprising baboon hauling in the plank and seizing the banana when it has reached safe haven on the cliff top. My imaginary baboon has arrived at this sagacious resolution by a neat piece of simulation of her own, but as for whether this would be true of a real baboon, your guess, your prediction, your simulation, is as good as mine.

The imagination, the capacity to simulate things that are not (yet) in the world, is a natural – emergent – progression from the capacity to simulate things that are in the world. The weather model is continually updated by information from weather ships and weather stations. To this extent it is a simulation of conditions as they really are. Whether or not it was originally designed to run on into the future, its ability to do so, to simulate things not only as they are but as they may turn out to be, is a natural, almost inevitable, consequence of the fact that it is a model at all. An economist's computer model of the economy of Britain is, so far, a model of things as they are and have been. The program hardly needs to be modified at all in order to take that extra step into the simulated future, to project probable future trends in the gross national product, the currency and the balance of payments.

So it was in the evolution of nervous systems. Natural selection built in the capacity to simulate the world as it is, because this was necessary in order to perceive the world. You cannot see that two-dimensional patterns of lines on two retinas amount to a single solid cube unless you simulate, in your brain, a model of the solid cube. Having built in the capacity to simulate models of things as they are, natural selection found that it was but a short step to simulate things as they are not quite yet – to simulate the future. This turned out to have valuable emergent consequences, for it enabled animals to benefit from 'experience', not direct trial and error experience in their own past history, nor the life and death 'experience' of their ancestors, but vicarious experience in the safe interior of the skull.

And once natural selection had built brains capable of simulating slight departures from reality into the imagined future, a further emergent capacity automatically flowered. Now it was but another short step to the wilder reaches of imagination revealed in dreams and in art, an escape from mundane reality that has no obvious limits.

ACKNOWLEDGEMENT

I thank Helena Cronin for numerous helpful discussions concerned with the writing and revising of this paper.

BIBLIOGRAPHY

1  J. Gleick, *Chaos: Making a new science* (Viking, 1987).
2  H. B. Barlow. The coding of sensory messages. In W. H. Thorpe & O. L. Zangwill (eds), *Current Problems in Animal Behaviour* (Cambridge University Press, 1961), pp. 331–60. Also, Possible principles underlying the transformations of sensory messages. In W. A. Rosenblith (ed.), *Sensory Communication* (MIT Press, 1961), pp. 217–34.
3  F. Attneave, Informational aspects of visual perception. *Psychological Review*, **67** (1954), pp. 183–93.
4  V. Dethier, *The Hungry Fly* (Harvard University Press, 1976).
5  D. H. Hubel and T. N. Wiesel, Receptive fields of single neurones in the cat's striate cortex. *Journal of Physiology*, **148** (1959), pp. 574–91.
6  D. J. McFarland, *Feedback Mechanisms in Animal Behaviour* (Academic Press, 1971).
7  J. Y. Lettvin, H. Maturana, W. S. McCulloch and W. H. Pitts, What the frog's eye tells the frog's brain. *Proceedings of the Institute of Radio Engineers*, **47** (1959), pp. 940–51.
8  Barlow, loc. cit. p. 227.
9  R. L. Gregory, *Eye and Brain: the psychology of seeing*. Second Edition (Weidenfeld & Nicolson, 1976).
10  R. Dawkins, *The Blind Watchmaker* (Longman, 1986, republished Penguin, 1988), pp. 33–5.
11  R. A. Rescorla, Two perceptual variables in within-event learning. *Animal Learning and Behavior*, **14** (1986), pp. 387–92.
12  K. J. W. Craik, *The Nature of Explanation* (Cambridge University Press, 1943).
13  J. Maynard Smith, *The Problems of Biology* (Oxford University Press, 1986).
14  R. D. Walk, The study of visual depth and distance perception in animals. In D. S. Lehrman, R. A. Hinde and E. Shaw (eds), *Advances in the Study of Behaviour* (Academic Press 1965), **1**, pp. 99–154.

# Muller on History –
# And on Conscience

## In Defence of the Historical School

*After that, I felt it incumbent upon myself to explain why I looked upon an historical treatment of religious ideas as the one most likely to lead to results of permanent value. I had to defend the Historical School against a very common misapprehension, as if the historian cared only about facts, without attempting to interpret them; and as if his interest even in these facts ceased the moment he approached his own time. The true object of the Historical School is to connect the present with the past, to interpret the present by the past, and to discover, if possible, the solution of our present difficulties, by tracing them back to the causes from which they arose...*

*This is the position which I felt bound to defend against that other school of philosophers who seem to think that our own inner consciousness... should be looked upon as the one and only source from which to draw a knowledge and understanding of Natural Religion. They seem to forget that even that inner consciousness of theirs is but the surface of human intellect, resting on stratum upon stratum of ancient thought, and often covered by thick layers of dust and rubbish, formed of the detritus in the historical conflicts between truth and error.*

*Natural Religion*, pp. 572–3

## Conscience

*Even in our own language there are survivals of psychological mythology... There is a well-known line quoted from Menander, Monost. 654:*

*To all mortals conscience is a god.*

*...Because I am conscious of having done what seems to me either right or wrong, I am supposed to possess a... conscience, which tells me what is right or wrong. But why should a man be supposed to possess such an organ or faculty, or why should we appeal to a man's conscience, as something apart from the man? If a man is tall, he does not possess something called tallness... We are justified, therefore, in saying that we are conscious of having done wrong; but as soon as we go a step further and say that we have a conscience which tells us what is right or wrong, we go beyond the facts, such as we know them... Nothing is more common now than to call conscience an inward monitor, or even the voice of God; to speak of conscience as the arbiter of right and wrong, nay, even as the source of all truth, and the highest witness of the existence of God. But all this is philosophical mythology. If we possessed within us a faculty, or an oracle, or deity to tell us what is true, and what is right and wrong... how could there be that infinite diversity of opinion as to what is true and what is right or wrong? We must learn that from other sources, and when we have learnt it from our teachers and by own experience and judgement, then and then only do we become conscious of having done what is right or wrong. If we like to call that consciousness, or that shame or that joy, conscience, we may do so, provided that we remember that we use poetic and mythological language, and that such language, unless properly guarded, may exercise a powerful influence on our character, whether for evil or for good. That almighty conscience may be a god to all mortals, as Menander says, but it may likewise become a dumb idol.*

*Natural Religion*, pp. 177–82

# 5
# History as Environment

## John Roberts

### I

In an earlier lecture in this series, criticism was directed against the idea that any final distinction, let alone separation, between the environment and objects (such as human beings) which it contains, was tenable. Though it may surprise philosophers, historians have of course long been aware that such disjunctions were logically improper, perhaps even impossible. But historians have to get on with the study of the concerns of real men and women in the real world. And we all know that in the general, everyday sense, we habitually and usefully distinguish 'environment' from some individual entity of which it is the setting. We see environment as that of which the individual entity, actively or passively, has to take account, to which it has to respond, even if that only means by accommodating itself to it. If we are thinking of ourselves – human beings – as the individual component of the relationship, environment is the world with which we have to grapple and cooperate. We know that the distinction is artificial and that it is a model which does not fit all the facts. Across that convenient boundary all sorts of currents flow, and many filaments run. Still, in the many ways in which the word 'environment' is used, there seems to be always inherent a useful idea of contrast, of otherness, of encounter or confrontation (in a neutral sense).

One might go further. From time to time there seem to be inherent in that antithesis certain implications of antagonism, exploitation, dialectical interplay. Put most bluntly, and in human terms, environments may master us if we do not master them. Even cooperation with environment is a form of mastery of it. And, of course, human beings have long collectively demonstrated a unique power to be masters. Before he is long on his island, Robinson Crusoe begins first to modify his environment and then to create a new one. The history of the natural sciences is a long story first of the understanding and then of the manipulation of Nature to produce desired environmental change. We are now even able to create friendly environments in space: people can live floating in constructed settings in that vast hostility for months on end.

It is obvious that environment itself is, in many ways, the product of history. (I speak of 'history' here not as mental activity but in the sense of 'what happened through human action', *res gestae*, of what is sometimes called the 'historical past'.) Such facts as topography, chemical and physical structures and climate are for the most part pre-historical. But there are other things in human environments which result from human agency in the past, from history. What is more, because of history they matter at some times more than at others. To delineate them, though, is not easy. They sprawl across the boundaries which separate old antitheses like mind and matter, objective and subjective. Take landscape. One such as the English, formed by centuries of human management, is clearly historical; it is a part of our environment which has been made by people. But what about the cultural and aesthetic assumptions with which we confront that landscape? They, too, are 'historical', made in the past but conditioning our life now, part of what I call historical environment. They exist in people's minds, but not all of them are consciously 'made' by people.

Is our human-made, or largely human-made, or partly human-made, historical environment susceptible to mastery, use, misuse as the natural phenomena of our human world have proved to be? Could one ever envisage the sort of total manipulation of the historical environment which seems to be attainable in the natural world? We are used to the idea of understanding Nature and working with the grain of it to achieve human purposes: could one 'manage' the historical past in the same way? The problem seems to be that, in the way I have been using the term, environment is not merely external. It is inside us, too. Right at the outset one meets what some philosophers would no doubt see as a merely verbal problem, but one which is, for historians, deeply disturbing (or should be). One can begin at a very material, physiological level. Our genetic pool can be traced back, I understand, to little tree-dwelling primates and even beyond them to the prosimians, sixty million or more years ago. To the changes brought about in their genetic legacy by millions and millions of accidents of selection in the hazardous, oddly-lit world of the primeval forest, we owe many human characteristics – for instance, the oppositional thumb, a way of seeing things as visual images and a certain nervous organization. Here, then, is an internalization of environmental factors which must be a part of our story – history.

This, though, is a matter of *pre*historic environment. Let us move on to the internalization of the historical. Philosophers used sometimes to speak of the 'contents of minds'. In these lectures I shall often touch on 'contents' with which historians are familiar – such things as attitudes, ways of understanding, categories, mythologies, hopes, fears, expectations, forebodings. All of these are truly part of our historical environment and they have an ambiguous aspect. They embody a problem. While they provide us, on the one hand, with tools and methods for the understanding (or misunderstanding) of the historical environment, they also form part of it; they are part of the 'other' which humans confront. They seem to me quite the most difficult part of our environment to grapple with.

Now in its other strugglings with environment, the human mind has been very successful. The evidence lies in humankind's demonstrated and unique power of making change. Uniquely among animals, humans have had built-in indeterminacy. Another way in which we might put it would be to say that humankind can have a history. Other animals do not have histories. Other animals have adapted to their environments and that might be taken as one sign of what it is not to have a history. The most momentous change in the evolution of our own species happened long ago when the human animal broke step with blind and casual selection and began to show it could modify its own environment. The oldest windbreak – which represents, I believe, the oldest evidence of building – has been dated to the era of *australopithecus* and may be a million years old. The old disjunction of Nature and Culture is clearly too sharp to be of much help here. Perhaps even before there was language to conceptualize it, the natural environment was being worked upon by humans, or human-like creatures. But when culture does come along it does not operate autonomously or without restraint, but in contexts which define its capacity to bring about change, and a part of those contexts is always the determining, self-enclosing nature of the culture itself. The vague term, 'environment', has to embrace historic culture both in its change-making and its determining roles.

So far I have been preliminary and general; let me now try to be more particular. Much of our world bears the visible stamp of history. All around us are things which originated in human action at certain moments or in certain eras of the past. Some have long outlived the age that gave them birth, and are merely trivial or decorative – beefeaters, curious rituals like conducting university ceremonies in Latin, standing for Loyal Toasts, or beating parish boundaries, some ancient ruins. Others are (like the Monarchy, Parliament, old universities such as Glasgow, and the Papacy) functionally much more important, even if not in the same way as once they were. We sometimes talk about such things in some such phrase as 'our heritage' or 'the legacy of the past'. Yet that does not take us very far. There is much else in the past which has big determining effects on what we can do now, even if those effects are exhaustingly difficult to define.

For example, in considering the British historical environment, you have to begin with prehistory, however boring you find it – with a group of islands on the edge of the Atlantic wind and water systems. They are, essentially, collections of navigable inlets and good harbours with easy access both to hinterlands enjoying good rainfall and moderate temperature and to the high seas. Men and women made use of these facts. They set up relations with some places rather than others, developed certain diplomatic and strategic views, evolved principles and traditions, and did many other things. The experience of insularity silently worked away at the shaping of institutions: the virtual absence of military invasion from English history in modern times is, I am sure, crucial to the hardening of certain social and political forms and to a certain gentleness over such matters as civic behaviour and the proper use of police power.

With that we arrive (too quickly, I fear, but I have little time) at ideas as a constituent of environment. They are central to it. One country is Christian, one is Muslim, one is Confucian: the people of each will, in consequence, behave differently in addressing themselves to reality. Then there are more specific ideas, present in some environments and not in others. The idea of the clearly delimited and sovereign territorial state, for example, though now almost everywhere taken for granted, is one which most societies, for most of recorded time, have been able to do without. It is historically contingent. It is true, also, that different societies have had very distinctive ideas about history. One may show a somewhat vague but widely held notion that history is more or less the story of a broad current of amelioration and improvement occasionally interrupted or diverted by bursts of folly and wickedness. In another, history is formally and explicitly defined as a story of progressive advance in the same general direction but by means of violent struggle, above all of social classes. Other societies virtually do not think about history at all. Yet even they may in practice accept quite uncritically certain summary statements about the past. Ideas about history can in fact affect the mentalities of whole societies (even, perhaps, of civilizations). They are part of the historical environment. They can have, that is to say, an effective role in shaping what people do.

Unfortunately, explaining the part played by ideas even in one historical environment (and delimiting one raises problems, too) is technically often very difficult. Many ideas come, so to speak, well wrapped up. History shows them lying about almost, unobserved. Let me cite a trivial case. The *maire* of a French town wears a tricolour scarf or sash, while his English equivalent wears a chain of office. Now it is not easy to read what those facts say. One has to know quite a lot of history to appreciate the difference between them. By his sash, the Frenchman is designated the representative of the nation-state; he is the local embodiment of its authority. The English mayor's chain, though, almost certainly supports a pendant jewel incorporating a coat of arms which is the symbol of the local community which he or she represents. To explain the sash you have to understand that the French had a revolution in 1789; to explain the coat of arms you should know something about the Middle Ages and its notions of civic liberties. Day to day, of course, it does not much matter whether you know any of this or not. Questions about the effective authority and duties of the two officers can be settled much more simply and straightforwardly, by consultation of the law. But those laws, too, would be very different, if the legacies of historical attitudes had been different.

The idea of unconscious associations also suggests a different instance. One notion which for a long time appeared to serve our country well, was that politics naturally organizes itself in confrontational mode, with two sides in conflict and debate striving to win the support of the public. The House of Commons has twice been rebuilt to conform to this idea, so it is evidently a potent one. Roughly, it has been dominant in this country from the early nineteenth century, when the concept of legitimate, loyal Opposition appeared, to the present day. In both this country and the United States, its plausibility was endorsed by long periods of effective restriction of political competition to two huge party interests (to whose consolidation, of course, it also contributed). Now some other countries which have taken up constitutional politics have assumed that this institutional model was intrinsic to it (Spain and her former colonies in the last century; post-colonial countries in this). Yet they have not found it workable. It does not seem to fit environments to which violent ideological disagreement, a lack of settled respect for law and precarious economic conditions are intrinsic. That has caused much disappointment. It arises because, although often unrecognized, such ideas about the typical organization of political activity carry with them a penumbra of history, cultural potential and assumption which does not suit all historical environments. They are not automatically transferable elsewhere, though superficial analogy and quick judgement may tempt people to try to transplant them. The environments in which they were shaped permit some things, ease and favour others, but also clog up, complicate and generate friction when such categories are applied in another setting.

They carry an enormous amount of history with them, and it is very hard to recognize what that means, or, indeed, to delineate its extent, until there has been a failure.

Consider, though, something apparently much simpler, political colour coding. It can acquire huge evocative power – orange and green, for example, or the red of the flag of revolution. This last has in fact undergone a curious transformation, for the red flag first emerged as an anti-revolutionary signal. The legislators of the French Revolution prescribed that a *drapeau rouge* should be displayed as the sign that the military would soon use force to disperse a crowd which was out of hand. Red was, of course, by then already a constituent of the Tricolour. In neither instance, though, had red any revolutionary associations. The famous flag of revolutionary France was derived from adding the traditional white of the Bourbons to the red and blue of the heraldic arms of the city of Paris. Within a short time, the Tricolour became the symbol of the Revolution and these origins were forgotten. It was eagerly taken up – in different national colours – by revolutionaries elsewhere and is still the basis of, for instance, the flags of Italy and Belgium. No French regime after 1800 ever felt able to abandon it: the flag had become a symbol, a sign of acceptance of, if not of commitment to, the revolutionary side of the French past. But often such phenomena (as the origin of the Tricolour shows) do not merely set previous history aside: they also come to terms with it, incorporate it, and that can show the weight of the unconscious past, too.

Detail often shows the operation of this weight more vividly and strikingly than the broader perspective. I hope therefore that you will tolerate a further example drawn from the era of the French Revolution. I have drawn attention to it elsewhere, but I make no apology for that, for I think it revealing.[1] In 1796 much of France was disturbed. Some of it was formally and actually in rebellion against the central revolutionary government in Paris, and the west of France was specially troubled. One day in that year, a young girl from a village on the edge of the Sarthe, of a family who were, like herself, committed to the revolutionary cause, was attacked and murdered by ruffians. The word went round, quickly, that she died because of her revolutionary sympathies. It was said that her attackers were royalists, though it is hard to believe they were anything but casual rapists. Still, she began to be spoken of as a republican 'martyr'. Soon, people began to gather at her grave, to lay flowers and little gifts there; miraculous cures were reported. The girl was alleged to have been seen rising to heaven, an angel with wings of red, white and blue (the colours of the Revolution). That seems odd. Angels were usually regarded as the stock-in-trade of reaction and counter-revolution. For the revolutionaries, who was not for the Revolution was against it; you were reckoned to be committed either to the reactionary, superstitious past or the revolutionary, progressive future. The local inhabitants, nonetheless, though committed to the Revolution, found it easiest to express that commitment in forms of traditional religion usually associated with the anti-revolutionary cause.

This paradoxical little episode says much about the power of historic environment to define the limits of action. History does not only leave passive legacies of objective problems, events, institutions, but legacies of ways we can think about the past. We have a degree of freedom, but it is very incomplete, to select and define the past which we choose to recover and use. We may speak of it explicitly, but often do not realize the extent to which language, argumentative structure and imagery limit and control our freedom to deal with the past and to understand it. We are often (one might say) 'used' by the past whose weight we do not feel, but find comfortable, as easily taken for granted as a familiar suit of clothes.

I do not wish to suggest that such facts must be deplored. The weight of history can be valuable social ballast; it can help individuals in confusing situations. It is often something we can applaud as a sensitive awareness of tradition. I recall that in 1961 I spent a very happy semester at the University of South Carolina. The year was, I need hardly remind you, a very special year for the whole South. It was the centenary of what (according to your point of view) was called the Civil War, or the War between the States. Nowhere in the whole United States, I suppose, was its importance more apparent than in South Carolina. Even though a terrible tragedy had begun in 1861, it merited commemoration as a great historical event. The year 1961 therefore brought with it a deal of good-humoured and sometimes elegant masquerade. Luxuriant whiskers and beards sprouted from beneath locks of a length not to be seen again until the late sixties and the era of Woodstock. But their purpose, of course, was very different from the hirsute hippiness of *Hair*. The aim was not to distinguish the wearer from society, but to identify him with it; this was a part of celebrations which involved dressing up and riding about in buggies with ladies arrayed in bonnets and long dresses. The aim was to remind people that South Carolina had a particular tradition of its own. Many people felt able to join in the pageant with a clear conscience.

Though dressing up emphasized the continuity of tradition it did not, of course, mean that anyone wished to go to war again. The citizens of South Carolina simply wished to re-affirm their pride in a common history, and to remember with affection and admiration the deeds –

especially the brave deeds – and the sufferings of their forbears. They were aware of a past which distinguished them from their contemporaries in other parts of the Union who also celebrated that centenary. They felt that past was important enough to have something to say about why they were still in 1961 different from other loyal Americans. It was, so far as an outsider could judge, a very innocent exercise, and if it indulged a somewhat one-sided and perhaps a little magnolia-tinted view of the past of the Confederacy – well, no great harm was done. Indeed, just because their sense of the past – even their preoccupation with it – might nerve people the better to meet the challenges of today with a broader and more sensitive view of what might lie behind them, such a preoccupation with it might even be, for a time, a positively good thing.

Such were my first simple thoughts about 1961. But let me now mention a second fact which then struck me about the weight of the past as it appeared in South Carolina in 1961. What was observable was the *indirect* influence of the past through a particular vision or view of it. It came to us, that is to say, through the minds of people, where it had been imaginatively transmuted into something which may not have been altogether like what actually could have been seen there a hundred years before. Yet it was still very important in shaping behaviour – it was a myth about the past, in short. This is clearly different from the way the past exercises its weight directly, through the sheer inertia and intractability of legacies. South Carolina provided an example of that, too. Also in 1961 a busload of Freedom Riders came to Columbia, on their way to the troubled city of Montgomery, Alabama. Whatever the rights or wrongs of their particular response to the weight of the past, those riders felt that weight in the second, more direct way. The problem of the black American certainly did not begin in 1861. But the past of which the war of 1861 was a part left to the future a complex of problems which was still determining people's lives a century later. Emancipation, as we all know, released black Americans into formal legal equality and the possession of certain rights, but also into a particular historical environment, cluttered up with ancient principle and prejudice. Developments in the economy, technology and education then slowly operated upon society and this took place alongside – among other things – a persistent social segregation which had still been an issue in the South in the 1950s. Worse still, they led to the possibly more appalling, because less easily categorized, troubles of the ghettos of the northern cities in the 1960s. There you have examples of the inertia of the past on the doorstep; America could not run away from the social and economic facts which her history had bequeathed to her, and they were there, inescapable, whatever historical mythology people chose to adopt about the way those facts arose.

Let me offer one further macrocosmic example of the dual operation, conceptual and actual, of historical legacies. Though it is usually easier to see them at work in detail in particular incidents and places, we have, after all, to think about and deal with the problems of whole societies, and sometimes very large ones. It is harder in such cases to be precise, and I am no expert, but let us for a moment, even if it can only be very briefly, think about China.

For most of the last century and much of this China was engaged first in resisting another, alien, civilization and then in coming to terms with it. That brought change and adaptation in Chinese life at every level. Some urged on the process; some resisted it. It was given different names by different observers: 'reform', 'revolution', 'modernization', 'westernization', for instance. After the revolution of 1911 there was always a strong likelihood that the process would be successful. Doubt persisted only about how long it would take and by what route change would come about. After 1947 that, too, seemed clear, although there were still surprises to come. Yet the labels were often misleading. At every stage (including the forty years since the Communist regime took power as a national government) the process of change in China has been far richer, more complex and more subtle than any mere substitution of one set of norms and institutions for another. People talked as if that was all that was going on, of course. They spoke of introducing democracy, of the triumph of nationalism or socialism, and pointed to specific changes such as the emancipation of women and the appearance (at times) of a free press. Yet the outcome never seemed to be quite what was meant by such words and institutions in the civilization they came from. Of course, it could not be. Though successful, the innovative, aggressive ideas of Western civilization underwent change as they rooted themselves in China, for they had to come to terms with the specific Chinese environment and Chinese history.

One crucial fact about the environment and that history was China's long centuries of comparative isolation. This partly arose from physical remoteness. China was a long way from the Mediterranean civilizations of Greece and Rome, or their later European successors. Even India and the Islamic world were usually to be reached only along a few, long, often very high land routes. China could be easily approached only from the northern deserts and plains. By sea, a few Arab descents apart, she was not much visited until the seventeenth century. Once reached, moreover, though her great river valleys offered ways inland, China's topography was discouraging: the 'vast jumble of mountains' was virtually impenetrable except from the north.[2]

Yet this long remote and inaccessible land was for virtually the whole of its history the largest political unit governing a single society of human beings in the world. It must be left to Sinologists to say what this meant in internal government, but it is clear that the empire was effective as an idea. Ideology reinforced isolation. A major act of policy in the fifteenth century symbolizes this. China was then a great sea power, able to send fleets of hundreds of ships as far as the Persian Gulf and East Africa. Chinese shipyards could then build ocean-going junks which were the largest people-carrying vehicles anywhere in the world. Yet the Ming emperor stopped the building of such vessels and forbade such maritime enterprise. That choice, so contrasted with those of the Iberian monarchies at the same time, had as its background a consciousness of superiority to the rest of the world. China, it was thought, could well get on without it. Until the nineteenth century China was to have no ministry of Foreign Affairs (as we should call it), because she was believed to be the centre of the world, to whose emperor all other peoples owed deference, obedience and tribute, as a universal ruler. The reality was that neighbouring lands – Korea, Burma, Indo-China – acknowledged Chinese suzerainty, while so little that was true and certain was known of lands further away that a vision of the world as a concentric system, perhaps in varying degrees of dependency, appeared quite plausible.

A high culture of outstanding refinement and a technology in many ways manifestly more advanced than anything available elsewhere (silk, printing, gunpowder) long reinforced the sense of superiority of China's educated class. For a long time it gave them a very sceptical view of what other civilizations had to offer. Even this is not the whole explanation of Chinese conservatism, though. There was also always a deep resistance to innovation arising from Confucian tradition, with its emphasis on the fulfilment of the duties of one's station and preservation of the *status quo*. Finally, Chinese government had to deal with very large numbers of people. This presented big problems, but also promoted an acceptance of social disciplines and a willingness to subordinate the individual which were much more marked than in, say, Western or European tradition. The Chinese historical environment was not to be propitious to the toleration of individual deviants from accepted norms. Opposition found it hard to legitimize itself: it represented a potential disruption of society and was innately distasteful to Chinese elites.

It followed from such facts that when some Chinese came to think change was needed, at least one path towards it was hard, perhaps impossible, to take. In Chinese society the ideological and social roots of the constitutionalism and democracy to which some reformers aspired could find little nourishment. So, in the 1920s and 1930s, it emerged that revolution would be needed to change things. In due course, that revolution proved to be very violent and demanding. But it, too, has turned out to be distinctively Chinese (and never more so, it may be remarked, than in its recent attempts to find a role for traditional Chinese merchant entrepreneurship). Although there were times when Chinese communist rhetoric suggested a blanket imitation of Soviet communism, swings in policy showed in the long run that what was happening was that another tradition was being drawn upon in order to use it for the better securing of China's own integrity and individuality. Of course, the nature of the forces playing on China mattered, too. Of alternative European models, communism rather than another had been chosen as a means and it was communism of a very special kind, the Soviet version, which had its own historical baggage to cope with.

China is an outstanding example of the weight and complexity of historical environment. The virtually irresistible comparison with Japan has been made too often to repeat it now; it is enough to recall that although Japan and her culture owed much to China's, the Japanese historical environment somehow disposed that nation to an earlier, more rapid, and at the same time more consciously controlled and successful response to challenges similar to those faced by the Middle Kingdom. The Japanese were accustomed to cultural symbiosis. They could accept categories which were different from one another (and even opposed to one another), as if they stood in functional, productive inter-relation. Co-existence and cooperation between what we may call 'Western' and Japanese civilization did not have to be excluded as a possibility, therefore.

I hope I have now justified at least my view that the general phenomenon of historical environment merits attention. I shall limit myself by way of summary to three brief concluding comments. The first is that history cannot be separated out of an environment. History is an indispensable component of the circumstances which appear to push a society in one direction rather than another, making certain outcomes more likely and certain others impossible *a priori*. This, obviously, is not to say very much: it may barely go beyond tautology, beyond saying that everything in the past goes to make the present, and so we should study the past as hard as we can in order to see it more clearly and realistically, both as a creative and an inhibiting force. That may not seem very helpful. Most of us have to grapple with a very specific present and that requires hard distinctions within the total world of historical phenomena in order to decide what is relevant to its understanding.

But that is my second comment: we always have to distinguish within the historic environment in order to deal with it. And the fact that such distinction is possible is intrinsic to it. We have already seen, for instance, that some parts of the past are human-made, while others have a priority arising from their more or less aboriginal nature. But this does not take us very far, and we must again be careful to avoid a false dichotomy; human agency determines the way in which nature is made effective. Minerals are not made by humans, but their discovery, extraction and exploitation by humans are what make them historically relevant. Disease is not human-made, and the relative absence of certain endemic levels of disease in medieval and early modern Europe, while Asia contained great reservoirs of infection, must owe something to such facts as climate and the availability of certain foods. Yet, as time goes by and more is learnt about agriculture, quarantine, medicine and much else, the contribution of human action (or the lack of it) to the persistence or eradication of disease is fairly obvious. The line between the human-made and natural past is always blurred.

My third comment is about another distinction we need to consider in dealing with what is presented to us by history: it is time for historians to give as much attention to the observer as to what is observed. It may be that the historical environment is best seen not as objective reality but as a selection of the past which historical judgement can determine to be relevant and influential. At any one moment some of it will be actually present to us, some of it only there *in posse*, awaiting revelation and authentication. It is not always easy to pin down for study. The environment as history is also partly constituted by selections of the past which are culturally dominant from time to time. In the commonsense view, our past is a shared past, yet people see it in different ways. So it is not perhaps shared, after all. The resonance of 1688 could be very different in Somerset, where it awakes only dim notions of the end of Monmouth's rebellion a couple of years earlier and the legend of Judge Jeffreys, and in a city which has football teams named Celtic and Rangers.[3] And, in spite of commonsense, we usually admit this. When we look for a common past to try to agree about it, there is usually rapid agreement that a common past is hard to find. There is not some one thing out there, waiting to be uncovered: we can only identify particular pasts, selected pasts about which people want to make judgements of value and meaning, even if coincidences of view between important groups of people do turn out to be possible from time to time.

After all, we all readily acknowledge that views of the past change in time. The Middle Ages were invented by the men of the Renaissance: they needed the concept to explain their own relation to Antiquity. Subsequently, that idea (and the associated notions of medieval character, style, culture) underwent many re-evaluations and reconsiderations. It has been idealized and despised. Its once-sharp boundaries are now irrevocably blurred. At one time one aspect of medieval history has been singled out as crucial, at one time another. One might remark, too, that similar re-evaluations have taken place in the idea of the Renaissance itself, of Antiquity, and (in a narrower, but still wide context) of the pasts of individual nations. No one now wants to emphasize the constitutionally progressive nature of British history as Macaulay was sure he could do. We know, too, that differing views of the past have been exploited and even invented so as to make possible action in the present. Individuals have sought to ride to power by exploiting particular views of history on the backs of the Jewish threat, the Spanish legend of the Reconquest or the Popish Plot. Some groups have sought definition and have invented history to provide it. Seventeenth-century Dutch burghers commissioned paintings of barbarians whom they saw as their forbears struggling with Romans and spoke of the ancient *Batavi* as their lineal ancestors. The historic reality of black African nationalism has led to much groping after the shadows of the medieval kingdoms of Ghana and Mali. There is always a possibility of a creative construction of a false past, a deliberate elaboration of a historical environment. At this point, though, I am beginning to touch on topics for later discussion. Let me not try to take the matter further today. Let me suggest simply that we can agree that the human environment is importantly shaped by history in all its aspects, mental as well as material, internal as well as external, and can exert very strong influence on our behaviour, not least through its shaping of categories with which we attempt to grapple with the world; that in order to escape that influence, it will be best if we are aware of it, because that may make it easier to avoid being its victims; that, finally, in dealing with the difficulties this presents, we should not expect it to be easy to arrive at shared judgements about the past – though historians have often been expected to deliver them.

## II Problems Posed by Historical Environment

Almost every day reminds us that a measure of frustration is part and parcel of human life. Each of us feels from time to time that our wills are thwarted by the wills of others or by a certain intractability in things. Some of those things, whether we recognize it or not, are historical constructs – ideas, attitudes, habits, institutions and many other things which have come into being through human action. Often, they are those big cultural determinants which, I suggested in my first lecture, are never more powerful than when they are not recognized, never more influential than when we undergo their influence unconsciously. Sometimes, then, our historical environment contains much that is either actually or potentially frustrating, placing restraint on our freedom. That is one of the problems history poses as environment, its power to frustrate people's aspirations.

Now we incline to believe that if we could only see our historical environment more truly and justly, in a more balanced and objective way, we might find ways of escaping its thrall, of enlarging our freedom, in fact. But, as I have already suggested, it is very difficult to do this. In the first place (as we noticed), our standpoint as observers is determined by the process we observe: history. The assumptions and stereotypes in our minds, the categories we bring to the understanding of our material, are themselves shaped by historical environment. Perhaps, we might think, this means that we may have a better chance of getting things right, or at least of not going so badly wrong, if we study times and societies remote from our own; at least in them, we shall not take so much, unexamined, for granted. On the other hand, a moment's reflection should remind us that there is no guarantee down that line that we shall not find anachronism or ignorance invalidating our judgements. Almost the only assumption we can ever confidently make is that the past remains much more alien than what those judgements convey.

There is also a danger (if we start from the hope or wish to overcome frustration through historical understanding) of over-simplifying the problems of historical environment by reducing them to a single, straightforward antithesis, a confrontation of inertia and innovation. But the model is one-sided. That is not the way history works. The past can force change on us as well as stand in the way of it. If we see the past always as inertia in opposition to innovation, the historical and determining in conflict with the non-historical, freely-willed, we are blinkered. The internalizing of history of which we have already spoken removes the ground for making any confident, clear-cut distinction between the historically-shaped and the freely-willed, even if (as I doubt) such a distinction is conceivable in principle. Everyone knows that Marx said that the task of philosophers is to change the world. We also know that whatever divergences and contradictions are grouped together under the general name of 'Marxism', its exponents have always claimed for that ideology a revolutionary power to change things, to innovate, and that its founder was a great innovator. So, in some ways, he was. Yet Marx himself, at his most innovatory, often only brought forward and emphasized values already championed in the eighteenth century, as part of the general movement of thought we call the Enlightenment. 'There is nothing specifically Marxist about them', one (Marxist) authority goes so far as to say, pointing out that Marx' principles are derived from a long tradition culminating in humanitarian, liberal ideology, and whose earliest phases are religious.[4] Marx' inheritance goes far beyond Hegel and British Political Economy. Nor is it just an inheritance of formal ideas. It is also marked by a certain cataclysmic and inspirational view of the French Revolution, by assumptions about the superiority of German culture and the power it gave to 'subdue, absorb and assimilate' the Slav peoples,[5] about the inferiority of Oriental civilization and much, much more. Strange to say, Marx' thought is even more rooted in history than is usually allowed, and its power to disturb and innovate certainly came from within history as much as from outside it.

To cut history off, to achieve a true break in historical continuity, a break where there can be discerned no connection except the accidental with what went before, is, of course, logically impossible. Almost the only occasion on which innovation comes even mainly from 'outside' history in any comprehensible sense is when technological or scientific advance presents unanticipated new opportunities; a new use for a raw material, for instance, or a new medium of communication. Then, of course, opportunities have to be taken; but they are taken by people whose minds are shaped by history. When the moon was first explored, the symbolic objects left behind by the first explorers and unmanned probes were national flags and ideological texts; the Bible and the works of Lenin. We might remark, too, now that one of the transforming forces of our day, television, has been let loose for forty years or so on America, that one of the earliest beneficiaries has turned out to be one of the most deeply-rooted and conservative forces in American society, religious fundamentalism, given new scope by the electronic church of TV religion. People often make the new serve the old.

The danger of simple words like 'innovate' and 'inertia' is that they give too passive and too undifferentiated an impression of the 'weight of the past' (to use another cant phrase). Historical environment is not uniform. It offers resistance to change in some directions and promotes it in others. Working with its grain is much easier than working against it. Different environments respond to the same new forces in different ways. We all know that the arrival of printing in Europe in the fifteenth century marked an epoch. It not only led to many specific changes, of which the growth of literacy among the laity was the most obvious, but it contributed to an immense acceleration and increase in the circulation of information. It affected, that is to say, both outcome and process, and both had huge importance. Well before the fifteenth century, though, China had printers. Yet no such dramatic changes followed the adoption of printing in the Chinese sphere of civilization. There, literacy did not spread beyond a narrow class; no such acceleration in the circulation of information occurred as had done in Europe. This is not the place to explore the reason why. But it seems reasonable to guess that it was not just a technical problem posed by a written system of characters which was absent in printing alphabetic languages. A language itself is, of course, one part of the historical environment. But it is only one and there must be others which help to explain so great a difference.

My first observation today, then, is simply that we should beware of over-simplified expectations. Innovation and consequent discontinuity has a way of popping up out of the most unpromising historical environment. If we consider the changes to lives brought by it, the most revolutionary event in Ireland's history in the nineteenth century must be the Great Famine. Yet that disaster was rooted – I am not intending to be facetious – in history, in the introduction earlier of the potato to Ireland, and its successful establishment as a staple of the Irish diet. More people could get a living from a given area of land if it grew potatoes. In Ireland, therefore, the historic role of the potato was revolutionary, for it encouraged population growth to the point of entailing catastrophe if the crop failed in conditions where other food was not readily available. In England, the role of the potato may have been profoundly conservative, helping to keep wages down (though if the matter were further pursued, I dare say one could argue that low wages had important innovatory significance in allowing the accumulation of new capital for investment). In either country, though, the explanation of a single episode or process has to take into account the historical setting which includes the introduction of a new food, though that came many years earlier.

There are some major difficulties in the way of understanding such complex processes. What is more, given the new extent, complexity and volatility of the world we must live in, we now probably face even greater difficulties than did our predecessors in grappling with historical environment. Ours is a world which is for the first time truly one human system. It is also one in which change is more rapid and more accepted than ever before. For all its turbulence and teeming variety, though, it also sometimes looks more uniform than ever before. It is characterized by a superficial standardization of terminologies and formal institutions drawn from Western sources. This may lead to misunderstanding, and certainly leads to a widespread, destabilizing phenomenon: the internalization in other cultures of aims and values which are Western and European in origin, and therefore exotic. Here, then, are particular difficulties which face us in trying to deal with our own historic environment. Yet it is more important than ever to try to grapple with it just because unanticipated change now poses the possibility of greater dangers than in the past, through its scope, rapidity and complexity.

In addition to such difficulties, moreover, there are still old and solid obstacles in our way in some societies. Many parts of the world display the human propensity to deny need for change. That, of course, implies that any possibility of useful consideration of history and its effects on us is set aside as pointless at the outset. The historic environment is, unconsciously, accepted as a datum and, equally unconsciously, formalized in one specific reading of what it may mean. In societies which still do not accept the possibility of historic change, there is a widespread presupposition that vested interests and routine perceptions are all that is needed. The historic environment is seen as protection. Such conservatism has sometimes worked well, it must be said: perhaps the outstanding example is that of ancient Egypt, where even stylistic change was very limited for thousands of years. But, as the nineteenth-century history of China and Japan, and the even more recent experience of such social fossils as Tibet, all show, external forces often now present conservative societies with irresistible pressures. This may well prove true of some modern Islamic societies which have drawn on the memories of past glories and the brotherhood of the Faithful when faced with challenge and disappointment.

But there are problems even within societies which are prepared to envisage change. The obstacles they pose to an effective handling of the historical environment tend to be more disguised. One which is common is the prevalence of general theories which are part of their historical environment. Racialist theories of history, to take a crude example, have often been used as a way of coming to terms with the historical reality of alien, minority presences. Few in this room would be likely to be taken in by them, but in many parts of the world, they still awake resonances and contaminate the present. More intellectually respectable and pretentious schemata, though, also lead to failure. Classical Marxism (by which I mean the somewhat mechanical, evolutionary form of historical materialism which was the core of European socialist ideology from the death of Marx to the death of Stalin) was a wonderfully effective generator of very specific answers to problems about the direction which history was taking. Unfortunately most of the answers were wrong. Whatever may have been its precise origins, Soviet Russian policy in China in the 1920s could be justified theoretically by an analysis which said that, in accordance with Marxist principle, a backward country like China could not contemplate socialist evolution until the nationalist bourgeoisie had carried out its own historic role of creating the conditions for proletarian revolution. The sad result was the delivery to destruction of the urban cadres of the Chinese Communist Party. This in due course promoted the emergence of a very Chinese form of communism under leadership distrustful of the Soviet Union's self-proclaimed right to leadership.

Old-fashioned Marxism was a very explicit matter. The schematization which it favoured is always pretty obvious. But other general theories are no less encumbering because less clearly articulated. No one nowadays, I suspect, believes in the 'inevitable' stages of social development which were commonplaces of eighteenth-century sociology. But the notion of progress which lies behind them is a different matter. Many people still retain this idea at their historical centre of gravity, so to speak, in the sense that they assume that, in default of some visible reason to the contrary, there is a normal evolution of institutions in a particular direction. Americans seem often to have acted on this assumption in making foreign policy. Democracy, in the sense of formal provision for wide participation in the suffrage and an electoral process generating representative organs and ensuring the periodic validation of rulers, has often been seen and prescribed by American statesmen as, self-evidently, the path all nations and peoples should and would, if history had its way, follow. This has led to much disappointment in practice, but misgivings and reflection on failure do not seem to weaken the belief. It appears to me to owe much to ways of looking at the past with an assumption that progress is the norm. Of course, that is to say it owes much to American history. That history, though, did not lie behind the post-colonial 'new nations' of the 1950s and 1960s. They have often been vexed in recent years to reconcile the expectations awoken by the promise of 'democracy' with the realities imposed by the local environment. The uncritical assumption that there is a 'normal' pattern of political development has also helped to graft on post-colonial states the idea of nationalism, the belief that political legitimacy only exists where the state-structure is based upon the will of a nation. (Of course, I do not mean to suggest that political tactics and propriety did not count for just as much, or more, in the process.) Nationhood is seen as the appropriate and inevitable outcome of history, and not merely (as it should be) as one of the master ideas or myths of the age. This has often been disastrous, because of the frequent indifference and irrelevance of the frontiers of post-colonial states (based as they are on the agreements of former colonial powers) to actual community and social identity.

Even when a concern exists to understand and learn from history without distorting it, all too easily this can give rise to false parallels and analogies. There is no need for schematic principles or grand theory on the basis of which the past can be read and misunderstood; there can simply be a false assumption that all the relevant facts have been considered and are understood. Much of the conduct of British foreign policy in this century seems to me to have been dogged by the perception of false analogies and public misconception.

These somewhat brief and summary illustrations all concern false ideas which are believed to be true. They can be articulated. When they are, we are tempted to believe that criticism can reduce their distorting power. We should not be too confident. Beyond the somewhat hazy border of quasi-rational theory, though, we confront myths. By this term I mean ideas which, whether rooted in objective reality or not, are effective. They provide satisfactory imaginative resolutions of complexity so as to release emotion for action. They operate very directly and immediately, certainly below the level of conscious thought, though they may blur into it. It is difficult in describing Marxism, for instance, to be sure just where the borders of observation, theory and myth should be traced. Ideas like that of the revolutionary vanguard, or the class struggle, as they are set out in Marx' writings, seem to me almost incapable of satisfactory reduction to empirical terms. Yet as striking and evocative images it cannot be doubted that they show enormous vigour and effectiveness in spurring people to act.

Most of us, though, are likely to distrust historical myth when we can detect it. We are well aware of its potential for harm. Myths can bring on disaster. The perverse historical consciousness of Hitler, say, is too complicated to explore here, but some place in the decisions which brought his unhappy country to needless ruin, and to a much more terrible fate than the one which would have followed a much earlier surrender when the war was already visibly lost by Germany, was surely played by his mythical conception of German history, of the German nation's historic task, of the racial eugenics made possible by the drive to the East, and many other mad ideas. Of course, a Hitler is very unusual. Yet it can hardly be doubted that the onslaught on Russia – evocatively code-named 'Barbarossa', in a reminiscence of a medieval crusading German emperor – awoke for many Germans vague feelings about participation in a centuries-old struggle of Slav and Teuton. In that myth, the physical advance of German settlement since the Middle Ages, the Christianizing of pagan peoples since the days of Charlemagne, and the superiority of Germanic culture all came to bear. No nation is without some elements in its historical sub-conscious which are better left unaroused (the Germans are certainly not alone in that) but the same sources would not have been available to sustain, say, British or French public opinion, even if other, equally misleading, mythologies can be seen to operate upon them from time to time. It was a possible creation of a particular historical environment.

But let us consider less alarming kinds of historical mythology. One example might be found in one major organizing myth of our political culture, the political antithesis of Left and Right. This mobilizes energy by reducing complex political issues to a simple model. It implies and sometimes asserts that all political differences can be expressed on a single spectrum. At one extreme (the Left) lie beliefs such as the rights of the individual, equality, democracy, progress and so on; in some circumstances, therefore, *Pas des ennemis à la Gauche!* On the extreme Right can be found a cherishing of order, discipline, duty, hierarchy, the authority of the existing regime. This schematic concept is not a scientific hypothesis, but a historical by-product, formed in 1789 in the early French Revolution. One of the accidents of that time was that in the first National Assembly those who wanted to carry the Revolution forward sat together on the President's left, and those who opposed them sat on his right. Other accidents then further shaped and enriched the antithesis this distribution expressed. The Revolution quickly so divided people that more and more issues seemed to fit into larger conflicts; the past versus the future, democracy versus aristocracy, enlightenment versus superstition, the will to change versus historic right, progress versus reaction, and so on. As time went by, blood was shed, property was violated, injustice was done. Moderates found their positions suspect (from both sides), their lives more and more difficult. If you were for the Revolution, you were against all those who opposed it, and vice versa. All issues seemed to reduce to one, and all that was needed to clarify people's political position was to specify how strongly they felt in relation to well-defined extremes. Every political difference, or difference which could be politicized, was visualized as a function of a basic division of political outlook. Eventually, it was believed to reflect also one of ideas, taste, emotion, character and even personality.

This is, of course, a great encouragement to a feeling of mastering history; it makes much of it an intelligible process. This was one reason why the idea that politics could be reduced to the opposition of Left and Right was exported with such success from France in the nineteenth century to countries where issues could be stated in terms not dissimilar to those of French politics. In the twentieth century it achieved even further-flung success; many non-European countries now talk in terms of Left and Right, too. Attempts were even made to employ it in the two great Anglo-Saxon democracies and we hear it taken for granted (though not very illuminatingly, it is true) in television discussions about the Conservative and Labour parties in Britain. This is surprising, because even as shorthand, it does not fit very well. We all know that Mrs Thatcher is an innovator[6] and many fervent members of the Labour Party are not. Indeed, it hardly ever has fitted British politics. But there is much else it does not fit, too. The idea of fraternity, for instance, can be associated with principles usually thought to be irreconcilably far apart on the spectrum. And that is because the idea of a Left/Right division is a myth, a concept which is significant as a means of mobilizing emotion for action, rather than as a theory explaining facts, and a myth which did not arise in our historical environment, but in an alien one. When now applied by those who do not understand this (or perhaps by some who do), it can present an obstacle to the understanding of historical reality. That it can make a difference to behaviour is not in question. If you really believe that to align yourself today with Mr Arthur Scargill implies that you are aligning yourself in some ideal sense with the Tolpuddle Martyrs, then it may well make a difference to how you behave. But it does not say much for your understanding of British history or of the real historic legacies we have to cope with today.

Let me now take a somewhat different tack. So far, I have been discussing what might be called conceptual barriers to understanding. They distort or complicate our perception of events and make it harder to see the historical environment in a proper light. The difficulty to which I now wish to turn concerns less the just estimation of historical events and forces, than the conclusion drawn from such estimation. I want to spend the remainder of this lecture talking about the myth of historic guilt.

People often show concern for what they see as responsibility for things done in the past. Sometimes (if they tend to view the past rather with regret than with satisfaction) they feel guilt about it. Although they used to, nowadays they rarely show pride. This, it appears to me, shows that we are confronting something arising from the very historical environment we seek to understand. It is a matter of particular environments: the Americans and the English show lots of guilt about the past, the French hardly ever do. The aim of the doctrine of historic responsibility is not understanding, but emotional release and action now. And because of this, it gets in the way of understanding.

Let me specify. We often hear assertions that, for instance, white Australians should feel guilty about what has been done to the aboriginal Australians, not only recently but from the arrival of the first white settlers; that modern Americans should feel guilty about the history of those we used to call 'Red Indians'; that all white people should feel guilt about the slave trade in Africa; that Germans – and perhaps the rest of the world – should feel guilt about the Holocaust. Merely to set out such a list will, of course, set your minds working about important differences even between these few cases. What they have in common, though, is that, emerging inescapably from the past, they are alleged to confront living men and women with moral responsibility and, explicitly or implicitly, to place on them the onus of acting in some way. The acts envisaged may be acts of reparation, of contrition, of simple intellectual correction of what is seen as false historical record, or even of retribution – their nature does not matter. What they reveal is a specific demand or plea to come to terms with and master or exorcize the past by doing certain things now.

I believe that moral passion and guilt tend to drive people to false perspectives on the past, to obliterate much that is significant in it. As a result, we are likely to misunderstand our historical environment and behave unwisely if our approach is dominated by a sense of our own moral involvement. But there is a long history of such thinking. Although our own century has heard more about historic responsibility than earlier ages, it is not a new idea. In early times, if I recall the Old Testament properly, collective guilt, descending from generation to generation, was often attributed to individual peoples and tribes. In medieval Europe it was the core of anti-semitic thinking that all Jews continued to share in the guilt of those who crucified our Lord. To take less sinister and yet now equally unacceptable examples, medieval Europeans also believed that a specific historic act such as acceptance of lordship or a commitment to allegiance might be irrevocably binding not merely upon those who made the act, but upon their descendants and successors. Until the emergence of a clear notion of popular sovereignty, such commitments were long regarded as a firm basis for attributing responsibilities and duties. (This was, I suppose, essentially what was at stake between Locke and Filmer.) Later, it came to be accepted that duties and responsibilities thus allegedly incurred could be cast off at will by those who had no part in the original transactions (if, indeed, those transactions ever actually took place). As late as 1776, though, a burgeoning 'new nation' thought it at least incumbent upon it to show 'a decent respect' for the opinions of humankind and to plead justification for the severing of ties and a rejection of historic allegiance. So there is nothing new about the idea that people can share and bear responsibility for what was done by others long ago. But that does not warm me towards the notion or lead me to believe that it is to be taken as self-evident.

Let me say something about my reasons for finding unconvincing the doctrine that because certain people did certain things in the past those identifiable in some sense as their successors should do certain things today. At the outset we face complicated historical questions (often begged): can we certainly establish what was actually done? Set that aside; can we then decide what 'identifiable' as a successor means, or who enjoys the relevant relationship? Then there are the separable but even more complicated factual questions of context: what was known to, likely to be in the minds of, or felt by those who did the deeds we believe to have occurred? What, as a matter of historical fact, did they – what did those who were their contemporaries – take for granted as normal, as moral, as good or evil?

Such questions are factual or quasi-factual. But there are more fundamental difficulties. The first argument for questioning the notion of historic responsibility must surely be that it flies in the face of commonsense. Obviously, that is not philosophically decisive. Nonetheless, the fact has to be faced. Responsibility in the present is usually thought to be incurred in three ways: by action (or non-action), by the authorizing of action (or non-action) by an agent, or by voluntary acceptance of responsibility for acts even without having had a part in them (it would not be thought ridiculous for me, for example, to apologize for or to endeavour to make recompense for, an act done without my authority by some members of my family, football club, college, regiment or so on). Now it is characteristic of attributions of historic responsibility that, before much time has passed – perhaps a half, or three-quarters, of a century – they relate to people who cannot, physically or logically, have had any actual influence whatsoever on the relevant events. So at least two acceptable grounds for attributing responsibility crumble away as mortality takes its toll. Unless persons can be found who wish to assume responsibility, therefore, none exists.

This is a big reduction in what can be spoken of as historic responsibility. It leaves us (in pursuit of the present line of argument) confronting at any moment only a dwindling number of survivors of fairly recent events as those who may be thought of as possibly responsible agents. So, at present, the Holocaust, Katyn and area bombing would remain within the scope of the doctrine, but the Atlantic slave trade does not. In those relatively few cases from the years of recent history where we can find survivors, we can now proceed to ask what look like straightforward historical questions: for instance, could Germans now alive who lived then have reasonably been asked to resist orders which led to the monstrous crimes of the Nazi regime? We know that some could, because they did. But we also know that others, who have left us records of their thinking, found it hard and in some cases impossible to make the decisive step to refuse to obey. A background of professional formation, uncertainty about the consequences of such an act, deep cultural conditioning, fear of defeat as a greater evil, and much else, held them back. Some of their motives may be thought to have weight. Of course there were time-servers, cowards, villains. We cannot confine responsibility to surviving party members, senior officials or any other single category. We know that not only the *Waffen-SS* but many units of the German army deliberately committed atrocities in the field. All that is certain is that the empirical question of responsibility even of the living, while attributable in principle, is not easy to settle. And, I should add, in seeking to fix it it is desirable that those conducting the search should not assume that they would be braver or clearer-sighted than the actors they scrutinize.

The attribution of responsibility for recent events, nonetheless, is actually irrelevant to my proposition that preoccupation with the idea of guilt interferes with historical understanding. I am afraid, though, that some of you will already be muttering to yourselves one of Acton's dicta: 'After the strong man with the dagger, comes the weak man with the sponge'. It is not my intention to dissolve responsibility in some historicist porridge, grey and tasteless. The point about the actual limits of the responsibilities of contemporaries, though, must not be lost to sight. Acton thought the historian should judge (and indeed, he seems to have thought he should be a hanging judge), but it is an implication of that role that the historian should do justice. That involves taking into account all relevant circumstance. Consider the position of Britons alive while the Atlantic slave trade was going on. There were quite a lot of them altogether, for inhabitants of these islands were personally engaged in the trade at least from the reign of Queen Elizabeth I to the start of the nineteenth century – for, say, 250 years. At the outset, we might note that in so long a time there would be many changes of circumstances modifying people's views of the trade. Yet, at the very least, to deal in slaves during that time was not in itself illegal. Those who took part in the business were therefore not legally culpable. Though some people came to think that the trade should be made illegal, and were eventually successful in convincing others so that they achieved their end and it became illegal, for a long time many, perhaps most, English people could have argued that slavery was justifiable because legal. Not all of the arguments actually used to defend the slave trade now appear to us of equal weight, and none, presumably, appears to be of sufficient weight, but many of them were then good enough to ease people's minds. After all, the first Portuguese slave-traders – who appear to have been the real initiators of the European African slave trade, as opposed to the European trade in whites to Islamic countries which had gone on for centuries and is usually overlooked by moralists – found it easy enough to persuade themselves that they were following conventional practice towards prisoners taken on crusade. That we find such arguments unconvincing is beside the point; the arguments for witchcraft once seemed as persuasive as those for the germ theory of disease. We cannot say that people have a moral obligation to be right, only that they should try to be. The status of past acts which we incline at first sight to condemn is not always clear.

By way of side-stepping one line of argument already set out, it is sometimes said that responsibility descends with enjoyment of the fruits of crime and that, therefore, so does guilt and the responsibility of reparation (which often cannot be provided, of course). To this it may be replied that this has not in fact been recognized as a doctrine consistently and limitlessly applicable. Occupation of property, at the time wrongful, in due time is not taken to inhibit a good title. But a more interesting point, to a historian, may be the elucidation of what such apparently factual matters as 'enjoyment' and 'benefit' might mean.

Again we face a double problem: first the factual one about consequences, and then that of deciding on their moral significance. The first (establishing finally what consequences are) is almost impossible. Who could have said what, in 1757, would be the consequences of the Battle of Plassey? Who can say now what they have been? A summary judgement is not hard, and I would agree that the British acquisition of fiscal rights over Bengal was the 'crucial step which led by inevitable stages to the British conquest of the entire subcontinent'.[7] But that judgement could be contested. And even if it is not, it does not mean that every detail of the history which followed is to be attributed to what Clive did at Plassey. It is only the total past in which, in this case, the historical environment of India must loom large, which totally explains what follows.

It follows, too, that we must try to assess benefits and costs, and to say precisely on whom they fell. This is very hard. To speak of English people who never went to India as 'enjoying' the benefits of conquest is clearly figurative. Without careful regard to context, I think it improper. No doubt, one can identify people who may be thought to have benefitted from British rule in India: those thousands or hundreds of thousands of Indian girl babies, for instance, who survived, thanks to British legislation against female infanticide, or the Hindu widows saved from the fire by the campaign against suttee, or the shareholders (not all British or Indian) in companies able to exploit low-cost labour, or the Indian elites who so effectively used the apparatus of the British Raj to resist structural changes which would undermine their own position and have now come into its inheritance. One could compile a similarly diverse list of losers. But this would and could tell us nothing about the collective responsibilities of an imperial people's successors towards India today. Perhaps this is because such responsibilities do not exist. That people alive today have responsibilities, I do not doubt, but I am sure they are not derived from history. They arise from contemporary reality, from undertakings given and received, from others understood informally, from emotions and ties felt here and now, from love of our fellow men and women, from the wish to oppose evil and promote good, and much, much else. If those responsibilities are more easily met because people are swayed by mythologies of historical guilt then that is fortunate, but, of course, historical mythologies often work otherwise and actually encumber the recognition of duties and the taking of steps to discharge them. I should prefer to do without such adventitious and improper aid.

Coming to the second aspect of the problem, what would now follow supposing (as we cannot) that it were possible to say at all precisely who were the beneficiaries from British rule in India? It is fairly easy to invoke a rudimentary notion of justice and say that debts should be repaid but that, of course, presupposes that what we are talking about *are* debts or similar forms of obligation. And even then, we must again note that there are dangers of anachronism: the old debate about the moral significance of usury showed as it went on important changes in the way people thought about a due return. Some might think, even today, that the provision of capital to a developing country at a tolerable charge is always an unqualified benefit, so that no disparity of obligation exists. It is also to the point that weighing benefits and costs quickly takes us into imponderables. The large salaries paid by the East India Company were justified by the restraints which were steadily imposed on the Company's servants in the matter of trading on their own behalf and by the considerable hazard, extending to health and life, of serving in India at all before the age of modern medicine. That might be thought, roughly, to be a balanced equation. But some of those servants were disinterested, hard-working and, whatever we may think of some of their ideals, idealistic, while others may have been slackers or undetected criminals. Prima facie, there is at least a possibility that the latter should be seen as exploiting the country from whose revenues they derived their salaries. But what of the others? One famous case is Macaulay; he, you will recall, took up a post in India in order to save enough from his substantial salary to support his family on his return. It is hard to believe that his service to India did not more than repay any monetary benefit his family may have drawn from his service there.

So far, I have avoided the case of responsibility for deliberate, unequivocal evil. What of the atrocities? it will be asked. The primary case in the minds of most of us may well be one already touched upon, the Holocaust of European Jewry. Soon, discussion of it must leave the area of contemporary moral judgement about what is due to survivors and perpetrators because there will be none. It will pass into that of historical moral judgement and even so appalling a series of crimes raises delicate questions. It is at times a useful legal fiction that nations are responsible for their rulers' actions: it justifies fighting wars by means calculated to arouse opposition to those rulers, for instance. We may also feel that the evidence of the treatment of the Jewish population of Germany itself by the German authorities (setting aside the dreadful things done to Jews of other nations) was sufficiently widely known in that country to make it reasonable to say that many, possibly most, Germans then living can be deemed to have shared in responsibility for the Holocaust. Yet there were some Germans, even if only a few, who must be free of such responsibilities. Some opposed the regime or its measures, and some must escape blame because they were too young to understand their situation.

Still, when such observations are made, and when due allowance has been made for fear of the Gestapo, in 1945 the world felt so deep a revulsion for what was found in the camps that it approved the victors' prosecution in court of specific 'war criminals', and expressed a virtually universal condemnation of Germans for the abominable things which had been done. (I seem to recall that in this country Victor Gollancz stood out against this trend, publishing his views in pamphlets which brought some odium upon him.) Subsequent events, of which the most important was the establishment of the state of Israel, in due course led German governments to pay sums by way of compensation for Jewish sufferings not only to survivors of the Holocaust and their relatives, but to the new nation. Besides indictable war criminals, there still must be Germans alive who somehow participated, even if only passively, in wicked acts against Jews between 1933 and 1945; no doubt it is therefore reasonable for German governments to try to discharge their guilt vicariously, at least so far as it can be done by compensation. But how long can that go on? One day, every German born before 1945 and every Holocaust survivor will be dead. What will then be the collective responsibility of Germany and the Germans? Surely, the only one they can then have will be one which they freely will to accept, for whatever reasons seem cogent to them. The world will not be right to seek to impose a special obligation on them from which other descendants of other participants in other wartime horrors will be exempted.

We must never forget that the idea of collective historic responsibility easily becomes an instrument of injustice and cruelty. Jews themselves were long persecuted for what were doubtless superstitious and materially interested motives (as well as simple cruelty), but under the cloak of moral justification provided by the attribution to their whole people of guilt for the murder of Christ. If we wanted to look nearer home, has the fostering in Ireland of cults of historic guilt done anything but encumber and embitter the solution of Ireland's problems? There seems to me to be plentiful evidence of immoral and wicked action by Irish people now alive to take account of: to postulate historic guilt only makes things worse by breeding misunderstanding, self-deception, self-righteousness. It is unreasonable that the events of the sixteenth century should be a matter of guilt to anyone today. This is a sombre topic, but a light-hearted remark attributed to Lloyd George seems to me to put the matter in the right perspective. Some time after peace talks began with Irish representatives in London in 1922 he was asked by a reporter how they were going. 'Oh, very well', he said: 'We've been at it two days and have already got back to Cromwell'.

Let me conclude. Though the conception of historical responsibility may sometimes be useful in promoting good behaviour (and I am inclined to think that such actions as the compensation offered to Israel by the German government owes more to a wish to stand well in world opinion than to a sense of guilt, which it would be unreasonable for all Germans to share) I find it invalid and an unhelpful, sometimes dangerous idea. It seems to me another example of the weight of a particular historical environment upon us. What ought to be at stake is present behaviour. We may look at the past and find what men did in it offensive, morally, aesthetically, or just because we know what it led to. That can tell us things about responsibilities which we, now, ought to recognize. We can learn from history the danger of a disregarding attitude towards our successors. We cannot dispense with the idea of a present responsibility for our planet, even, perhaps, for our universe. But we owe nothing to the past except, perhaps, respect and gratitude. The men and women who lived in it are dead and beyond our power. We should try to be beyond theirs. In my last lecture, I shall try to be a little more positive about approaching the historical environment so as to achieve that.

# III Overcoming History

Early medieval town dwellers picked up Roman bricks and masonry and used them to build their churches (which they often modelled on Roman law courts), Moorish builders in Andalucia took Visigothic and Roman columns to make up the numbers they needed for the great mosque at Córdoba. Such appropriations did not mean they were overcoming the past; nevertheless, they were using it. The limitations those old materials imposed on them were much less important than the scope and scale they made possible. When we are dealing with ideas and assumptions, though, and not with concrete objects, the question of limits on freedom in using the past is more important. To decide where they fall is a question which may have become more difficult to answer in our own day because of certain characteristics of the modern historical era; the global scope of its processes, its vast information flows, its huge recent accelerations and its striking embodiment in technological change. The novelist Hermann Hesse has said that 'There are times when a whole generation is caught... between two ages, two modes of life, with the consequence that it loses all power to understand itself and has no standing, no security, no single acquiescence'.[8] Something like that seems to be going on over much of the world today. One consequence is that disagreement about the implications of the historical environment often breaks out when ideas jump from one culture to another. Whether in the form of liberalism, nationalism, Christianity or Marxism does not seem much to matter; what matters is that they soon prove to be deeply at odds with the environment into which they are introduced. Discomfort, disappointment, disaffection follow. In one place a strong man – an Ataturk, say – will triumph over the difficulty. Another – a Reza Shah – is (almost to the world's surprise) unable to do so and fails, delivering his country to reaction by his defeat. Such historic dislocations justify thinking about ways of 'overcoming' history, the subject of this last lecture.

We have already glanced at attempts to manage the past by succumbing to it, by clinging to it and shunning the new. Another technique is the exact opposite: you ignore the past altogether. Inspired by confidence, ignorance or both, you simply refuse to see that there is a historic problem at all; you rely on technical solutions to the problems of your society. It is often thought that more investment, more food, better technology will by themselves meet all the needs of some poor societies. But it often turns out that certain patterns of investment conflict with existing notions of social hierarchy, that food is not acceptable unless it takes account of local dietary habits, that technology cannot easily be harnessed within existing social structures. It is shown, in fact, that people are not always very flexible or adaptable. At present, one of the most likely consequences of the failure to take account of history is a failure to manage effectively the transfer of technology to undeveloped countries. The new technologies which are permeating the globe's economies cannot simply be injected into any social system. A capacity for learning and mastering them has to be present; there has to be a pre-existing capability to accept new ideas and an amenable and responsive system into which to introduce them. Soon, there will also be a need for a new spread of training opportunities to create an open-minded workforce adaptable to new ways, and a ready supply of capital to spread the new technologies and ensure their best deployment. Most developing countries have no such prerequisites; their history has just not provided them. Consequently, there can be no benign, silent spread of new technology in most of the Third World. It is more likely that there will be violent shocks, affronts and challenges to old ways and perceptions, dangers to the social order. It would be better to recognize the huge scale of investment in infrastructure (often in immaterial infrastructure like education) which the effective management of historical environment will require in such societies, and, perhaps, that more growth in the advanced economies is the only way to provide the capital for it. And that might mean, in a world already divided between haves and have-nots, an inexorable further widening of the gap between them. Given such prospects, it might be thought that at least as much thought should be given to the adaptation and preparation of the cultural environment shaped by history, as to economic, technical and administrative innovation.

Political solutions, in particular, are notoriously liable to failure or abortion when history is overlooked and there is too great a reliance on technical answers to problems. Woodrow Wilson at the Peace Conference of Paris in 1919 once faced an Irish delegation which recalled to him earlier remarks he had made about self-determination. Plaintively, he observed that when he gave utterance to those words 'I said them without the knowledge that nationalities existed which are coming to us day after day'.[9] Paradoxically, the rulers of the conservative empires whose dissolution was posing so many problems to the leader of the world's greatest democracy at that moment, had been much more aware than he of such historic facts as the existence of Wends, Serbs, Ukrainians, Croats, Ruthenes, Uzbeks, Letts, Bosnians and many other peoples. Not that those defeated people had drawn the right conclusions from their knowledge: knowing the history is not in itself a solution. But it can help.

Some who have turned their backs on the past have, of course, wanted to do so in order to break with it. They have acted from will, not ignorance. This is a solution often embraced by revolutionaries. Not all of them, of course; those of 1688 positively clung to history, even representing their own actions not as revolutionary but as continuous with history – James 'haveing Abdicated the Government and the Throne being thereby Vacant', William and Mary are assumed to have succeeded by right.[10] Ninety or so years later, American revolutionaries took rather more complex views of their own relation to the past. Some of them made what they were doing sound very historically-based: they proclaimed their wish (and right) to be treated like other subjects of the British Crown (to enjoy, that is, the benefits of 1688). Others, of whom Jefferson may be the outstanding example, took a truly revolutionary view. It came out in his quarrels with Hamilton. 'The Hamiltonian view', says one commentator '...was a call for a new manipulation of an old and valid history' (or, as we might say, a myth which would still work). 'The Jeffersonian was a rejection of that history – indeed, it called for periodic revolutions to make certain that history might never again have the opportunity to inhibit intelligent responses to scientifically perceived needs'.[11]

I think that a broadly acceptable summary, and it helps to explain Jefferson's later enthusiasm for what occurred in France in 1789 and afterwards. The French Revolution, much more unambiguously than the American, was a rejection of history. Yet it too began with an essay in historical resurrection, the assembling on 5 May 1789 of the ancient Estates General. Out of the lumber-room of French history was trundled this venerable device. It had not met for over a century and a half. It embodied in its tripartite structure of Clergy, Noblemen and non-nobles (the Third Estate) not only convenient representative arrangements, but a whole theory of society and the relations between people and their rulers. But the event which struck everyone as the real coming of revolution, the event that mattered, came a couple of months later and was one of rejection of the past. This was the attack upon and destruction of the Bastille, a royal prison which symbolized much more than the oppression of any individuals incarcerated there. It came to stand for all of the old, bad past. This past, not completely, not all at once, and not by all French people, but very largely, quickly, and always with the authority of the National Assembly, was demolished wholesale in the next few years. The established Church and the Monarchy disappeared; so did distinction of birth, the indissolubility of marriage, chartered corporations, the ancient provincial divisions of France. The best symbol, perhaps, came when it was decided to make explicit the total nature of this rejection by stopping the calendar and starting all over again. Not only was the year to be reconstructed around twelve equal months each of three weeks of ten days, but chronology was deemed to have begun on September 21, 1792, with day One of the first month of the year One and the foundation of the French Republic.

It is instructive to consider what followed. The Revolutionary Calendar (as it was called) was used officially for ten years or so, as late as the Consulate of Bonaparte, and just survived into the nineteenth century. People had ceased to use it well before it was officially wound up, though, and before the Christian calendar was officially reintroduced. At least in that respect, the Revolution did not succeed in cancelling the past. Nor was it the only one. Much else came back and now we know, too, that much never went away. Undeniably the nineteenth-century history of France was irremediably marked by the Revolution. The tremendous effort of national will made between 1789 and 1794 deeply impressed both foreigners and the French. For the next three-quarters of a century France tended to be seen as (it is not too strong a word) a revolutionary nation. French people (especially if they lived in Paris) were thought prone to disturbance and sedition, difficult to govern. Their governments were regarded with suspicion lest they use revolutionary nationalists in other countries as the instruments of France's own national interest and policy. Nor could any French government, even at the Restoration, disown much of what had been done. The Great Revolution had become part of French history, of the historical environment, something which had always to be taken into account, always to be allowed for by France's rulers and neighbours. A French king might still, in 1824, be crowned in the historic way in the traditional place, the cathedral of Rheims. But the prelate who anointed him could not use the historic vessel, handed down from Merovingian times, in which the sacred oil of consecration had always been contained, because it had been smashed in the Revolution. A half-century later, that king's grandson, the man called 'Henry V' by his supporters, wrecked their hopes by refusing to return to take the French throne unless it could be under the white flag of the Bourbons – the flag, as he put it, of Joan of Arc. He would not accept the tricolour which was the symbol of the Revolution and which every regime since 1800 had adopted or tolerated. Yet that symbol had by then to be accepted by any would-be ruler of France, because the Revolution was now part of French history for most French people, not a deviation or aberration from it.

That is one side of the French nineteenth century. Now consider the other side. Much of the texture of everyday life was profoundly unchanged and long remained unchanged by what had happened. Old provincial feelings undermined the new departmental boundaries. French was spoken less than patois. In everyday life, metric measurement was virtually ignored over much of the country a half-century after 1789. So was the new currency; people still spoke of *Louis d'or* and *livres*.[12] This suggests, I believe, that a revolutionary dismissal or dispersion of the past can have only a limited success. It attempts to cut off the past and make arrangements to do things differently. This is what Joseph II tried to do in the diverse settings of the Habsburg dominions, and what some British evangelicals and utilitarians tried to do in India. The material with which such reformers seek to work – society – is cluttered with landmarks and features with which people find it very hard to dispense (all the more so if they are not altogether conscious of them). Even those who want change (let alone those who have to operate new arrangements) are people whose minds are already shaped by that past. Turning your back on the past always proves to be an illusion. It is almost always better to taper away the past by working with the grain, rather than to try to saw it off.

Yet that course, too, can have unfortunate consequences if it encourages a response into passivity, in which history is seen merely as something to be endured. Christians have often sought to deal with history by interpreting it as the kingdom of this world, a story of sin and failure, to be put up with and lived through by the Christian whose real goal lay elsewhere. Underlying such an attitude is an implicit statement that history has been scrutinized and understood; so this is overcoming history by putting it in its place. Christians had (in this view) only to make such allowances for it as enabled them to control or evade its ever-present potential for corrupting them or distracting them from their proper task, the pursuit of salvation. Although this seems likely to be an enduring attitude within Christianity, it was probably most widespread in the first centuries of the Church. Most Christians would now reject it. Other interpretations soon appeared, even in early times, which made it possible to see history in a different, but still Christian, way, as the embodiment of divine purposes and even divine instrumentation. The great name which springs to mind in this connection is that of St Augustine. To recall that his greatest work sprang directly from the need to grapple with a specific event – the sack of Rome in 410 – throws into relief his concern with the understanding of the past as a guide to action. If the history of Rome is properly understood, says Augustine, and, indeed, the history of pagan civilization, too, then the Christian will be able to deal with the actual world.

Similar approaches can also be set out in non-Christian terms. They can and have been put in some which are uncompromisingly secular and materialist. They are all variants of what may be called the General Design view of history, a view which postulates an intended or innate and necessary course which it would be foolish or impious (and probably both) not to take into account in settling one's own actions. Whether history is seen as the unfolding self-revelation of free, rational spirit – as, I take it, Hegel thought – or the evolution of relations of production so as to permit the inauguration of the classless society, as Marx thought, is of less moment than that both views point to a very specific relationship between the subject of the historical process and that process itself. We should try to understand history if we are not to be crushed or thwarted by it, and the way to understanding it is (such interpretations say) to grasp the design or teleology which informs it.

No doubt such approaches can be personally suggestive and even illuminating. But they are of limited value and in the end misleading. They are mythological, always in their nature and sometimes in intention.

They draw their conclusions from hypotheses cast in terms which cannot ultimately be sustained by historical argument, nor are dependent on it. The examples glanced at all hold out promises of more successful management of our condition; they stress that knowledge of the past makes possible more successful management of the present. Many myths do not overtly offer so much, and look forward, not back – an idea like that of the Chosen People, or the Second Coming, while illuminating the meaning of what is going on, does not necessarily suggest that any more is called for here and now than courage and endurance. But, of course, we all know that the idea of the Second Coming, whatever might be its logical and necessary connotations, in fact inspired early Christians to very specific and vigorous practical action (or abstention from action) of many kinds.

Yet though professional historians usually ignore them, we find it helpful to have categorical views of a large kind about the nature of the past and its significance. We want to understand history, because it makes it possible to act with greater confidence here and now. Moreover, if we do not have good historical ideas – meaning, by that, ideas which stand up to critical scrutiny by those thought competent to offer it – we shall still have to make do with bad ones. As Newman once put it in another connection, 'We cannot do without a view and we put up with an illusion when we cannot get a truth'.[13] Myths are (among other things) a way of dealing with the historical environment, and so of acting. Can we manage them, bring them under control?

Myths I take to be complexes of mental images. They act as co-ordinates, usually somewhat large in scope and vague in outline, around which people order their ideas of reality – by which I mean the world as they perceive it. When they are felt to provide satisfactory explanation, they mobilize energy for action. Sometimes these co-ordinates are not clearly grasped by those who employ them. They can be hidden, implicit in the result to which they tend. Nor, even when they are present to the consciousness, are they necessarily capable of satisfying defence. In their many forms, those which are mainly concerned with history have included some which are about what has happened and its meaning, some which are about what is going to happen. They can be very important in determining the possibility or impossibility of action.

Historians are used to noting the presence of such myths as phenomena of the societies whose pasts they study. But not a great deal of systematic attention has been given to them. Partly, this is because history has long been dominated by a concern to examine what it was that underlay rational, conscious action. Of course, irrational behaviour is noticed from time to time. The great Gibbon gave it much attention. But while the irrational looms large in his narrative, its role is clearly delineated and subordinate. It illustrates a story whose assumptions relegate irrationality to the category of aberrant phenomena. Gibbon gives much weight to superstition, but with a polemical and didactic purpose, not for its own sake as a subject worthy of historical understanding. We may regret this, but need not be hard on Gibbon: with less excuse, many of his successors did not even show the interest he had shown. Yet this, too, is understandable; after all, there is so much history to be done. That means that the pull exercised by any apparently well-defined, clearly-structured subject-matter, approachable through plentiful and apparently unproblematic documentation, is bound to be great. So (to limit the question solely to the matter of religious history) historians until very recently eagerly pursued the history of the Papacy, of relations of Church and State, of canon law, ecclesiastical institutions, monasteries and religious orders, rather than the more mysterious, slightly disreputable topics of hermits, dancing mania, witches, flagellants, Cathars and crackpots, or the reality of the mass of superstition in the shadows behind such spectacular achievements as the twelfth-century 'Renaissance'. We long tended to launder out the unmeasurable, the non-institutional, the inexplicable. This is not just because of a lack of documentation; as Sir Keith Thomas has shown, ample material (though not always of a very formal nature) exists to assess the weight of superstition and magic. We have not tended simply to take such things for granted as inexplicable, but – more important – as disregardable, marginal. They were not understood to be effective, and that was a very grave error.

All this has now begun to change. Historians are now much more interested in the irrational. We have begun even to see that some of the roots of science lie in superstition. We have now learnt to look harder and longer at superficially trivial ritual, custom, symbols, artwork. Myths, and historical myths in particular, form a natural topic for investigation as a result of this swing of interest. But not much has yet been done. While we vigorously pursue the study of some irrational forces playing upon humankind in its history (the external forces of climate, epidemics, even volcanic eruptions, for example) the history of ideas is still very much dominated bibliographically by the study of conscious, formal mental activity, rather than of unreason and passion. If I may cite one small example because it is known to me from personal investigation, the history of politics and society in eighteenth and nineteenth century Europe is not to be fully understood (I believe) unless due weight is given to explaining the extraordinary but neglected fact that thousands of educated, supposedly sensible people then believed that the real explanation of even the most important events of the age was to be found in the plots of wicked conspirators. Now that this bizarre image of the social process should ever have seemed plausible seems to me to merit explanation (as does, say, the witch craze of the seventeenth century). It is also an example of what I mean by a historical myth, for although it had very little basis in reality, it was convincing enough to move people to decisive action.

The bearing of this on the understanding of the historic environment is that many such myths still provide widely accepted ways of handling the past. They are there, whether we like it or not, and have to be taken into account. But because of that, they can be subjected to historical study and criticism. Now since we are to have myths anyway, let us decide which are good, which bad. This appears to me to be one of the most important tasks of history. Fortunately, whether they know it or not, historians are at least indirectly engaged in it much of the time.

Consider the nature of some of the mythology which clusters about the idea of nationalism and which both needs, and is undergoing, daily criticism by historians. Much energy has been put into discovering or manufacturing national pasts. Thus, in recent years, African nationalists have sought to press back alleged national identities into the preliterate past, no easy task. This has led to exaggeration and distortion, as great social and cultural achievements have been claimed for medieval Ghana, or the peoples who built the ruins we now call Zimbabwe. An exotic, alien myth of nationality, drawn from Europe has been thought helpful in handling the problems of post-colonial Africa. It has followed, as it did in Europe, the creation of new states which have sought to mould their subjects in a nationalist cast of mind. Not surprisingly, they have not always been successful, any more than were successful, say, Italian governments in making Italians out of Neapolitans, Romans, Tuscans, until long after the governmental unification of Italy.

Even the African landmass itself now shows signs of turning into a historical myth whose major purpose – the establishment of identity – is the same as that of national myths. In this case, the ground of identity was laid by non-Africans. Historically, the name of Africa comes from outside. Once the designation of a province of the Roman empire along the northern coasts, it was extended by later Europeans to the continent as a whole. Because most of the continent was long unknown to them except at scattered places along its coasts, the name concealed the vast diversity of reality. Other Europeans gradually came to be aware that not all the inhabitants of the continent were Moslems, and one of its biggest single diversifications remains that between Islamic Africa and the rest. But it was a long time before Europeans began to make further significant distinctions among Africans. It was easy, too, to think of

'Africa' as in some sense a whole because of its historical passivity. Since the days of ancient Eygpt, African cultures have had virtually no influence on the rest of the world except as a result of external agency. Europeans took black slaves across the Atlantic and with them went practices which left some marks on Western culture; in, for example, agriculture, cuisine, music and entertainment. Whether the same was true of the comparable numbers of Africans taken by Arabs to the Islamic lands of Arabia and the Gulf, to Indonesia and Canton, I cannot say. In time, the continent also came to exercise a profound indirect influence on a growing world economy, as a source of minerals and other natural resources. But almost no effect was produced on the outside world by Africans themselves; their continent's resources were tapped and mobilized by outsiders. The most substantial branch of trade in which Africans were engaged, after all, was for a long time the supply of other Africans to European and Arab slavers. The continent has long been, historically, a theatre into which shaping, exploiting, manipulating and stimulating forces flowed from the outside. She did not supply to Europe mathematics such as came from India or the Islamic world, technical processes such as came from China. Instead to Africa outside Egypt most transforming forces came from outside – the wheel, literacy, new crops. No doubt this passivity and the sense that the continent has been used by outsiders for their own purposes, flowed together with the temporary sense of common political cause in the post-colonial period to encourage a sense of common identity which has expressed itself rhetorically and in (largely unsuccessful) organizational efforts in recent years. But it has also led to the cultivation of myths about African history.

Examples of European creations of mythical pasts are of course plentiful. At the time of the Greek revolt against Ottoman rule early in the nineteenth century, much was made by some Greeks of a distant past. The fall of Constantinople to the Turks nearly four centuries earlier was evoked as the extinction of the national liberty of those who were addressed by their leaders as 'Hellenes' or 'Romans'.[14] There was, that is to say, a conscious attempt to attach a nineteenth-century political movement to a historic symbol of great prestige and inspirational value: the heritage of the Roman empire. This had often been done before. In 550, amid the ruins of the empire in western Europe, the first barbarian king we know to have done so put on his coins an image of himself wearing imperial insignia. An earlier barbarian leader, Theodoric, had said to the Romans 'our royalty is an imitation of yours', had held games in the imperial style in the circus when he went to Rome, and had put *invicta Roma* on his coins.[15] The urge to associate with the myth of Rome has been recurrent in European history. The mystery attached to *imperium* appears to have been prized by Charlemagne. Reminiscences of Roman antiquity (mingled with those of Greek) haunted people in the Renaissance, dictated artistic style in the West for centuries and surfaced yet again in a political sense, only a few years before the Greek revolt, in the neo-classicism of Revolutionary and Napoleonic Europe.

Sadly, mythology of this sort has often been the cloak and justification for crime. There can be few clearer instances than the myth of Crusade. Whatever the initial appeal of the idea when preached by Pope Urban, the notion of Crusade seems quickly to have built up a potential for emotional release and justification which was capable of enduring for centuries. It sustained not only the long effort towards the Holy Land to which it had first been directed, but struggle in the Languedoc, in Spain, in Prussia and Africa. It flowed on into the age of European expansion, too: Henry the Navigator not only took part in a crusading expedition to Ceuta, but saw his exploratory expeditions down the West African coast in the crusading context, and the Cross went to the Americas with the *conquistadores*. And their example recalls the crimes and cruelty the crusading idea could cover. It eased consciences, as, no doubt, it had eased the consciences of those who followed Simon de Montfort to despoil the Albigensians of their lands and property, or the Teutonic Knights who enslaved the Slavs and Letts. It was a myth with a long life.

I believe it is the danger inherent in some myths which makes the role of academic history, 'real' or 'scientific' history, important in the management of our historical environment. Bringing historical myths under criticism may well be the most important social function of my discipline. It is the civic justification which we can add to our intellectual and aesthetic reasons for pursuing it. I take it to be important, after all, that we do not think we can merely invent the past, or tolerate for long one which is invented. There would be real danger in doing that. It could produce conflict of aspiration and practicality by falsifying our view of the historical environment within which we must work. It is dangerous, for instance, to see history as progress if that stops you recognizing that confidence in progress has led men and women astray and into blunders. It is dangerous to celebrate material achievement, if that then disguises the costs of the problems it created. Scholarly history's first public duty is the elaboration and criticism of simplicities. The typical stance of the professional historian must be critical. 'Yes, but', he or she says, when confronted with a view, 'it was not quite like that' – or 'not at all like that', perhaps. Because what we say about history cannot be absolutely and completely true, it does not follow that some historical statements are not certainly more true, or more false, than others. We must always try to pull down the unacceptable, even if we can only replace it with the provisional.

I have made no systematic survey, but I am sure that there are more historical statements than we think which are non-specific, imprecise. Not all take the form of the hard, clear assertion 'Adam Smith studied at Glasgow University'. Most of the time, History moves towards generalization. Historians aspire to valid summary statements about the past. By 'summary' I do not mean that such statements are necessarily brief: they may, even about a relatively short episode, stretch to volumes. But what comes out is inevitably a summary statement of what was once the complexity of real life, which took up twenty-four hours a day of the lives of possibly millions of people. Such statements are validated by professional standards which uphold such practices as the consideration of all relevant evidence, the avoidance of anachronism, the exclusion of invalid criteria and so on. The result almost always turns out to be damaging to widely and long-accepted historical myths.

Let me offer an example. There has been much reconsideration (amid violent debate) of modern German history in the last twenty years or so. This has not been simply a matter of coming to terms with the recent past – the episode of Nazism, above all – although this was central in bringing about reconsideration. It extended also to earlier periods, to the assessment of Germany's role in Europe, to judgements about policy in the approach to and during the First World War, to the allocation of responsibility for that international calamity, to questions about social justice in the Second Reich, and about the benefits, costs, methods and nature of the nineteenth-century process of unification which was for so long seen as a liberal and progressive triumph. To all this reconsideration German historians – and particularly the younger among them – have made a large and splendid contribution (often quarrelling violently with one another as they did so). And, as a consequence, they have advanced the re-education of Germany about its past. It is difficult for the British, who seem to me unusually unconcerned about their history, to understand the importance of what was going on. But the German historians' demolition of such deeply-rooted stereotypes as the 'stab in the back' which brought defeat in 1918 (Siegfried, we should remember, was stabbed in the back by Hagen), or of the myth of the deliberate exclusion of Imperial Germany from a 'place in the sun' by other colonial powers, or of the idea of a historic mission to civilize the Slavs running from the *Drang nach Osten* of medieval German settlers to the attack of 1941 – all this has surely been unquestionably healthy. It shows that it is possible, after all, to create new visions of the past and to release the present from fiction long taken for granted. That must be valuable.

It must be said that such changes are not usually easy to achieve. The Germans had the advantage – if that is the word – of stimulus by national trauma. At any one moment there is a huge gap between widely-held, popular views of the past, and what is known by scholars to be true. Sometimes this gap is both too gross and too trivial to matter. Whether Sir Francis Drake was actually playing bowls when the Armada was sighted does not really matter: only one man's reputation for cool-headedness is somewhat affected by the historian's verdict. Sometimes, though, it is very large and important. Yet the excellent work of Irish historians has blown away much misunderstanding of recent Irish history among specialists, without much disturbing the entrenched views of bigots and fanatics. So we should not expect too much. The advance of mental hygiene is a slow business. Nevertheless, I believe it to be visible. Nowadays it is difficult to write or promote drum and trumpet, patriotic, glorifying history in this country, though it remains popular elsewhere. That is a gain, even if there sometimes seems to be a danger of toppling the other way, so as to set up new denigratory, disparaging myths in the place of those of the past.

The muse of 'History' is something of a maid-of-all-work, capable of being pressed into service on many fronts and in many ways. This is because, among the humanities, Clio is involved in practical decision, in action, as other disciplines are not. So far as her cleansing function is concerned, every obscurity removed from the past, every misleading perspective altered, actually also alters our capacity to act because it alters the historical environment. It delimits the context of action in a new way. Of course it is true that other human disciplines change our lives. Only the unimaginative could deny that the study of literature and language, or of the arts, or the pursuit of artistic activity, may have social and practical effects. But such effects tend to be, by and large, indirect. They are diffused though many channels to contribute – mixed up with much else – to the shaping and colouring of public taste and the stimulating of thought. Their direct operation is only sporadic and occasional. Few people move straight from a judgement about (say) Keats or Baudelaire to a practical conclusion about action. Philosophy, it is true, has always been thought to be more engaged in the real world than literary study. Clearly the business of serious thinking encourages its practitioners to bring to light implications of all sorts, and to expose false reasoning and anomaly in all sorts of thinking, including thinking about practical matters. Moreover, there have always been some philosophers (in spite of what Marx said) who have hoped or sought to change the world and to have practical effect. They have often been preachers; there is, in the warehouse of philosophy, a great deal of explosive, combustible, sometimes toxic waste lying about in the form of unstable ideas left by some of them. Systematic thinking can actually have direct and obvious good social, political and institutional effects, too. Yet History, among the humanities, is the most likely of them to be found in direct relation with the sphere of practical action. In the background of all social decision, necessarily even if only implicitly, lies a view of history. That view sets the stage for, and limits and determines the nature and extent of, discussion. Useful progress in history is achieved through the ability of good historians to change this background, and so change the argument taking place against it. Even great historians, it is true, rarely exercise this power to affect fundamental thinking consciously. Yet as we remake our past, so we make our future. No one now has any right any longer to believe that history predicts. But it is mixed up in making a future, even if it cannot define one. What historians do, therefore, may be of enormous importance.

History, then, like myth, turns out to direct us towards the present – to action – and a part of that present is confrontation with the past, grappling with our historical environment. The study of History is our best instrument for managing the past, by making it more intelligible. It strives to reduce the sheer irrationality and untruth of much of what is said about the past. No doubt, when it has cleared the ground a little, new myths will spring up to encumber it again. But they, too, can be brought under criticism. As I have said elsewhere, society cannot do without history, it will have, willy-nilly, bad history if it does not have good. To use a disjunction put forward by an Oxford professor some years ago, there must be an available lay history, and if specialist history does not illuminate and irrigate, criticize and control that, then it will be bad lay history. Society needs historical-mindedness, which in the end comes down to seeing that, contrary to what most people believe, the past was very unlike the present. This is not just a cognitive matter, it is a moral stance.

In these lectures I have argued that the weight of our historical environment – history as environment – is substantial, and that we are foolish if we do not take account of that. It followed, I suggested, that there is an important role for historians to discharge in articulating and criticizing views of the past. *A multo fortiori* and for the last time, there can be no question in our society of *not* returning to the past again and again to think about it. The reason for doing so is not even that we ought to know about it, it is, paradoxically, that we already do 'know' about it. Whatever attitude we take towards it, even one of dismissal, implies a view, a state of knowledge. It will always be dangerous to take that necessarily imperfect knowledge for granted, and not to question it. We shall always need articulated readings, evidently illuminating visions, of the past. Their usefulness will lie in the versions they offer, against which other versions can be compared, so that, if less satisfactory, they can be rejected. Scientific rigour has to be pressed in such versions as far as it can go. Beyond that, we shall be into judgement, but judgement, too, can be shown to be soundly or unsoundly based, good or bad. The aim must always be to understand the past, and to base that understanding on knowledge. Such understanding of history reveals us to ourselves. This is why, finally, history is not scientific or is only quasi-scientific in approach and method, not in its nature. It is essentially a speculative and critical activity, whose function is direct, personal and illuminating. Through it we learn about ourselves. It is always collective autobiography, or perhaps, on a bad day, collective psychoanalysis.

NOTES

1  The attention of historians was first drawn to this episode by A. Soboul, in 'Sentiment religieux et cultes populaires pendant la Révolution: Saintes pat-riotes et martyrs de la liberté, *Annales historiques de la Révolution française*, xxix (1957), pp. 129–213.

2  The phrase is J. Needham's. *Science and Civilisation in China*, I, (Cambridge University Press, 1954), p. 63.

3  [Editor's note.] Non-Scottish readers may appreciate the explanation that Celtic are an essentially-Catholic football club with strong support among the descendants of nineteenth-century Irish immigrants to Glasgow, while Rangers are the leading Protestant Club. The accession of William and Mary in 1688, followed by the attempts of the deposed James II to use Ireland as a springboard from which to regain the British throne, fomented sectarian strife in Ireland from the effects of which we are arguably not yet free. The Battle of the Boyne (1690), at which William decisively defeated James, is still celebrated annually by 'Orange marchers' through the streets of certain parts of Glasgow.

4  M. Rodinson, *Islam and Capitalism* (Penguin Books, 1977), p. xvii.

5  *Karl Marx* [and] *Friedrich Engels Collected Works*, XI (Lawrence & Wishart, 1979), p. 71.

6  [Editor's note.] Mrs Thatcher was Prime Minister of Britain when this lecture was delivered.

7  A. Lamb, *Asian Frontiers* (Pall Mall Press, 1968), p. 55.

8  Quoted by Z. Brzezinski, *Between Two Ages, America's role in the Technetronic Era* (Penguin Books, 1976), p. 1.

9  E. Holt, *Protest in Arms* (Putnam, 1960), pp. 181–2.

10  The Bill of Rights (I Will. and Mar., Sess. 2, c. 2).

11  B. D. Karl, in N. Hagihara (ed.), *Experiencing the 20th Century* (University of Tokyo, 1985), p. 290.

12 See E. Weber, *Peasants into Frenchmen: The Modernization of Rural France 1870–1914* (Chatto & Windus, 1977), pp. 30–5.

13 J. H. Newman, in T. Ker (ed.), *Idea of a University* (Clarendon Press, 1976), p. 70.

14 See, for example, H. Lidderdale (ed.), *Makriyannis: The memoirs of General Makriyannis 1797–1864* (Oxford University Press, 1966), pp. xliii–xliv, and *passim*.

15 D. Bullough, in D. Talbot Rice (ed.), *The Dark Ages* (Thames & Hudson, 1965), p. 158.

# Muller on Concepts – And on the Cosmological and Related Arguments

## From Sensation to Name

*All that we have or know consists of sensations, percepts, concepts, and names. But though these four phases of knowledge may be distinguished, they cannot be separated as entirely independent functions of our mind. They form parts of one whole, members of one living organism. In the actual work of thought... we deal with names as embodiments of concepts, we deal with concepts as the result of percepts, and we deal with percepts as the residue of sensations. The process which changes sensations into percepts, and percepts into concepts and names belongs to the very earliest age in the history of the human mind. In learning our language we enter at once on an inheritance which has been amassed by our predecessors during thousands of years, and to which we ourselves may add something, but very little in comparison to what we receive ready-made. It has been argued that even with us sensations may exist by themselves, as when we feel a blow, taste what is bitter, smell what is nauseous, see what is dark, hear what is loud. They exist, no doubt; but as soon as we become conscious of them, know them, think them, they are more than sensations; they have become percepts, concepts, and names... Real thought (antahkarana, inward-doing) begins when we... do what no one can do for us, namely combine the percepts of sensations into concepts by discovering something they share in common, and embody that common property in a sign or a name.*

*Natural Religion*, pp. 115–16

## The Problem of Creation

*The question which the Vedic poet asked when he said...*

> *What was the wood, what was the tree whence they fashioned heaven and earth?*
> *Search, O sages, in your mind for that on which he stood when establishing the worlds.*

*...is in reality the same question which we ask today, and which has received ever so many answers from century to century, and will receive as many more, so long as heaven and earth remain... We are the descendents of those Vedic poets, their language is essentially our language, their thoughts are essentially our thoughts, the world we live in is much the same as their Aryan home, and whatever discoveries have been made in other branches of knowledge, no new facts have been discovered since their time to help us to solve that old and yet always new question, whether there is an author of the Universe, whether there is a Creator and a God.*

## The Cosmological Question

*[In the Rig-veda] the poet asks:*

> *Who knows the secret? who proclaimed it here,*
> *Whence, whence this manifold creation sprang?*

*That it sprang from somewhere, or, as we should say, that it was contingent on something non-contingent, is taken for granted. There is as yet no cosmological argument. But yet the question is there, and to my mind that question is far more important than all its answers. It is in that question, in the power of asking that question, that the true nerve of the cosmological argument lies.*

## Teleological Argument

*Ask yourselves, Can you imagine the craving of hunger in nature unless there is something in nature to satisfy that hunger?... Neither can we imagine this craving for the Unseen, the Unheard, the Unperceived, or the Infinite, unless there was something to satisfy that craving, if only we look for it where it can be found...*

*As soon as this non-phenomenal is represented in the likeness of man, – and man knows nothing better in the whole world, and in his whole mind than man, – the teleological argument comes in by itself. The author and creator of the universe, if once conceived, cannot be conceived except... as the wisest being, and man claims the right to look for his wisdom in his works. Thus one of the Vedic poets exclaims:*

*Wise and mighty are the works of him who... stretched out apart the starry sky and the earth.*

*...Unless it was possible to conceive anything wiser than wise, or better than good, the author and creator would always to human beings retain these human qualities, and his work, the phenomenal world, would always be scanned for proofs of his purposes and his wisdom.*

This is the teleological argument in its most rudimentary form.

## *Ontological Argument*

As to the ontological argument we may discover traces of this also in the very earliest speculations of the Indian sages:

> *How could that which is, be born of that which is not?*

This is the question asked by the author of the Brahmana, and the very question supplies the answer, It could not.

This may seem a very crude form in which to state the ontological argument, but it is its very crudeness that makes it instructive.

*Natural Religion*, pp. 239–52

# 6
# The Kingdom of the Mind

## *Anthony Kenny*

### The Geography of the Mind

The invitation to participate in this centenary series of Gifford Lectures encouraged speakers to talk about the environment, whether physical, spiritual or social. In accepting the invitation I indicated my intention to talk about the spiritual environment. It is from that angle that I approach my topic: the kingdom of the mind.

Some people think of the mind as an inner environment, the polar opposite of the external environment of the physical Universe. I believe, and shall argue, that this is not the correct way to think of the mind: the boundary between the spiritual and the material is not the same as the boundary between inner and outer. But I will take as my topic the nature of the mind, and the bounds which that nature sets to our spiritual environment.

The spiritual environment in which we live must include, as a supreme point, the concept of God. This is true whether God exists in reality or whether God is a fictional upper bound to the powers of the human imagination. So in lecturing about the mind and the spiritual environment I shall be fulfilling the testamentary wishes of Lord Gifford.

In replying to the invitation of the Senatus I declared my intention also to lecture about the relationship between philosophy, theology and poetry. These three disciplines are related to each other not so much by a common subject as by a characteristic feature of their use of language. In virtue of this feature these disciplines all stand, in a way which I hope to explain, at the frontiers of the mind.

My three lectures will have the overall title *The Kingdom of the Mind*.

The first of them will be entitled *The Geography of the Mind*. It will delineate the different mental faculties such as the intellect, the imagination and the fancy. It will explain how the concept of an inner environment is misleading, even though the mind can be said to operate within a bounded world.

The self which is the inner bound of the mind is not a feature of any interior world. The limits of the spiritual environment are set by the purview of our mental powers, whether we consider the capacity for seeking and finding explanation, or the faculty which consists in the mastery of literal discourse. The second lecture, treating of these matters, will be called *The Frontiers of the Mind*.

At the boundary of explanation we find God; at the limits of literal discourse we break into poetry. The third lecture will explore what happens when we try to go beyond the frontiers of the mind, to talk about God and to leave behind the conditions which give sense to our literal discourse. The third lecture will be called *Seas of Thought*.

In this first lecture, then, I will explore the everyday geography of the mind: the relations between the senses and the intellect; the contrast between outer senses and inner senses; the two kinds of imagination, fantastic and creative. I shall speak of the intellect as the capacity for operation with signs, and the will as the capacity for the pursuit of rational goals. I shall speak of the relation between the mind, the brain, and the body.

But first, why speak of the mind in these geographic terms at all?

> My mind to me a kingdom is:
> Such perfect joy therein I find
> That it excels all other bliss
> That God or Nature hath assigned.
> Though much I want that most would have,
> Yet still my mind forbids to crave.

So wrote the Elizabethan poet Sir Edward Dyer in a lyric set to music by Byrd exactly four hundred years ago. The theme of Dyer's poem is contentment with one's lot: he seeks of life only a bare sufficiency, aims not at wealth and power:

> ...what I lack my mind supplies
> Lo! thus I triumph like a king,
> Content with what my mind doth bring.

Other poets besides Dyer[1] have imagined the mind as an inward territory; but not all have seen it as a private kingdom secure from the buffets of the outer world. For Gerard Manley Hopkins it was sometimes a region of terror:

O the mind, mind has mountains; cliffs of fall
Frightful, sheer, no-man-fathomed. Hold them cheap
May who ne'er hung there.

All of us, at one time or another, are inclined to think of the mind in similar, though less articulate, terms as an inner landscape, whether we look on it with delight like Dyer or with despair like Hopkins. Let us try to evaluate philosophically this metaphor. Let us ask whether, in prosaic truth, there is an inner region within each of us for us to explore; and if so who is the guide who will best help us with the exploration – the philosopher, the poet or the theologian.

It is not easy to give a non-controversial definition of the mind as a starting point for the evaluation of the metaphor of the inner kingdom. Different philosophers would delineate the boundaries of the kingdom in different ways. Historically, there was one conception of mind which dominated philosophical thinking in the centuries when Aristotle was accepted as the doyen of philosophers, and there has been a different one since Descartes inaugurated a philosophical revolution in the seventeenth century.

The Old, or Aristotelian, kingdom of the mind had rather narrower boundaries than the new or Cartesian kingdom. For Aristotelians before Descartes the mind was essentially the faculty, or set of faculties, which set off human beings from other animals. Dumb animals and human beings shared certain abilities and activities: dogs, cows, pigs and humans could all see and hear and feel, they all had in common the faculty or faculties of sensation. But only human beings could think abstract thoughts and take rational decision: they were marked off from the other animals by the possession of intellect and will, and it was these two faculties which essentially constituted the mind. Intellectual activity was in a particular sense immaterial, whereas sensation was impossible without a material body.

For Descartes,[2] and for many others after him, the boundary between mind and matter was set elsewhere. It was consciousness, not intelligence or rationality, that was the defining criterion of the mental. The mind, viewed from the Cartesian standpoint, is the realm of whatever is accessible to introspection. The kingdom of the mind, therefore, included not only human understanding and willing, but also human seeing, hearing, feeling, pain and pleasure. For every form of human sensation, according to Descartes, included an element that was spiritual rather than material, a phenomenal component which was no more than contingently connected with bodily causes, expressions and mechanisms.

Descartes would have agreed with his Aristotelian predecessors that the mind is what distinguishes human beings from other animals. But for them what made this true was that mind was restricted to intellect, and only humans had intellect; for him what made it true was that though mind included sensation, only humans had genuine sensation. Descartes, that is to say, denied that animals had any genuine consciousness. The bodily machinery which accompanies sensation in human beings might occur also in animal bodies; but a phenomenon like pain, in an animal, was a purely mechanical event, unaccompanied by the sensation which is felt by humans in pain.

By introducing consciousness as the defining characteristic of mind, Descartes in effect substituted privacy for rationality as the mark of the mental. The intellectual capacities which distinguish language-using humans from dumb animals are not in themselves marked by any particular privacy. Whether Smith understands quantum physics, or is motivated by political ambition, is something which a third party may be better able to judge than Smith himself. In matters such as the understanding of scientific theory and the pursuit of long-term goals the subject's own sincere statement is not the last possible word.

On the other hand, if I want to know what sensations someone is having, then I have to give his utterances a special status. If I ask him what he seems to see or hear, or what he is imagining or saying to himself, what he says in reply cannot be mistaken. Of course it need not be true – he may be insincere, or misunderstand the words he is using – but it cannot be erroneous. Experiences of this kind have a certain property of indubitability, and it was this property which Descartes took as the essential feature of thought. Such experiences are private to their owners in the sense that while others can doubt them, they cannot.

Privacy of this kind is quite different from the rationality which pre-Cartesians took as the defining characteristic of mind. It is thus that human sensation falls, for Descartes, within the boundaries of the mental, whereas for the pre-Cartesian it fell without.

In addition to intellection and sensation there are other human capacities and activities which philosophers have identified as mental: memory, for instance, and imagination and the passions or emotions. Some philosophers have classified memory and imagination as inner senses: they have regarded these faculties as senses because they saw their function as the production of imagery; they regarded them as inner because their activity, unlike that of the senses, was not controlled by external stimuli.

The theory of inner sense was common to both Aristotelian and Cartesian accounts of the mind. It took, however, different forms within the different traditions. In one interpretation of Aristotle the inner sense of imagination was seen as active not only in the absence of external stimuli, but also whenever the outer senses themselves were active: the operation of the senses, on this interpretation, consisted in triggering off the imagination to produce the appropriate inner image. In the post-Cartesian psychology of Hume, the deliverances of the outer senses are impressions, the deliverances of the inner senses are ideas; the whole content of our minds, the phenomenal base from which the whole of the world is to be constructed, consists of nothing but impressions and ideas.

Most importantly, for the post-Cartesian empiricist tradition which flowers in Hume, the meaning of the words of our language consists in their relation to impressions and ideas. It is the flow of impressions and ideas in our minds which make our utterances not empty sounds, but the expression of thought; and if a word cannot be shown to refer to an impression or to an idea it must be discarded as meaningless.

Though the theory of the inner sense can be found both in medieval Aristotelianism and in post-Cartesian psychology, it took radically different forms in the two traditions. In particular, the relation between imagery and language was conceived quite differently by an Aristotelian such as Aquinas and a British empiricist such as Hume. Aquinas agreed with the empiricists that wherever there was thought there must be a flow of imagery: but for him it was not the images which gave content to the thought, but the thinking activity of the intellect which gave meaning to the images in the imagination.

For reasons which have been presented convincingly in our own time by Wittgenstein, I believe that Aquinas was correct, against the empiricists, in his view that when we think in images it is thought that confers meaning on the images, and not vice versa. We do much of our thinking by talking silently to ourselves; but the procession of imaged words through our imagination would not constitute a thought, would not have the meaning it does, were it not for our mastery of the language to which the words belong, a mastery which is an achievement of our intellectual power, not of our image-making faculty.

We can convince ourselves of this if we reflect on what happens in these cases where our imagination is concerned with symbols such as spoken or written words. If I call to mind the image of an advertisement in an unknown tongue, seen on a hoarding in a foreign city, the presence of that image in my imagination does not mean that I have in my mind the thought the imagined words express. But the point is not restricted to where the images in our minds are images of symbols. When our private thoughts are embodied not in imagined words, but in other visual or aural images, here too, as reflection will show, the image carries no unambiguous meaning on its face. My mental image of Napoleon may or may not resemble Napoleon; but my mental image of Abraham certainly does not, since I have not the faintest idea what Abraham looked like. An image does not get its significance by any resemblance to what it is an image of; to have meaning it must be employed in a particular way by the intellect. In the book of our thoughts, one might say, it is the intellect that is the author who provides the text; the imaging faculty is no more than typesetter and illustrator.

An empiricist philosopher might be willing to accept the claim that images possess the meaning they do only when they are in the mind of a language-user. But she might maintain that the mastery of language is something which is itself to be explained in terms of laws of association between images in succession. Whereas Aquinas, in the Middle Ages, and Chomsky, in our own time, would insist that language acquisition can only be explained if we postulate a species-specific ability in human beings. Domestic animals live in the same sensory environment as human babies, yet seem unable to achieve the mastery of abstract and universal terms which the child acquires as it grows. Aquinas was willing enough to attribute inner senses to animals no less than to humans; but for language-acquisition, he insisted, an inner sense was not enough, an intellect was necessary. In the empiricist account of mind he would have failed to recognize anything which he would call the intellect: the empiricist programme might be described in his terms as the endeavour to eliminate the intellect in favour of the inner sense.

In fact, I believe that the notion of 'inner sense' is misleading, whether in the scholastic or the empiricist tradition. It is not, in my view, the appropriate concept with which to grasp the nature of a faculty such as the imagination. How then are we to characterize the imagination? We must begin by making a distinction.

By 'imagination' there are at least two things which we can mean. We may mean simply the ability to call up mental images; an ability which each of you can exercise now simply by shutting your eyes and imagining what I look like, or by sitting in silence and reciting the Lord's prayer to yourselves. Much work in modern psychology and philosophy has gone to show that the imagination, in this sense, is incapable of performing the explanatory tasks which empiricist psychology attributed to it, and is unamenable to scientific study by introspection. I believe that these contentions of contemporary behaviourism are justified: but it would be foolish to be led by them to deny the very existence of the imagination in the sense of the power to call up images. The imagination, in this sense, is a power that is generally shared by members of the human race.

There is another sense of the word in which imagination is a much less evenly distributed faculty. The ability to imagine the world different in significant ways; the ability to conjecture, hypothesize, invent – this is a second form of imagination, creative imagination. Creative imagination is what poets, storytellers and scientists of genius have *par excellence*.

Neither of the two kinds of imagination we have distinguished can be identified simply with the human intellect in the sense of the ability to master language. Take first the capacity for imaging, which gives us the ability to talk to ourselves. This is a gift which is minor in comparison with the ability to talk at all: there could be a race just as intelligent as us which could think only aloud, and not in privacy; their lives would be both more honest and more noisy than ours, but there would be nothing in the world which would be beyond their ken without being also beyond ours. But if the imagination, in this first sense, is something inferior to the intellect, the imagination, in the second sense, is something superior to the intellect: it is the ability not just to understand language, but to use language creatively, to form new thoughts and discover new truths and build new worlds.

In tribute to Coleridge, but without claiming fidelity to the criteria by which he makes his distinction between two faculties, I will call the imagination in the first sense the *fancy*, while reserving the word 'imagination' for the creative imagination.

Like Coleridge, too, I shall feel the need to make a further subdivision within the realm of the creative imagination. Such imagination, I have maintained, is exhibited by geniuses both in science and in poetry. Both scientific and poetic imagination involves the mastery of language. Language is used in the framing of hypotheses no less than in the writing of drama. But when Darwin framed the hypothesis of evolution by natural selection, he did not need to use language in any non-literal manner. But it is one of the characteristics of the literary imagination that it is intimately linked with the ability to use language figuratively, in symbolic images, so that the literary imagination is called 'imagination' by a double title.

Not only poets, but prophets and divines have claimed that there is a special link between their calling or craft and its expression in imagery. Sometimes the claim takes the following form. Language in its literal sense is adapted to cope with material objects, with bodily entities. But the poet, the prophet, the divine, are concerned with matters spiritual, not bodily. Therefore they can use language only figuratively. An argument of this form sometimes seems to lurk behind some theological presentations of the theory of the analogical nature of religious discourse.

In my second and third lectures I will return to the topic of the creative imagination and its relation to metaphorical or analogical language. For the present I wish to dwell a little longer on the more humble faculty of the fancy. It is the imagination in this sense which philosophers have been inclined to call an inner sense. It was a faculty which differed from outer senses like sight in having an organ and an object inside the body (in the brain) rather than an organ at the edge of the body (like an eye) and an object outside the body (like the trees I see).

In fact, the fancy is a faculty quite different from senses such as sight or smell or touch. Sense faculties are faculties for discriminating between public objects which different subjects, depending on their circumstances, may be in better or worse positions to observe. Sense faculties operate by means of organs, that is, parts of the body which can be voluntarily controlled in characteristic ways which affect the efficiency of the discrimination. But the objects of the fancy are created, not discovered; there is no such thing as gradual approximation to their optimal discernment, or control by one observer on another's acuity of discrimination. The eye may be screwed up to see more clearly, or the ear cocked to hear more sharply; but there is no organ which can be deployed to capture an image more vividly. Using one's fancy is not discriminating between images: it is fantasizing discrimination between objects.

The fancy is not, then, a sense. Is it a part of the mind? According to the Aristotelian tradition, no; according to the Cartesian tradition, yes. The answer to the question, if the fancy is not a sense, must depend on its relationship to the intellect. And that cannot be decided until we have offered some attempt to delineate the intellect itself.

The human intellect is the capacity for intellectual abilities. It is a capacity, not an activity: babies have minds even though they do not yet exhibit intellectual activities. It is a second-order capacity: an ability to acquire abilities. To know a language is to have an intellectual ability: the ability to speak, understand and perhaps read the language. To have an intellect is to have a capacity one stage further back: the ability to acquire abilities such as the knowledge of a language.

Intellectual abilities are abilities for intellectual activities. Intellectual activities are ones which involve the creation and utilization of symbols. Mathematics, philosophy, portrait painting and poetry are clearly intellectual activities by this definition. The definition, you will have observed, has an indistinct borderline; this is a merit of the definition, since the concept it is aimed to capture is a fuzzy concept.

The most important intellectual skill is the mastery of language. Others, such as knowledge of mathematics, are acquired by human beings through the languages they have mastered. So the study of the acquisition and exercise of language is the way *par excellence* to study the nature of the human mind. To study knowledge of language you have to consider what the exercise of linguistic knowledge is. The exercise of linguistic knowledge is linguistic behaviour: but 'behaviour' here must be understood broadly, so that, for instance, reciting a poem to myself in my head imperceptibly to others will count as an instance of linguistic behaviour.

I have delineated the senses, the fancy and the intellect. Where now are we to place the boundary of the mind? The geography of the mind, it is clear, is not a simple matter to discover. Already we have seen that its most basic features are a matter of dispute between philosophers. It cannot be explored simply by looking within ourselves at an inward landscape laid out to view. What we see when we take this inner look will be partly determined by the philosophical viewpoint from which we look, or, we might say, by the conceptual spectacles we may be wearing.

But at this point I should make my own position clear: I believe that the clearest insight into the nature of the mind is to be obtained from the Aristotelian viewpoint. The mind is to be identified with the intellect, that is, the capacity for acquiring linguistic and symbolic abilities. The will, too, is part of the mind, as the Aristotelian tradition maintained, but that is because intellect and will are two aspects of a single indivisible capacity, as I will shortly go on to explain.

It may be argued that the definition of the mind as an intellectual capacity is too austere and abstract. Some may feel that it is a perverse denial of the reality of the mind. Surely the mind is not just a faculty: it is an immaterial and private world, the locus of our secret thoughts, the auditorium of our interior monologues, the theatre in which our dreams are staged and our plans rehearsed.

Now it would be folly to deny that human beings can keep their thoughts secret, can talk to themselves without making any noise, can sketch figures before their mind's eye instead of on pieces of paper. But the capacity for mental imagery of this kind – visual, audio-motor and other imagery – has already been described and named: it is not the intellect, but the fancy.

Moreover, the fancy, no less than the intellect, is a capacity or faculty. Particular exercises of the imaginative fancy are psychological events, occurring at particular times and places; they are experiences, in relation to which the subject is in a uniquely authoritative position. (The authority she has, though, is the authority of the judge, not of the witness.) These psychological events occur with great frequency in our lives; they may play a greater or lesser part in our lives according to the active or contemplative nature of our temperament and vocation.

To understand the nature either of the intellect or the fancy the philosopher has to reflect on the nature of ability in general. Abilities are distinct from their exercises: an ability is a more or less enduring state, the exercise of an ability will be a datable event or process. Whisky, for instance, even while standing harmlessly in the bottle possesses the ability to intoxicate; it only begins to exercise it after being imbibed.

Abilities must be distinguished not only from their exercises but also from their possessors and their vehicles.

The possessor of an ability is what *has* the ability: in this case of human abilities, the human being in question. It is I, and not my mind, who know English and am exercising this ability in giving this lecture.

The vehicle of an ability is the physical structure in virtue of which the possessor of an ability possesses the ability and is able to exercise it. The distinction between abilities and their vehicles is not something which is peculiar to human beings and their abilities. The vehicle of the whisky's power to intoxicate is the alcohol the whisky contains. A vehicle is something concrete, something which can be weighed and measured; an ability, on the other hand, has neither length nor breadth nor location. This does not mean that an ability is something ghostly: my front-door-key's ability to open my front door is not a concrete object, but it is not a spirit either.

Though the distinctions we have drawn are not restricted in their application to the abilities of human beings, they have many applications in the human realm and are vital to our attempt to delineate mental geography. An important instance of the distinction between possessor, ability and vehicle is the distinction between people, their minds and their brains.

Human beings are living bodies of a certain kind, with various abilities. The mind, as we have said, is *par excellence* the intellect, the capacity to acquire or possess intellectual abilities. The vehicle of the human mind is, very likely, the human brain. Human beings and their brains are physical objects; their minds are not, because they are capacities. Once again, to say that the mind is not a physical object is not to say that it is a ghostly spirit. If I insist that a mind is not a physical object with a length and breadth and location, that is not out of devotion to spiritualism, but simply out of concern for conceptual clarity.

The distinctions which I have been making are not novel: they are developments of distinctions which go back at least as far as Aristotle. However, philosophers have been tempted in every age to blur the distinctions: they like to reduce potentialities to actualities. Some philosophers attempt to reduce powers to their exercises: thus, explicitly, David Hume, who said the distinction between a power and its exercise was frivolous. Some philosophers attempt to reduce powers to their vehicles: thus, implicitly, Descartes, who wanted to identify the powers of bodies with their geometrical properties.

Philosophical errors about capacities in general show up particularly vividly when they occur in the philosophy of mind. Applied in this area, exercise-reductionism becomes behaviourism: the attempt to identify mind with behaviour consists in treating the complex second-order capacity which is the mind as if it was identical with its particular exercises in behaviour. Applied in this area, vehicle-reductionism becomes material- ism: the attempt to identify mind with brain consists in reducing my mental capacities to the parts and structures of my body in virtue of which I possess those capacities.

Materialism is a grosser philosophical error than behaviourism because the connection between a capacity and its exercise is in truth a more intimate one than the connection between a capacity and its vehicle. In the case of the mind, the connection between capacity and exercise is a conceptual connection: one could not understand what the mind was if one did not understand what kinds of thing constitute the exercise of mental capacity. The connection between capacity and vehicle, on the other hand, is a contingent one, discoverable by empirical science.

If the mind is not a physical structure how can one talk, even metaphorically, about the geography of the mind? Can the mind have a structure at all, if it is not a concrete object? The answer is yes, provided that we are clear what kind of structure we are talking about.

The set of abilities through which the mental capacity is exercised have relationships to each other, and these relationships between abilities form the structure of the mind. There are, for instance, relationships between the ability to multiply and the ability to take square roots. Once again, this is not something peculiar to minds, and the structure in question is not a ghostly partitioning. Not only human beings have abilities which are structured in this way: we can discover the structure latent in the operations of a pocket calculator by identifying the algorithms it uses (which we might do, for instance, by identifying the different kind of rounding errors which occur in its output).

There is a distinction between the structure of the mind, in this sense, and the structure of the brain which is its vehicle. Here again, the analogy with the calculator helps to make the point clear, because there too there are different kinds of structure: it is the mathematician who identifies the structure of the algorithm, the engineer who is the expert on the structure of the electronic hardware.

I have several times denied that the mind is to be identified with the brain. There is a venerable tradition which denies that the intellect has a bodily organ at all: for Aquinas, for instance, the brain was the organ of the fancy, but there was no organ of any kind for the intellect. The thesis which I have been defending needs to be distinguished from Aquinas' theory.

Aquinas does not, as I do, make a systematic distinction between the organ and the vehicle of a faculty. I use the word 'organ' in a way suggested by its etymology and consistent with the use of the word to describe the eye as the organ of sight. On my view, a sense organ is something like a tool, a part of the body which can be voluntarily moved and used in characteristic ways which affect the efficiency of the discriminatory activity which it serves. In this sense there is no organ of the intellect, nor of the fancy either: I cannot move my brain in order to imagine better in the way that I can turn my eyes to see better. Even if brain activity is a necessary condition for thought, this does not make the brain an organ of thought in the way that the eyes are organs of sight and the tongue and palate are organs of taste. But if we distinguish between organ and vehicle, then we can say that the brain is the vehicle both of the fancy and of the intellect.

What, now, is the relation between senses, fancy and intellect: how are these faculties which we have distinguished interrelated with each other? Let us consider first the relationship in the context of the acquisition of concepts, and then in the context of the exercise of concepts.

In order to possess a concept of something which can be an object of experience, it is not sufficient simply to have the appropriate experience. Young children see coloured objects before they painfully acquire colour-concepts; dumb animals can see and taste a substance such as salt but they cannot acquire the concepts which language-users can exercise in general judgements about salt. A special ability unshared by animals is necessary if human beings are to acquire concepts from the experience which they share with animals.

The mind is not just the ability to acquire abilities such as concepts: it is the ability to exercise them in appropriate conditions. It not only harvests ideas from experience, it gathers them in: it is the storehouse of ideas. Varying the metaphor, the intellect when it commences its activity, is an unwritten tablet, a *tabula rasa*. As concepts and beliefs are acquired by the operation of the specifically human intelligence, the tablet becomes covered with writing, the empty barn fills up. The mind has contents as well as powers. To find out the contents of a person's mind at a given time, you must find out what she understand, what she knows, what she believes at that moment.

The ideas, that is to say the concepts and beliefs, of the intellect are exercised in various ways. Just as the senses are necessary but not sufficient for the acquisition of ideas so, too, sense and fancy are necessary for the exercise of ideas. If there is to be an exercise of concepts, or the application of knowledge, there must be some exercise of sense or fancy, some application to a sensory context.

This necessity obtains whether the concepts are concrete or abstract, whether the truths known are necessary or contingent. For a man to be exercising the concept, say, of red, it seems that he must be either discriminating red from other colours around him, or having a mental image of redness, or a mental echo of the word 'red' or be talking, reading or writing about redness, or something of the kind. He may indeed be able to *possess* the concept *red* without this showing in his experience of behaviour on a given occasion, but it seems that without some embodiment in sensory activity there could be no *exercise* of the concept on that occasion. Similarly, with the knowledge of a general truth, such as that two things that are equal to a third are equal to each other. For this knowledge to be exercised it seems that its possessor must either enunciate it, or apply it say in the measurement of objects, or utilize it in some other way even if only in the artful manipulation of symbols.

Once one has described the intellect and the fancy and grasped their relationship to each other, it does not greatly matter what answer one gives to the question earlier postponed: is the fancy a part of the mind? The Aristotelian tradition which I am defending is perhaps best expressed by saying that in the geography of the mind the homeland is occupied by the intellect. The fancy and the senses are regions which are not part of the mind strictly so called: they are colonies rather than metropolitan areas. They are indeed well colonized: the images which occur in the fancy have the meaning they have because of the intellectual skills of the person whose fancy it is; the senses of a language-user perceive the world structured by the categories of the language of which the intellect is master. But they are not strictly part of the mind.

One question remains which must be addressed before I bring this lecture to an end. One may ask: where, in all this geography of the mind, is the location of the affective side of humanity: the emotions and the will? A full answer to this question must await a later lecture. The contrast between cognitive and affective, in human life, cuts across the stratification of senses, fancy, intellect. But I promised in this lecture to consider the relation between the intellect and the will. Doing so will illustrate what we are about when we regionalize the mind into faculties.

Human beings do many things such as understanding, judging, feeling, desiring, deciding, intending. Philosophers ascribe these different states and activities to different faculties. Why? What is it to ascribe particular actions to one or other faculty? It is to group the actions together in virtue of common features of description and assessment which apply to them.

Among the characterizations we may assign to human mental states and actions, there are two which stand out as the most important. We may characterize certain states as true (or false); we may characterize others as good (or evil). Beliefs, most obviously, may be described as true or false; desires, most obviously, may be described as good or evil. Those states and activities which can be evaluated on the true/false scale belong to the cognitive side of the soul; those states and activities which are evaluated on the good/evil scale belong to the affective, volitional side of the soul. At the highest level, the truth-bearing (or falseness-bearing) items are actualizations of the intellect; the goodness-bearing (or badness-bearing) items are actualizations of the will.

States of the will and activities of the intellect may both be described as right or wrong; it is wrong to think that the earth is larger than the sun, and wrong to have vengeful strategies; but the wrongness in the one case consists in falsehood, and in the other case in evil. The right, we might say, is the genus of which the true and the good are the species. Similarly, the human mind is a capacity of which the intellect and the will are the primary faculties.

The intellect and the will can be thought of as two aspects of the ability to master language. We make use of language both to understand the world and to control and alter the world. The intellect is the power to receive and process linguistic input: to understand what we are told by others, to categorize the world we experience in terms of the concepts of our language. The will is what gives the linguistic dimension to our behavioural output: it is the power to pursue the long-term goals which can be formulated only in language, and to enroll other language-users, by command and request, in our pursuit of those goals. Intellect and will are therefore two aspects of the overall ability to master and employ language which is the essence of the human mind.

## The Frontiers of the Mind

In the previous lecture I sketched the geography of the mind by distinguishing between faculties, such as the senses, the fancy, the intellect, the will and the imagination. I accepted the tradition according to which the mind is *par excellence* the intellect, the faculty for acquiring intellectual skills such as the mastery of language. I insisted that the mind, like any other capacity, needed to be distinguished from its exercise (in behaviour) and its vehicle (including the brain).

I have said that my topic in these lectures could be called the spiritual environment. I have denied, however, that the spiritual environment is helpfully thought of as being an inward environment. The view which identifies the spiritual with the inner has been well described – and identified as a target for attack – in the lecture by Don Cupitt earlier in this series. For a certain tradition, Cupitt says, it was in the relation to God, and *only* in that relation, that my personal identity could be perfected. To constitute and perfect me I didn't need the world, nor the body, nor the passions, nor even other people. I needed only God. This spiritual individualism – which survives in the present century in a secularized form – is thus characterized by Cupitt.

> Put crudely and strongly, its three principal doctrines are that the self is a substance, that the self is spiritual or immaterial, and that the self's relations with its physical environment are merely external to it, contingent, and not constitutive of it. Consciousness is seen as the primary philosophical certainty, and the conscious self, observing and deliberating, stands back a little from the world. It is a little sub-world on its own. It is not unaffected by natural events; on the contrary it registers them all the time. But it is not *constituted* by what it does and what happens to it, so that the familiar jibe, 'the ghost in the machine' is fair enough as an epitome of how the mind-body relation is seen.[3]

Like Cupitt, I reject the tradition he thus describes. However, I believe that the limits of the spiritual environment can be defined by a consideration of the two poles of spiritual individualism: the self and the creator. In this lecture, on the frontiers of the mind, I will consider first the self, the inner bound of mind, and then the concept of God, the outer bound of mind.

What can be more intimate or important to each of us than our self? The poet Thomas Traherne wrote

> A secret self I had enclos'd within
> That was not bounded with my clothes or skin.[4]

The self of which Traherne speaks is what is most personal and private to each of us. Most people never see beyond our clothes; a few intimates have seen the uncovered nakedness of our skins; but no human being other than myself has seen my self. Other people – each of us may feel – can know me in a sense, but what they can know of me is only what is exterior; however familiar they may be with me, however hard they may try, they can never reach to the real self within.

*The Oxford English Dictionary* lists a special philosophical sense of the word 'self' which it defines as follows: 'That which in a person is really and intrinsically *he* (in contradistinction to what is adventitious); the ego (often identified with the soul or mind as opposed to the body); a permanent subject of successive and varying states of consciousness.'

It is the purpose of this lecture to claim that the self of the philosophers is a mythical entity, and so likewise is the self of the poets and dramatists to the extent to which it is modelled on the philosophers' myth.

At one level, 'the self' is a piece of philosophers' nonsense consisting in a misunderstanding of the reflexive pronoun. To ask what kind of substance my *self* is, is like asking what the characteristic of *ownness* is which my own property has in addition to being mine. When, outside philosophy, I talk about myself, I am simply talking about the human being, Anthony Kenny; and my self is nothing other than myself. It is a philosophical muddle to allow the space which differentiates 'my self' from 'myself' to generate the illusion of a mysterious metaphysical entity distinct from, but obscurely linked to, the human being who is talking to you.

The grammatical error which is the essence of the theory of the self is a deep error and one which is not generated by mistaken grammar alone. The error has a number of different roots, and these need to be pulled up if the weed is to be eradicated. We may concentrate in the present lecture on two of the roots: the epistemological root and the psychological root.

The epistemological root of the notion of the self is Cartesian scepticism. Descartes, in the *Meditations*, convinces himself that he can doubt whether the world exists, and whether he has a body. He then goes on to argue, 'I can doubt whether I have a body; but I cannot doubt whether I exist; for what is this I which is doubting?' The 'I' must refer to something of which his body is no part, and hence to something which is no more than a part of the human being Descartes. The Cartesian ego is a substance whose essence is pure thought, the mind or *res cogitans*. This is the self in the second of the philosophical senses identified by the *OED*, 'the ego identified with the soul or mind as opposed to the body.'

Attempts to give content to the notion of a Cartesian ego run into two insoluble problems. The first problem concerns the relation of that ego to the body from which it has been distinguished. The second concerns the relation between the underlying mental substance and its successive conscious states. I shall not develop either problem in this lecture, but simply record my opinion that the two problems prevent any coherent content being given to the notion of *res cogitans*.

When Descartes asked himself 'What am I?' he gave the answer 'A mind'. A medieval Aristotelian would have answered, 'I am not my soul any more than I am my body; I am a person, but no part of me is a person. My body is a part of myself, and my soul is a part of myself. When I die, even if my soul leaves my body, I shall no longer exist; and I shall not exist again unless there is a Resurrection of the body.'

The epistemological route to the notion of the self takes us to a self which is much more circumscribed than the Aristotelian notion of the soul or intellectual mind. For the Cartesian ego is the substratum of those states of mind about which doubt is impossible. But there are many states of the intellect, as that was conceived by scholastic philosophers, which are not exempt from doubt and where the first person is in no position of infallible authority.

The intellect is the faculty whereby I understand, judge, know, believe. It is far from being the case that whenever I think I understand, judge, know or believe something I do in fact understand, judge, know and believe that thing. If Descartes wishes to say that we are infallible about the contents of our own minds, the most he can claim with plausibility is that we know what we are thinking at a given moment. No one, he may say, is better placed than yourself to answer the question, 'A penny for your thoughts?' and while in answer to that question you may lie you cannot be mistaken. Surely I am infallible about what I am visualizing in my mind's eye, or saying to myself in my head! That is something which I *know*, and which *only* I know, or at least only I *really* know, since others will have to take my word for it and they cannot be sure I am not deceiving them.

Somebody with a scholastic training might reply that in that case what Descartes is identifying himself with is his imagination, not his intellect. The images of inner vision, and the words of inner monologue are *phantasmata*, exercises of the fancy rather than of the intellectual mind. Of course, as we saw in the first lecture, the intellect and the fancy are linked: these images have the significance they have because of the intellectual capacity of the imaginer. If I do not know French I cannot talk to myself in French any more than I can talk to you in French. But equally I am in no position of infallible authority about the correctness and coherence of my French, whether uttered aloud or only in my head.

Among the activities which the medieval tradition ascribed to the intellect was the activity of doubting. Here, surely, one might think, Cartesian infallibility applies. We may be mistaken about what we know or understand, but surely we know when we are doubting! But even this is wrong. The death-blow to the whole Cartesian programme was given when Wittgenstein made us realize that even the words used to give private expression to Cartesian doubt would not have any sense in a world which contained nothing but a Cartesian ego.

The Cartesian ego is one version of the myth of the self: the version which grows from an epistemological root. A different and richer version of the myth is to be found in empiricist philosophy after Locke. The root from which it grows is psychological rather than epistemological: it derives from a particular picture of the nature of introspection.

From the point of view of medieval philosophy the Lockean self no less than the Cartesian ego takes its rise from a confusion between the intellect and the imagination. However, it owes its particular character to an erroneous picture of the imagination which it must be admitted was shared by medieval scholastics no less than by seventeenth-century empiricists. According to this erroneous notion, when I conjure up a mental image, my relation to the image in my mind is similar to my relation to a picture I look at in an art gallery, except that in the one case I am looking at an inner image, and in the other case I am looking at an outer picture.

I argued in the previous lecture that the notion of an inner sense is a misleading one, whether in the scholastics or in the empiricists. It exaggerates the superficial similarities between sensation and imagination, and conceals the profound conceptual differences between the two: namely, that a sense is a faculty of discrimination, and the fancy is not. Because imagination is fantasized sensation, and because sensation is essentially discrimination, to imagine is to fantasize discrimination. But to imagine that one is discriminating is not the same thing as to discriminate between images.

The objects of imagination are misdescribed when imagination is conceived as an inner sense. But much more seriously, the notion of an inner sense misrepresents the subject of imagination too. The self, as misconceived in the empiricist tradition, is essentially the subject of inner sensation. The self is the eye of inner vision, the ear of inner hearing; or rather, it is the mythical possessor of both inner eye and inner ear and whatever other inner organs of sensation may be fantasized.

Hence, if the whole notion of inner sense is misconceived, then not only the objects of imagination are misunderstood when regarded as inner sense-data, but so also, more importantly, there is a misunderstanding underlying the idea that there is an inner subject of sensation, the self of empiricist tradition.

If I am right, the self of modern philosophical theory is a chimera begotten of empiricist error. But notoriously thorough-going empiricism has also had a problem in making room for the self. Empiricism teaches that nothing is real except what can be discovered by the senses, whether inner or outer. The self, as inner subject, can clearly not be discovered by the outer senses, which perceive only the visible, audible, tangible exterior of things. But can it be discovered by the inner sense either? It is well known that Hume, after the most diligent investigation, failed to locate the self.

> When I enter most intimately into what I call *myself*, I always stumble on
> some particular perception or other, of heat or cold, light or shade, love
> or hatred, pain or pleasure. I never catch *myself* at any time without a
> perception, and never can observe anything but the perception... If any
> one upon serious and unprejudic'd reflexion, thinks he has a different
> notion of *himself* I must confess I can reason no longer with him. All I can
> allow him is, that he may be in the right as well as I, and that we are
> essentially different in this particular. He may, perhaps, perceive something
> simple and continu'd, which he calls *himself*; tho' I am certain there is no
> such principle in me.[5]

Herbert Spencer stated clearly the reason why this failure to discover
the self was not merely a contingent matter, not something to be
attributed to the Scottish philosopher's inattentiveness or sloth. Self is, by
definition, the inner perceiver; therefore it cannot be anything that is
inwardly perceived. 'If, then, the object perceived is self, what is the
subject that perceives? Or if it is the true self which thinks, what other
self can it be that is thought of?[6] For empiricism, the self is an unobjec-
tifiable subject, just as the eye is an invisible organ. But just as the
Cartesian ego – as the locus of intellectual infallibility – dwindles to
nothingness when Cartesian principles are rigorously applied, so too the
empiricist self vanishes when subjected to systematic empiricist scrutiny.
It is not discoverable by any sense, whether inner or outer; and therefore
it is to be rejected as a metaphysical monster.

To Descartes' question, 'What am I?' my own Aristotelian answer is
that I am a human being, a living body of a certain kind. We sometimes
speak as if we have bodies, rather than are bodies. But having a body,
in this natural sense, is not incompatible with being a body; it does not
mean that there is something other than my body which *has* my body. I
am not a soul, but I am a body; but just as I have a body, so I also
have a soul or mind: that is to say, I have an intellect and a will.

To say that I have a mind is to say that I have the capacity to acquire
and exercise intellectual abilities of various kinds, such as the mastery of
language and the possession of objective information. To say that I have
a will is to say that I have the capacity for the free pursuit of goals
formulated by the intellect. The mind and the will, as I emphasized in
the previous lecture, are capacities. What are they capacities of? Of the
living human being, the body you see before you during this lecture.

When I die, my body will cease to be me and I will no longer exist.
Some people believe that intellectual and volitional capacities can be
exercised apart from the body. I find this difficult to understand. It is
true that in the present life there are intellectual and volitional activities
which do not involve any bodily activity, such as silent thought and

spiritual longings. No doubt even such activities depend on the activity of the brain, but this appears to be a contingent rather than a necessary truth. But it is not a merely contingent fact that the person whose thoughts and longings they are is a visible and tangible body; and I do not for my part find it easy to make sense of the idea that such activities can take place, and be attributed to individual souls, in the absence of bodies to individuate the souls. For in the sense in which it is undoubtedly true to say that I have a soul, the soul appears to be *my* soul simply and solely because it is the soul of *this body*.

I do not, however, in the present lecture wish to take issue with those who believe in disembodied immortal souls. For nothing I have said so far would necessarily be rejected by those who believe in such souls. We may take St Thomas Aquinas as a spokesman for such believers. Aquinas undoubtedly believed that each human being had an immortal soul, which could survive the death of the body and continue to think and will in the period before the eventual resurrection of the body to which he looked forward. None the less, Aquinas did not believe in a self which was distinct from the body, nor did he think that disembodied souls were persons.

This is made clear in a striking passage in his commentary on the First Epistle to the Corinthians, which was first drawn to my attention by Professor Peter Geach. Commenting on the passage, 'If in this life only we have hope in Christ, we are of all men most miserable', St Thomas wrote, 'A human being naturally desires his own salvation; but the soul, since it is part of the body of a human being, is not a whole human being, and my soul is not I; so even if a soul gains salvation in another life, that is not I or any human being.[7]

It is remarkable that St Thomas says not just that the soul is only part of a human being, but that it is only part *of the body* of a human being. Commonly he uses 'soul' and 'body' as correlatives, and often he writes as if soul and body are related to each other as the form and the matter of Aristotelian hylomorphism. But the formulation which he uses in this passage is in fact the more correct one from the hylomorphic standpoint: the human being is a body which like other mutable bodies is composed of matter and form; the soul, which is the form of the living body, is one part of the body, and the matter is another part of it, using 'part' in the very special sense which is appropriate in this context.

What is most clear from the passage is that St Thomas refuses to identify the disembodied soul, even a beatified disembodied soul, with any self, or ego. According to St Thomas, what I am, what you are, what everyone else is, is nothing less than a human being. He refuses to identify the individual with the individual's soul, as Descartes was to do. He would not disagree with the thesis I have argued that each of us has no self other than himself or herself.

In one very special case, it might be thought, St Thomas would agree that a human being had a self which was distinct from the soul and body which made him a human being. According to the doctrine of the Incarnation, Jesus Christ is who he is not through the soul and body which constitute his humanity, but because of the divine personality incarnate in him. As Cardinal Newman put it in the hymn 'Praise to the Holiest' the special feature of the Incarnation is that

> ...a higher gift than grace
> Should flesh and blood refine
> God's presence and his very Self
> And essence all divine.

But it would be quite wrong to think that the doctrine of the incarnation involves the thesis that in Jesus the Divine Self occupied the place occupied in the rest of us by the human self. For the philosophers' self was meant to be something central and important to each human being; and someone who lacked such a self would be no real human being, so that if God was to become incarnate as a human he would need to take on a self as well as a soul and a body. If, on the other hand, we accept that the philosophers' self is mythical, then the concept of self cannot be used to mark out a locus for the divine to occupy in the case of incarnation. Just as my self is nothing other than myself, so God's Self is just God himself: it is he, and not any distinct self, human or divine, which, according to the Christian doctrine, took on human nature.

For the poets whom I took as the point of departure for these lectures, the self had two essential characteristics: first, it was a secret and private entity, and secondly, it was that part of a human being which was most lasting and essential, by comparison with superficial and accidental features. But it is a mistake to identify what is fundamental with what is private.

Much of my life is private in the sense that it consists of thoughts and feelings which I keep to myself and do not express to others. Like most people, I accompany much of what I do with fragmentary inner monologue; each day I have feelings, suffer moods, entertain fantasies which I do not trouble to inform other people about. Because these episodes in my life are not made public, they may seem to be peculiarly my own. Self-knowledge, according to the mistaken philosophy of the self, is the monitoring of this inward life.

It would be absurd, however, to claim that my private imaginings constitute that which, in the words of the OED, is 'really and intrinsically me in contradistinction to what is adventitious'. To be sure, someone who had access to all my private imaginings would know more about me than someone who was privy only to my public utterances. But the knowledge of what I say to myself or merely think of doing is much less important than the knowledge of what I actually say and do in the real and public world.

The really important questions about oneself, about what kind of person one fundamentally is, are not questions which can be settled by introspection. 'Do I really love her?' 'Am I the kind of person that would betray a friend to death to save my life?' 'Will I regret, in five years time, that I changed my job in midlife?' 'Am I getting more and more vain as I grow older?' These, and countless other questions of the same kind, are not questions which receive their definitive answer in private colloquy with oneself in the imagination. A close friend or spouse may well be able to conjecture in advance with greater perspicacity than I the answers they will eventually receive in the testing conditions of real life.

As with self-knowledge, so with self-love. When I am selfish, the good which I am pursuing is the good of the human being, Anthony Kenny; not the good of some inner entity in the theatre of the imagination. Those who pursue pleasure and power for themselves are seeking not pleasure and power in the inner world of the imagination, but in the public world of flesh and blood. Unselfishness, too, is measured not by interior acts of secret renunciation, but by the willingness to put first the interests of other human beings in the public world. The self that is cosseted or disciplined is not the inner observer of the mental theatre, nor the centreless subject of objectivity: it is the human being with all the parts and passions of a man.

The self, then, which is the inner bound of consciousness, vanishes upon philosophical examination. In its place we have the bodily, vulnerable, contingent, insignificant human being who possesses the mind with which he or she explores and seeks to understand the vast Universe about us. Is there an outer limit to the exploration and understanding of the Universe?

I shall argue, at the end of this lecture and in the next, that the concept of God can be seen as a concept of the outer limit of human understanding of the Universe. But before doing so, I must take some time to discuss a different view of how we acquire the concept of God: that is, the view that we encounter God as an item within our mental history. On this view, God appears not at the outer frontiers of the mind, but within these frontiers as an object of experience. Let us ask whether it is possible to have an experience of God, and in what sense.

If God is an immaterial spirit, and has no body, however ethereal, then God cannot literally be seen with the ordinary senses. Visions of God, such as those attributed to Moses in the Bible, must at best be regarded as the seeing of a miraculous manifestation or symbol of God, not as a literal seeing of an invisible divinity. But that would be accepted by many who claim, none the less, that God is known to us in experience.

They would argue rather thus. Some people have, and perhaps all people can have, religious experiences; and religious experiences put us in contact with God. It is true that God, since he has no body, cannot be perceived by the external senses, but we (or at least some of us) have an inner sense which can be trained to focus on God and thus provide irrefutable evidence of his existence.

I think that the expression 'religious experience' is an unfortunate one; not because of anything to do with religion, but because of the confusing nature of the relevant concept of 'experience'. The word is used to cover any item in a person's mental history, whether sense-experience, feeling, emotions, imaginations, dreams and reveries. It thus provides a catch-all which includes items of very diverse cognitive status. In particular, 'religious experience' includes many different kinds of things, ranging from sentiments of edification to mystical ecstasy.

Sentiments of grief, of guilt, of justification, forgiveness and exaltation in the context of a religious liturgy or on the occasion of the reading of a sacred text clearly play an important and valued part in the life of a religious believer. But religious experience in this sense is not something which can be regarded as an encounter with God, in the sense in which the sighting of a distant comet may be an experience of that comet. The sentiments get their significance and profundity from the institutions which provide their context and not vice versa. And the nature and point of these institutions depends crucially on whether or not there is a God who can be known by the human mind.

Religious experience in this common sense, therefore, is not experience of God. What of the rather different kinds of experience claimed by the mystics? Can the experience of mystics be regarded as a perception of God by means of a secret, interior, sensory capacity? The notion of an inner sense, I have already argued, is not a helpful one: the implicit comparison with the external senses is misleading. But there are special difficulties in the notion that God could be detected by any sense, inner or outer.

If there is a God with the attributes ascribed to him by Western theism, then he is everlasting, unchanging and ubiquitous. In relation to such an object there cannot be any activity of discrimination resembling the discriminatory activities of the senses: we cannot have a sixth sense which detects that God is here and not there, as we can see that something is red at one end and not at another, or which detects that God was around a moment ago and is not now, as we can hear a noise which suddenly stops.

If God is everywhere always, there can be no sense to discriminate the places and times where he is from those where he is not; the whole nature of a sense is an ability to tell differences of this kind. One cannot get nearer to or get further from God as one can get nearer to or further from a source of light or sound: one cannot be too early or too late to encounter him as one might be to see or hear something. The whole context within which talk of sense-experience makes sense is lacking in the case of alleged sense-experience of God.

Mystics themselves are as willing to describe mystical experiences in terms of unity of will with God as they are in cognitive terms. But whether the union with God is described in terms of love, or compared with a seeing, or a touching, or a tasting of godhead, it cannot be taken literally as the operation of a sixth sense. For the mode of operation of the alleged faculty differs too much from the mode of operation of genuine senses; and the essential attributes of the alleged object to be sensed differ too greatly from the attributes of any possible object of sensory discrimination.

Where, then, is God to be found in the mind? He is not an object of the senses nor within the fancy: is he to be found in the intellect or in the imagination? My reply – to be expounded in the next lecture – is that if he is to be found at all he is to be found, by means of the imagination, at the boundary of the intellect.

Consider traditional proofs of the existence of God, the different versions of the cosmological argument. All such proofs start from a phenomenon, or class of phenomena, within the world, which demand explanation. They go on to show that a particular type of explanation will not lead to intellectual satisfaction, however frequently it is applied. Thus, movement is not to be explained by objects in motion, nor can effects be explained ultimately by causes which are themselves in turn effects, nor can complexity be explained by beings which are themselves complex.

Proofs of the existence of God, if they are not to be mere appeals to ignorance and incomprehension, must not depend on particular features of the world which are as yet unexplained. They must depend on the necessary limits of particular types of explanation. The cosmological argument must depend on necessary, not contingent, features of the kind of cosmos to be explained, even if the cosmos is itself contingent. Otherwise they will be vulnerable to defeat by the progress of science. (I have argued elsewhere that the Five Ways of Aquinas are unsuccessful forms of the cosmological argument precisely because they depend, more than at first meets the eye, on particular theories of physical explanation).[8]

If there is to be a successful version of the cosmological argument, it must be an argument to show that a particular type of explanation must fail to render intelligible the class of phenomena to be explained, and that intelligibility can only be found, if at all, in a being which stands outside the application of that particular paradigm of explanation. Such a being, the argument may conclude in the style of St Thomas, is what all men call God; but we must wait until the next lecture to consider what the nature of that 'calling' may be.

In addition to the cosmological argument for divine existence there is also the ontological argument. This too is an argument pointing to a limit: but now the limit is not the limit of explanation, but the limit of conception itself. The premise of the ontological argument is that each of us, even the atheist, has the concept of God as that than which no greater can be conceived. From this premise, the ontologist offers to prove that God must exist in reality and not only in the mind. But St Anselm, prince of ontologists, goes on to show that that than which no greater can be conceived cannot itself be conceived. The corollary of the ontological argument therefore appears to cut off the premise on which it rests. Only if there is some sense in which we can conceive the inconceivable can we talk of God at all. In the next lecture, let us brashly set off from the coasts that bound intelligibility onto these strange seas of thought.

## Seas of Thought

At the end of the last lecture I claimed that God was not to be found in the mind. He is not the object of experience of any inner or outer sense; he is not the terminus of a process of intellectual explanation; he is not an object grasped by any normal concept. To grasp God, it seems, we have to cross the limits of our understanding.

God, we said, was not a terminus of any of the standard patterns of explanation in the world. Rather, the concept of God is invoked as a limiting case of explanation. If a proof of the existence of God is to take its start from an explanatory series in the world, it must aim to show that such a series, however prolonged, cannot arrive at a complete and intellectually satisfactory account of the phenomena to be explained. The argument must take a form similar to the demonstration that the addition of one half to one quarter to one eighth and so on, will never surpass unity.

If we are to have a proof of the existence of God it will not suffice to say that we do not know whether some pattern of explanation in the world will succeed in explaining everything that needs explaining; we have to aim to show that it cannot possibly do so. And that is indeed what the traditional proofs of God attempted to do: to show, for instance, that no explanation by one or more moving objects will suffice to explain motion, that no explanation of one contingent object by another contingent object will suffice to explain contingency.

It is possible to look at proofs such as Aquinas' Five Ways as providing not so much proofs as definitions of God. God is then that which accounts for what, in the motion series, is left unexplained by previous motors in the series. God is that which accounts for that which, in the causal series, is left unexplained by the individual members of the series. God is that which accounts for what is left unexplained in the series of contingent substances which arise from each other and turn into each other. God is that which accounts for what is left unexplained in the series of complex entities composed of simpler entities.

The way in which God accounts for the unexplained is not by figuring in some further explanation. When we invoke God we do not explain the world, or any series of phenomena in the world. The mode of intelligibility which is provided by the invocation of God is something of a quite different kind. In terms of a distinction fashionable in some philosophical quarters, the introduction of the concept of God provides not explanation but understanding.

It is worth dwelling on these points for a moment. In his book *The Blind Watchmaker* Richard Dawkins has some fun with Bishop Montefiore, late of Birmingham, who had, in his book *The Probability of God*, drawn attention to the implausibilities of certain evolutionary explanations. I quote from Dawkins.

> [Montefiore] makes heavy use of what may be called the Argument from Personal Incredulity. In the course of one chapter, we find the following phrases, in this order '...there seems no explanation in Darwinian terms... it is no easier to explain... it is hard to understand... it is not easy to understand... it is equally difficult to explain... I do not find it easy to comprehend... I do not find it easy to see... find it hard to understand... it does not seem feasible to explain... I cannot see how... neo-Darwinism seems inadequate to explain many of the complexities of animal behaviour... it is not easy to comprehend how such behaviour could have evolved solely through natural selection... it is impossible... how could an organ so complex evolve?... it is not easy to see... it is difficult to see.'

The Argument from Personal Incredulity, Dawkins insists, is an extremely weak argument. In some cases it is based on simple ignorance. Dawkins continues:

> Even if the foremost authority in the world cannot explain some remarkable biological phenomenon, that doesn't mean that it is inexplicable. Plenty of mysteries have lasted for centuries and finally yielded to explanation... But we aren't testing human ingenuity. Even if we found one example that we *couldn't* explain, we should hesitate to draw any grandiose conclusions from the fact of our own inability.[9]

I do not judge whether Dawkins' criticisms of Bishop Montefiore are well taken. But as criticisms of the general pattern of traditional arguments for the existence of God, they would be misplaced. As I have already insisted, according to this pattern of argument the appeal to God was not based on particular failures of explanation, but upon the provable inability of a particular pattern of explanation to give a satisfactory account of phenomena of a certain type.

There is a palmary example of this within Dawkins' own field. However successful explanation by natural selection may be in explaining the origin of particular species of life, it clearly cannot explain how there come to be such things as species at all. That is to say, it cannot explain how there came to be true breeding populations; since the existence of such populations is one of the premises on which explanations in terms of natural selection rest as their starting point.

To say this is not to say that Darwinians do not offer explanations of the origin of life; of course they do, and some of them are to be found in Dawkins' book; but they are explanations of a radically different kind from explanation by natural selection. Whether God must be invoked as the author of life, or whether one of the explanations of life in terms of chance and necessity can be made intellectually satisfactory, one thing is clear: natural selection cannot explain the Origin of Species.

I insisted earlier that God is not a part of any of the explanatory series from which proofs of God's existence take their rise. This point, too, is worth emphasizing against Dawkins. Elsewhere in *The Blind Watchmaker* Dawkins considered the following argument offered to show the difficulties of accounting for the origin of life and the existence of the original machinery of replication:

> Cumulative selection can manufacture complexity while single-step selection cannot. But cumulative selection cannot work unless there is some minimal machinery of replication and replicatory power, and the only machinery of replication that we know seems too complicated to have come into existence by means of anything less than many generations of cumulative selection.

This argument, Dawkins says, is sometimes offered as proof of an intelligent designer, the creator of DNA and protein. He replies:

> This is a transparently feeble argument, indeed it is obviously self-defeating. Organized complexity is the thing we are having difficulty in explaining. Once we are allowed simply to postulate organized complexity, if only the organized complexity of the DNA/protein replicating engine, it is relatively easy to invoke it as a generator of yet more organized complexity. That, indeed, is what most of this book is about. But of course any God capable of intelligently designing something as complex as the DNA/protein replicating machine must have been at least as complex and organized as that machine itself. Far more so if we suppose him *additionally* capable of such advanced functions as listening to prayers and forgiving sins. To explain the origin of the DNA/protein machine by invoking a supernatural Designer is to explain precisely nothing, for it leaves unexplained the origin of the Designer. You have to say something like 'God was always there' and if you allow yourself that kind of lazy way out, you might as well just say 'DNA was always there' or 'Life was always there', and be done with it.

A traditional theist would say that this paragraph misrepresented the notion of God in two ways. First of all, God is as much outside the series complexity/simplicity as He is outside the series mover/moved. He is not complex as a protein is; nor, for that matter, is He simple as an elementary particle is. He has neither the simplicity nor the complexity of material objects. Secondly, He is not one of a series of temporal contingents, each requiring explanation in terms of a previous state of the Universe: unchanging and everlasting, He is outside the temporal series.

Because God is not a part of any of the explanatory series which He is invoked to account for – He is first mover unmoved, He is first cause only by analogy – the vocabulary and predicates of the different explanatory series are not applicable to Him in any literal sense.

When we turn from the cosmological argument to the ontological one, the vocabulary at our disposal to describe God becomes even more constrained. The ontological argument, in contrast to the cosmological argument, concerns not explanation, but conception. In terms of the geography of the mind, it moves from the explanation of the outer world to the limitation of the inner. God, in Anselm's definition, becomes the outer limit of conception; because anything than which something greater can be conceived is not God. God is not the greatest conceivable object; He is himself greater than can be conceived, therefore beyond the bounds of conception, and therefore literally inconceivable.

But if God is inconceivable, does that not mean that the notion of God is self-contradictory, and God a nonsensical *Unding* which cannot exist?

That would be so if conceivability were mere freedom from contradiction; but there are many reasons for thinking that non-contradictoriness is not identical with freedom from contradiction. A notion is conceivable only if it is free from contradiction: that much is sure; but Kant, Wittgenstein and the positivists have suggested other, more stringent, criteria of conceivability. The conditions laid down by these philosophers seem unsatisfactory for reasons unconnected with theism; but they are right to say that freedom from contradiction is only a necessary and not a sufficient condition of conceivability.

If God is inconceivable, is it not self-refuting to talk about Him at all, even if only to state His inconceivability? The paradox here is one which is familiar in other areas of philosophy too. Bertrand Russell[10] gave currency to Berry's paradox, which invites us to consider the expression 'the least natural number not nameable in fewer than twenty-two syllables'. This expression names in twenty-one syllables a natural number which by definition cannot be named in fewer than twenty-two syllables. Clearly, to solve this paradox, we have at least to distinguish between different ways of *naming*. And the solution to the paradox of God, if there is to be one, must be found by insisting that while we can speak of God, we cannot speak of him literally.

If this is so, there cannot be any *science* of theology. My book *The God of the Philosophers*[11] was meant to be a refutation of this would-be science. The God of scholastic and rationalistic philosophy is an *Unding*, full of contradiction. Even in talking about God we must not contradict ourselves. Once we find ourselves uttering contradictory propositions, we must draw ourselves up. We can perhaps seek to show that the contradiction is only apparent; we may trace back the steps that led to the contradictory conclusion, in the hope that minor modification to one of the steps will remove the clash. Or we may claim that the contradiction arises because metaphorical language has mistakenly been taken literally. The one thing we must not do is to accept contradiction cheerfully.

To say that we cannot speak literally of God is to say that the word 'God' does not belong in a language game. Literal truth is truth within a language game. Some philosophers believe that there is a special religious language game, and it is in that game that the concept of God is located. I believe, on the contrary, that there is no religious language game, and that we speak of God in metaphor. And to use metaphor is to use a word in a language game which is not its home.

However, it is not peculiar to theology that it cannot be encapsulated in a language game. If Wittgenstein is right – and after all, the notion of language game is his coinage – there is no philosophical language game either: there are no truths special to philosophy. Finally, a certain kind of poetry is an attempt to express what is literally inexpressible.

I have said that theology speaks in metaphor. Theologians have preferred to say that theological language is analogical, and analogical discourse is not necessarily metaphorical. However, theological attempts to explain how non-metaphorical analogy applies to God have been, in my view, unsuccessful.

Scholastic theologians, drawing inspiration from cryptic passages in Aristotle, distinguished two kinds of analogy: analogy of attribution and analogy of proportionality.

Analogy of attribution was often illustrated by reference to the term 'health'. Strictly speaking, only living things such as animals and plants can be healthy. But a climate or a complexion may naturally be described as healthy. A climate was healthy, the scholastics explained, because it was a cause of health in animals, the prime analogate; a complexion was healthy because it signified, or was caused by, health in the prime analogate, the human animal. Thus, causality was the key to analogy of attribution. But this kind of analogy will not explain the attribution of predicates drawn from creatures to the creator. For in one sense God is the cause of everything (and therefore no one predicate of creatures belongs to him rather than any other) and in another sense, God, standing outside the causal series as *prima causa analoga*, is not the cause of anything.

Analogy of proportionality did not depend on causal relationships. It may be illustrated with reference to the analogous term 'good'. A good knife is a knife that is handy and sharp; a good strawberry is a strawberry that is soft and tasty. Clearly, goodness in knives is something quite different from goodness in strawberries; yet it does not seem to be a mere pun to call both knives and strawberries 'good', nor does one seem to be using a metaphor drawn from knives when one calls a particular batch of strawberries good. The explanation of this kind of usage, the scholastics explained, was a kind of arithmetical proportion, thus:

$$\text{Goodness of x} :: \text{essence of x} = \text{Goodness of y} :: \text{essence of y}$$

It is because we know the essence of knives and strawberries that we can understand what 'good' means applied to each of them, without having to learn a separate lesson in each case.

The difficulty in applying this pattern of analogy in the case of God, is that we have no idea what His essence is. Even those who have thought that we had, in a fairly strong sense, a concept of God, have fallen short of saying that we have any grasp of God's essence. So the analogous predicates which function as, according to the theory, 'good' does, cannot be applied to God in any meaningful way, if we insist on literal meaning.

The relation between literal and non-literal meaning will become clearer if we interpose some brief but very general reflections on the nature of language. The three great uses of language are to express, to describe and to prescribe. The use of language to express is the most primitive and basic, the one on which the others are built. The child's prelinguistic expression of its needs, wants and emotions is the primitive stock on to which the parents graft the more exotic growth of the language used in the community for description and prescription.

Descriptive speech, the use of language which is the exercise of the intellect, is evaluated on the true-false scale. Prescriptive speech, the use of language which is the exercise of the will, is evaluated on the good-evil scale. Expressive speech, which is the manifestation of the emotions, is evaluated on both scales: an expression of emotion may be criticized either for being inauthentic (and in that sense false) or inappropriate (and in that sense evil).

The geography of the soul which we sketched in the first lecture was incomplete because it did not assign any place to the emotions. There are, in fact, two principal kinds of emotion. First, there are those which are expressible non-linguistically. We may call these the passions – they are the ones related to hunger, thirst, lust, sleepiness. Passions which are expressible non-linguistically can also be expressed linguistically; as has been said there is a basic, expressive, use of language on which description and prescription are built. Then, secondly, there are those emotions which are expressible only linguistically, just as there are thoughts which are expressed only linguistically. It is in these regions of the mind that we must locate religious sentiments, such as awe, guilt, faith and worship.

Cannot, it might be asked, these emotions be expressed also in *action*? They can indeed motivate action; but there is a difference between behaviour which expresses emotion and action which is motivated by emotion. When these emotions motivate action, thought expressible in language is still needed to distinguish the motivation from other motives which might find vent in similar behaviour: to discriminate, for instance, love from lust, patriotism from bravado.

Just as the expression of the passions constitutes a basis for the primitive use of language, the expression of the higher emotions provides a dominant role for the creative imagination. This is particularly so in the case of the religious emotions. As the intellect is exercised above all in the two modes of explanation and understanding, so the imagination, which in the scientific mode is exercised in hypothesis, in the artistic mode is exercised in *dichtung*, in poetry and storytelling.

We denied earlier that God could be located in the operation of the fancy. Can God be discovered by the exercise of the creative imagination?

The imagination is clearly not a means of acquiring information about the world outside us in the way that the senses are. Still, the use of the imagination can increase our sensitivity to other people and thus our ability to inform ourselves about what they feel and are likely to do. Works of the imagination may teach us things about human beings; great works of fiction are means by which the human race extends its self-awareness. Could we say that knowledge of God could be acquired by the use of the imagination, in the way our knowledge of ourselves and of our peers grows through storytelling and poetry?

For imagination to be a genuine source of knowledge there has to be some way of distinguishing what is discovered by the imagination from what is created by the imagination. How can we settle whether God is discovered by the imagination or created by it? After all, if there is no God, then God is incalculably the greatest single creation of the human imagination. No other creation of the imagination has been so fertile of ideas, so great an inspiration to philosophy, to literature, to painting, sculpture, architecture and drama. But the very fact that an atheist can salute the idea of God as a magnificent work of the human imagination shows that whether God exists is something which the imagination itself cannot settle.

But the question was not whether the imagination could show that God existed, but whether, if by some other means we had reason to believe in a God who was beyond the use of literal language, the imagination could provide us with the means of discourse about Him. For it is the imagination which is the creator of metaphor and metaphorical language.

Metaphor, as has been said, is not a move in a language game. It is, in the standard case, taking a word which has a role in one language game and moving it to another. The predicates which we apply to God – predicates, for instance, concerning knowledge and love – are taken from other language games, and used in the absence of the criteria which give them their meanings in the language games in which they have their home. If there is such a thing as a religious language game, it is not a language game in which there is literal truth. In this, as was observed, religious language resembles philosophy and the kind of poetry which endeavours to express the literally inexpressible.

Not all poetry, of course, is of that kind. It would be foolish to say that 'Great Anna, whom three realms obey | Did sometimes council take, and sometimes tea' is an attempt to express the inexpressible. It would also be foolish to claim that the poetry of the inexpressible is bound to be of superior value to the poetry of the mundane. But in order to throw light on the problems of talking about God it is the poetry of the inexpressible to which we must turn.

I know of no philosopher who has described the paradox of talking about the inconceivable Godhead with such precision as the poet Arthur Hugh Clough. Consider, as an example, his poem of 1851 *Hymnos Aymnos* ('a hymn, yet not a hymn'). Its first stanza begins with an invocation to the incomprehensible Godhead:

> O Thou whose image in the shrine
> Of human spirits dwells divine;
> Which from that precinct once conveyed,
> To be to outer day displayed,
> Doth vanish, part, and leave behind
> Mere blank and void of empty mind,
> Which wilful fancy seeks in vain
> With casual shapes to fill again.[12]

The poem starts from the assumption that the place to look for God is in the individual's inmost soul. I have argued earlier that the search, so conducted, is bound to fail; and that, too, is the poet's conclusion. Attempts to give public expression to the God encountered in the soul yield only meaningless, self-contradictory utterances ('blank and void') or images unconnected with reality ('casual shapes')

The second stanza of the poem, which I omit, develops the theme of the impotence of human utterance to embody the divine. In the third the poet proclaims that silence – inner as well as outer – is the only response to the ineffable:

> O thou, in that mysterious shrine
> Enthroned, as we must say, divine!
> I will not frame one thought of what
> Thou mayest either be or not.
> I will not prate of 'thus' and 'so'
> And be profane with 'yes' and 'no'.
> Enough that in our soul and heart
> Thou, whatso'er thou may'st be, art.

The agnosticism is radical: the *via negativa* is rejected as firmly as the *via positiva*. Not only can we not say of God what he is, we are equally impotent to say what he is not. The possibility, therefore, cannot be ruled out that one or other of the revelations claimed by others may after all be true:

Unseen, secure in that high shrine
Acknowledged present and divine
I will not ask some upper air,
Some future day, to place thee there;
Nor say, nor yet deny, Such men
Or women saw thee thus and then:
Thy name was such, and there or here
To him or her thou didst appear.

In the final stanza Clough pushes his agnosticism a stage further. Perhaps there is no way in which God dwells – even ineffably – as an object of the inner vision of the soul. Perhaps we should reconcile ourselves to the idea that God is not to be found at all by human minds. But even that does not take off all possibility of prayer.

Do only thou in that dim shrine,
Unknown or known, remain, divine;
There, or if not, at least in eyes
That scan the fact that round them lies.
The hand to sway, the judgment guide,
In sight and sense, thyself divide:
Be thou but there, – in soul and heart,
I will not ask to feel thou art.

The soul reconciled to the truth that there can be no analogue of seeing or feeling God, that nothing can be meaningfully said about Him, can yet address Him and pray to be illuminated by His power and be the instrument of His action. But does not this presume that God can after all be described: at least as a powerful agent who can hear our prayers? No, the prayer need not assume the truth of that; only its *possibility* is needed. An agnostic's praying to a God whose existence he doubts is no more unreasonable than the act of a man adrift in the ocean, or stranded on a mountainside, who cries for help though he may never be heard, or fires a signal which may never be seen. Of course, the need for help need not be the only motive which may drive an agnostic to prayer: the desire to give thanks for the beauty and wonder of the world may be another.

If there is a religious language game, it is surely the language game of worship. This, too, has received magisterial description in a poem of Clough's: his early work *Qui Laborat, Orat*.

O only Source of all our light and life,
  Whom as our truth, our strength, we see and feel

But whom the hours of mortal moral strife
    Alone aright reveal!

Mine inmost soul, before Thee inly brought,
    Thy presence owns ineffable, divine;
Chastised each rebel self-encentered thought,
    My will adoreth Thine.

With eye down-dropt, if then this earthly mind
    Speechless remain, or speechless e'en depart;
Nor seek to see – for what of earthly kind
    Can see Thee as Thou art?

If well-assured 'tis but profanely bold
    In thought's abstractest forms to seem to see,
It dare not dare thee dread communion hold
    In ways unworthy Thee

O not unowned, Thou shalt unnamed forgive,
    In worldly walks the prayerless heart prepare;
And if in work its life it seem to live,
    Shalt make that work be prayer.

Nor times shall lack, when while the work it plies
    Unsummoned powers the blinding film shall part
And scarce by happy tears made dim, the eyes
    In recognition start.

But, as Thou willest, give or e'en forbear
    The beatific supersensual sight,
So, with Thy blessing blest, that humbler prayer
    Approach Thee morn and night.

The poem has appealed to many readers – Tennyson was among its
first admirers. It has been applauded by the devout no less than the
sceptic and it has subtleties which are worth attention. There is first the
paradox, obvious and surely intentional, that a poem which appears to
deny the propriety of addressing the Godhead in prayer is itself an explicit
second-person address to God. What is the inward bringing of the inmost
soul before God but that 'lifting up of the mind and heart to God' which
is one of the traditional definitions of prayer? The poet, therefore, is not
so much attacking the practice of vocal prayer, as urging the praying soul
to be aware of the limitations of human prayer, even at the moment of
uttering one.

The first two stanzas, in particular, in their majestic movement, could stand by themselves as a prayer that might be uttered without misgiving by a perfectly orthodox Christian. They would, no doubt, be most congenial to those traditions which have emphasized the inner light rather than the external revelation as the supreme source of our awareness of God. But the solemn rallentando forced by the alliteration of the last two lines of the first stanza makes the beginning of the poem remarkably apt for liturgical recitation.

The second pair of stanzas develops, now in a more radical fashion, the traditional themes of the spirituality and ineffability of God. Because God is spirit, he cannot be seen by human eye, nor pictured by any inner eye of the imagination. Because God is ineffable, his nature cannot be expressed in language, and therefore it cannot be grasped by any human thought, however abstract. Thus far many theologians of the most orthodox kind would agree with the sentiment of the poem. But must the conclusion be that the inner eye must be cast down and the inner voice be silenced?

The ineffability of God is given by Clough a moral as well as a logical element. We must not attempt to name God, as Adam named the animals; for naming is a claiming of power; when God named himself to Moses it was in a manner which was a refusal to give a name. To leave God unnamed, then, is not equivalent to disowning him; on the contrary, it is to refuse to claim an ownership which would be blasphemous.

There is another moral consideration which enters into the contention that it is impossible to talk literally about God. (This, too, is developed by Clough, in some of his prose writings.) The fact that theological language cannot be literal provides a reason for toleration in religion. That is to say, theological propositions cannot contradict each other in the straightforward way in which empirical propositions do. Hence, there is not that head-on clash between different theologies, and different religions, which has been used to justify the persecution and killing of one religious group by others.

To say that religious language is not literal, and to say that different religious creeds do not contradict each other, is not to say that all religions are of equal worth. The mode of utterance of Shakespeare and of Southey is poetic in each case; that does not mean that the writings of each of them display an an equal insight into human nature. Equally, the fact that Christianity and Hinduism each speak in metaphor does not necessitate that each of them has an equally valuable insight into divine nature, or the nature of the Universe as a whole.

The premises of Clough's *Qui Laborat, Orat* are profoundly orthodox; the guiding sentiment too is traditional. *Orando laborando* was Rugby's school motto; but a closer parallel to the poem's title is the motto of the

Benedictine order: *laborare est orare*. But from the ineffability of God orthodox believers have never drawn the conclusion that it is profane to use words to describe and invoke him. Rather, they have said, with St Augustine, *vae tacentibus de te* – woe to those who are silent about thee.

Some religious thinkers have attempted to show that coherent literal description of God is after all possible; others have simply claimed that there can be worse things than talking nonsense. Perhaps that is what lies behind Augustine's *vae tacentibus*. We may aim at a rational worship, and yet get no further than the babble of infants or the glossalaly of the possessed.

In the present century no one surpassed Wittgenstein in the devotion of sharp intelligence to the demarcation of the boundary between sense and nonsense. Wittgenstein finished the masterpiece of his youth with the words, 'Wovon man nicht sprechen kann, darüber muss man schweigen': whereof one cannot speak, thereof one must be silent. But within ten years he was putting forth his own gloss on Augustine's *vae tacentibus*. 'Was, du Mistviech, du willst keinen Unsinn reden? Rede nur einen Unsinn, es macht nichts.'[13] We may paraphrase thus: 'So, you don't want to talk nonsense, don't you, you cowpat! Talk a little nonsense, it will do you no harm.'

NOTES

1   Helen Gardner, *The New Oxford Book of English Verse* (Clarendon Press, 1972).
2   René Descartes, *The Philosophical Writings*, translated by John Cottingham et al. (Cambridge University Press, 1985).
3   Don Cupitt, *Nature and Culture* (this volume, p. 33).
4   Thomas Traherne, *Poetical Works* (Oxford University Press, 1903).
5   David Hume, *Treatise of Human Nature*, ed. Selby-Bigge (Oxford University Press, 1928), p. 252.
6   Herbert Spencer, *First Principles* (Collins, 1862), III, p. 20.
7   St Thomas Aquinas, *Super Epistolas S. Pauli lectura*, ed. Cai, (Marietti, 1953). '[C]onstat quad homo naturaliter desiderat salutem sui ipsius, anima autem cum sit pars corporis hominis, non est totus homo, et anima mea non est ego; unde licet anima consequatur salutem in alia vita, non tamen ego vel quilibet homo. In I ad Corinthios XV, 1.II', §924.
8   Anthony Kenny, *The Five Ways* (Routledge & Kegan Paul, 1969).
9   Richard Dawkins, *The Blind Watchmaker* (Longmans, 1986). Quotations on these pages are from pp. 38, 141 respectively.
10  Bertrand Russell and Alfred North Whitehead, *Principia Mathematica* (Cambridge University Press, 1910) I, 63.
11  Anthony Kenny, *The God of the Philosophers* (Clarendon Press, 1979).

12 *The Poems of Arthur Hugh Clough*, second edition, ed F. L. Mulhauser (Clarendon Press, 1974), pp. 311–12, 14 respectively.
13 F. Waismann and B. F. McGuinness, *Ludwig Wittgenstein und der Wiener Kreis* (Basil Blackwell, 1967), p. 69.

# Muller on Religions
# – And the Miraculous

### The Three Aspects of Natural Religion

*A study of religions has taught us... that, like the great rivers they may indeed have one source, but that their tributaries are so numerous that they often impart an entirely new colour to the original volume of water. It was this conviction that led me to treat of religion under its three aspects as physical, or inspired by the aspect of nature, as anthropological, or founded on the nature of man, and as psychological, or occupied with the nature of soul and its relation to God...*

*And... Religion, when looked upon not as supernatural, but as thoroughly natural to man, has assumed a new meaning and a higher dignity when studied as an integral part of that historical evolution which has made man what he is, and what from the very first he was meant to be.*

Preface to *Collected Works*, pp. xiii, xix

### Craving for the Supernatural

*Unfortunately, it is still with many of us, as it was with the Jews of old. They were always hankering for something exclusive and exceptional, for something super-natural and miraculous. They alone, they thought, were the chosen people of God. They would not believe, unless they saw signs and wonders, designed for their special benefit, while they remained blind to the true signs and wonders that appealed to them on every side.*

*And yet the founders of the three greatest religions of the world [Islam, Buddhism and Christianity], however much they may differ on other points, are unanimous on one point, namely in their condemnation of this hankering after the miraculous, and after the supernatural, falsely so called... 'Except ye see signs and wonders ye will not believe.'*

*Such utterances... should... make us pause and reflect what the true meaning of a miracle was in the beginning. It was not the supernatural forced and foisted into the natural; it was the natural perceived as the supernatural; it was the reading of a new and deeper meaning both in the workings of nature and in the acts of inspired men; it was the recognition of the Divine, reflected in the light of common day.*

*Physical Religion,* pp. 337–40

# 7
# Is There Reliable Knowledge About God?

## John Habgood

The key word in my title is 'reliable'. It is a word which falls short of 'certainty'. To claim 'certain' knowledge about God would be impious. But 'reliable' knowledge is knowledge adequate for the practical purposes of living; it is knowledge to which it is both possible and sensible to commit oneself.

This practical slant to the word is important to my meaning. I am not keen on the modern use of the word 'praxis', but at least it serves as a reminder that theory and practice are inseparable. Belief in God is not an idea which may or may not make a difference; it has no substance unless it makes a difference. Knowledge about God belongs within a total context of life, a total environment of doing, willing, thinking, feeling, relating, responding and historical conditioning, and if extracted from this context it becomes arid speculation.

Furthermore, reliability is not some kind of bonus within the religious life, but belongs to the heart of it. Religion *is* relying; the two words come from the same root. The phrase 'reliable knowledge' can therefore carry some faint religious overtones, even when used in a thoroughly secular context. It opens up the possibility that faith may have something to do with it. In fact the phrase can act as a kind of bridge between faith on the one hand and a hopelessly impracticable ideal of total objectivity on the other. And it is a flexible bridge. There can be degrees of reliability. There can be questions about when knowledge is reliable enough.

My title refers to reliable knowledge *about* God, and before I plunge into the main subject let me spell out the significance of that word 'about'. In some ways it is easier to defend knowledge *of* God rather than knowledge *about* him, because knowledge *of* him, where it exists, is mostly interior and incommunicable, and hence difficult to test or refute. It can be profound and wordless as in the mystics, or no more than a vague feeling as in the lady from East Barnet who was overheard saying, 'I don't actually believe in the Resurrection, but I do think that there's something going on up there.'[1]

If there is certainty at all in religion it seems to belong at this level of ineffability, at the point where philosophy and theology run out into silence. To try to express it can be to destroy it, or at least to distort it so seriously that all expressions of it become controversial. That at any rate is what it feels like, and why talking about God can seem so problematic in comparison with interior knowledge of him. There is a plausible view of religion which sees it as a response to an inexpressible something articulated in a variety of forms which are bound to differ from one another, not just because the subject matter is difficult and the basis of knowledge contested, but because description itself always to a greater or lesser extent falsifies what it is attempting to encapsulate.[2]

But how is this 'something' known, even inarticulately, unless there is some prior framework of understanding, some rudimentary language of thought, within which it can be recognized? Without language it is doubtful whether we could think at all. In saying this I do not want to deny the immediacy of religious experience. I believe that all our knowledge of God depends upon our having a prior relationship with God, a relationship in which God himself takes the initiative in making himself present to us. But we cannot know his presence as presence, indeed cannot even acknowledge a religious awareness, without a language and without thought forms in which to identify it. And a language always belongs to a historically conditioned culture and to a particular mode of rationality.

Thus, despite the incommunicable nature of claims to know God directly, there is no escape from trying to articulate knowledge *about* him. It is these articulate claims I want to concentrate on in this lecture, while recognizing that precisely because they emerge from a struggle to say something which cannot in the end be said, they are bound to be different from one another, and controversial. In what sense can such diverse and fragmentary knowledge claim to be reliable? A hundred years of Gifford Lectures show something of the multiplicity of answers.

There is plenty of evidence of unreliable knowledge of what God is like. Who now believes in Baal? Perhaps there are nature worshippers who respond in their own idiom to the same sort of reality as Baal worshippers once responded to in theirs. But Baal as a concept is dead, and so are hundreds of other gods who once formed the centres of cults, who exacted sacrifice and devotion, who engendered a theology however rudimentary, and who were believed to be powerful. As H. L. Mencken said of them in his memorial service for the gods in which he listed 100 or more now-forgotten names, 'They ranked five or six thousand years ago with Jahveh himself... yet they have all gone down the chute...'[3]

This carnage is a vivid reminder that religions are not closed immutable systems. They can lose their plausibility, die, be defeated; or they can develop, adapt to circumstances, reinterpret their basic tenets, and be radically transformed. It makes sense therefore to ask how far the knowledge of God can be seen to conform to some kind of empirical model. Do gods die because they no longer relate effectively to the world as it is perceived to be? And if so, is the corollary also true, that where perceptions of God have survived through many millenia and many transformations, there must be something in the nature of things which continues to make belief in them a plausible option? We can press the point further. If scientific knowledge evolves through a process of trial and error, is it possible to identify the same process at work in theology? After making allowance for very different subject matters, is there a valid analogy between scientific and theological knowledge?

I turn first to the character of scientific knowledge, and I do so deliberately through the work of a practising scientist rather than the philosophy of science. John Ziman is a physicist and his book *Reliable Knowledge* gave me the title of this lecture.[4] He sets out extraordinarily well what most ordinary scientists see themselves as actually doing and aiming for. Scientists can be curiously unreflective in philosophical terms, and some of the excesses of scientism spring from this lack of critical awareness. But most, I believe, would acknowledge the goal of reliable knowledge, the consensus of rational opinion, the idea of public knowledge which is in principle accessible to all who go through the requisite procedures.

In what then does its reliability consist? Apart from the process of trial and error to which I have already referred, Ziman spells out the need for unambiguous language, language which is universally translatable, language stripped of all its overtones and historical associations, language which carries its full meaning on its surface. The language of science need not always be mathematically precise, but it must be clear. Great moments of scientific advance have usually been linked with the forging of some new concept, like force, or mass, or charge, with sufficient clarity for it to become an organizing principle around which numerous ideas and observations can then fall into place.

Scientists cannot, however, avoid metaphor and analogy in the process of theorizing and pushing out the boundaries of knowledge, because these are usually the only means available for describing what cannot be directly observed. Indeed the function of scientific models is to explore ways of understanding which 'look right', and a certain imprecision may be positively helpful in stimulating the imagination and pointing up the limits of the analogy. Underneath the idea of 'looking right' lie unwritten assumptions or agreements about what counts as an explanation, and such assumptions may in their turn be developed further by the stimulus of good analogical thinking. Interacting particles, for example, do not behave like billiard balls; in fact as I discovered when asking a foolish question on a visit to CERN a few years ago, it becomes progressively more difficult to know what a particle is. But the billiard table is a marvellous place to begin.

Unambiguous language operating within potentially fruitful models can build up a network of concepts and interpretations which mutually reinforce each other. Ziman uses the familiar metaphor of a map. Crisscrossing fields of study can, over time, produce a reliable map of a major area of knowledge. It is the cross-checking, the ability to approach a subject from many different angles, and to travel round it intellectually by many different routes, which creates confidence. This is one reason why science can never be a solitary exercise. Maps are created by consensus. They are put together from innumerable travellers' tales. And they do not have to be final and perfect to be useful.

This is a deliberately modest account of what natural scientists are trying to do, seen from the perspective of a physicist. But even by these standards, says Ziman, the behavioural sciences fall at almost every hurdle. Sciences like sociology and economics, for instance, lack clear, unambiguous and universally recognized theoretical concepts. This is not due to any inadequacy in the researchers themselves, and the idea that there could be a 'Newton of the social sciences' who could identify such concepts and unify the whole field, is fantasy. The irreducible difficulty is that if human beings are to take account of the significance of their own actions they cannot do it in language which has been stripped of all its human associations. Metaphors, analogies and models exist in abundance, but for the most part they are limited in their application and fail to coalesce into the kind of large scale map which gives such strength and reliability to the natural sciences. Ziman questions whether behavioural maps are any more reliable than conventional wisdom. Perhaps we learn more about ourselves from novels and plays and poems and traditional rules of thumb, which are in many ways better suited than abstract analyses to handle the actual complexities and ambiguities of human living. I am reminded of the plea made by Howard Root in a seminal essay written in 1962 that natural theology should 'begin all over again'[5] by attending to 'the disturbing visions of human nature which find expression in serious modern literature.' Does this mean then that in such fields the process of building up consensus towards the goal of reliability has to be abandoned?

Thus far Ziman. I have used him at some length because I believe he gives convincing expression to a widely-held and basically pragmatic view of science, which gives content to the word 'reliable', which pinpoints some of the difficulties in the behavioural sciences, but which by implication leaves theology firmly at the unreliable end of the spectrum of knowledge.

Suppose, however, we take up his hint about literature and traditional wisdom, and ask how we understand and learn from these. We find ourselves engaged in a very different critique of knowledge, which in turn throws back some awkward questions to the natural sciences. I refer, of course, to hermeneutics and to the huge intellectual industry which has grown up around seemingly simple questions about how to read books intelligently and to grasp the meaning of what other people are saying. It rests on the insight that all knowledge is interpretation – which may seem fairly obvious. But its implications are dizzying.

At this point I merely want to note that hermeneutics began with the attempt to systematize interpretation of the Bible. I remind you of this because some months ago when I mentioned the title of this lecture to a clerical colleague his immediate response was, 'So you are going to talk about revelation'. In a sense, yes. But not in the sense that there is a given store of reliable knowledge about God in the Bible which can be painlessly extracted without difficult enquiry into how the Bible is to be understood and evaluated.

Gadamer,[6] a key figure in the development of hermeneutics on whom I shall be relying at this stage in what I am saying, does indeed talk about truth as a kind of revelation, a disclosure. Great art or literature or significant events can exercise a claim over us. They can uncover some part of our world or our lives which was previously hidden from us. But the claim is not a simple one. The disclosure depends also on ourselves, who we are and where we stand, our historical conditioning, in a word, our prejudices.

For Gadamer the starting point is prejudice, not in the pejorative sense but in the sense that none of us starts with a clean slate. Prejudice forms the perspectives from which alone the growth of knowledge is possible. We build on what is already there. But not uncritically. The so-called hermeneutic circle is a constant process of re-evaluation. In the interpretation, say, of a classic text the interpreters carry with them their own traditions and assumptions and first project these onto the text in order to begin to understand it. They may, for example, approach a particular biblical passage as theology, or history, or mythology, or liturgy, or fantasy or whatever, but they must also allow the text itself to modify and correct that original projection. So begins a kind of dialogue between the text itself and the developing understanding of the interpreter as initial apprehensions and assumptions are challenged and refined. There is no simple, objective, ultimately true meaning of a text abstracted from a particular place and time. A text belongs within its own time, and has to be interpreted in our time. But it does not follow from this that 'anything goes'. There can be what Gadamer calls 'a fusion of horizons' by the integration of different perspectives. There has to be a long process of dialogue, a continuing conversation. The goal of this conversation, whether between text and interpreters or between interpreters themselves, is understanding. The method is self-criticism and willingness to learn, together with openness to the subject matter, and the defining and testing of prejudices in relation to its claims. The validation of understanding is agreement.

I am bowdlerizing a complex story. My purpose in telling it is to make two simple points; first, that the study of literature or of any meaningful human communication can be as serious and self-critical as any other intellectual activity, including science; second, that there are partial ways of escape from the subjectivist trap in which mere prejudice, mere private opinion, have the last word. To acknowledge the conditioned character of all human thought and perception is not to be set loose on a sea of uninformed opinion. It may not be possible to substantiate claims to some ideal of total objectivity, always assuming that that is desirable. But there remain ways of being rational, of growing in understanding, and of acquiring more reliable knowledge. The heart of the process is dialogue. This is not a return to Hegelian dialectic because it does not presuppose, as Hegel did, that there is some point of absolute knowledge beyond which no further advance is possible. The process remains open. There is no escape from the possibility of being wrong, and the willingness to go on listening to others always threatens whatever interim conclusions may have been reached. But the process as a whole does lead on to a richer more developed rationality.

Gadamer's approach says more about the behavioural sciences than about the natural sciences. This is because the behavioural sciences, like the humanities, entail what has been called 'a double hermeneutic'. Not only are they constituted by their own traditions of interpretation, like any other rational enquiry, but their subject matter also includes the meanings which people ascribe to their own actions, and hence the traditions or prejudices by which they interpret these. There are thus two layers of tradition, one belonging to the science and the other belonging to its subject matter, and the interactions between these can be extraordinarily complex. So it is with theology. It is not a science in the same sense as the natural sciences whose goal, however remote and unattainable and, in Gadamer's terms inadmissible, is complete objectivity. The subject matter of theology is itself 'meaning'. It claims not only to be meaningful as an intellectual tradition, but also to characterize God as himself the focus of meaning, a meaning which can only be known by identifying with it and living by it.

At this level the practical dimension of hermeneutics becomes crucial. Knowledge about God is never simply book knowledge, though there are elements of book knowledge within it. There is a rational study of religion at the first level of hermeneutic which may or may not yield agreed public knowledge. At the second level of hermeneutics where communities and individuals have to face the meaning of their own existence, reliability takes a different shape. It relates more to what I described earlier as an interior certainty as glimpsed in whatever forms of expression are available. Yet even at this level such certainty needs to be tempered by continuing openness, dialogue and self-criticism.

This idea of a double hermeneutic helpfully distinguishes between theology, the humanities and the behavioural sciences on the one hand, and the natural sciences on the other. But it is important to grasp that all claims to knowledge, including the natural sciences, are subject to at least one kind of hermeneutic process. The sustained philosophical critiques of science throughout this century have led to the growing recognition that scientific data are not detachable from theory, and that theories are not detachable from the historical contexts in which they are formulated. *All* knowledge, in other words, is interpretation. Furthermore, the language in which the interpretation is given determines the character of the result. I made the point earlier that successful scientific language is clear, unambiguous and universal. For the study of many phenomena this is a *sine qua non*, and for the study of some phenomena the clearest, totally unamibiguous and most universal language of all, namely mathematics, is almost wholly sufficient. Ziman describes physics as 'the science devoted to discovering, developing and refining those aspects of reality that are amenable to mathematical analysis.'[7] Physics, in other words, is a mathematical fishing-net for capturing mathematical relationships.

As an ideal of language, though, and as a determinant by implication of what counts as reliable knowledge, clarity, precision and universality can be disastrous, as the recent history of British philosophy has revealed only too obviously. Alasdair Macintyre has described part of the heritage of the Enlightenment as precisely such a modernized sanitized language which achieves universality at the cost of uprooting itself from the cultural traditions in which different languages had hitherto grown. In his latest book *Whose Justice? Which Rationality?*[8] he makes the point, very much in the spirit of Gadamer, that it is not only moral concepts like justice, but concepts of rationality itself, which have been embodied in long intellectual and social traditions, and which cannot be fully understood apart from them. The Enlightenment thinkers, in deliberately cutting loose from such traditions, deprived rationality of its history, of that long process of refinement through constant debate which had given the criteria of rationality their stability. Bereft of such traditions we are left with the illusion that all which can be said significantly can be said within the confines of a modern universal language which uproots profound ideas from their contexts and puts them on display in a market place of opinions. Customer preference rules.

The word 'God' is a case in point. Part of the theological crisis of modernity lies in the difficulty of giving any actual content to the word. To attempt to describe God in purely conceptual terms is to be reduced to incoherence or banality. Martin Buber when challenged by a friend that all the evil which had been done in the name of God had ruined the word replied:

> Yes it is the most heavy-laden of all human words. None has become so soiled, so mutilated. Just for this reason I may not abandon it. Generations of men have laid the burden of their anxious lives upon this word and weighed it to the ground; it lies in the dust and bears their whole burden. The races of men with their religious factions have torn the word to pieces; they have killed for it and died for it, and it bears their fingermarks and their blood. Where might I find a word like it to describe the highest? If I took the purest, most sparkling concept from the inner treasure-chamber of the philosopher, I could only capture thereby an unbinding product of thought. I could not capture the presence of Him whom the generations of men have honoured and degraded with their awesome living and dying. I do indeed mean Him whom the hell-tormented and heaven-storming generations of men mean. Certainly they draw caricatures and write 'God' underneath; they murder one another and say 'in God's name'. But when all madness and delusion fall to dust, when they stand over against Him in the loneliest darkness and no longer say 'He', but rather sigh 'Thou', shout 'Thou',... and when they then add 'God', is it not the real God whom they implore...?[9]

A word with a history. And the meaning has to include the history. Reliable knowledge about this God cannot be abstracted from the anxious debates and the blood-stained controversies which have shaped the ascription of his name. The recent report of the Church of England Doctrine Commission, entitled *We believe in God*, referred to 'well winnowed traditions'.[10] Reliability has a time factor built into it. All traditions, including scientific ones, remain 'provisional, corrigible and incomplete' but to have become traditions at all they have to have achieved a certain stability over time. And in their time they can be adequate.

In a sense what I have been saying in these last few paragraphs is what any Bible-based Christian should know instinctively. The God whom Christians worship can only be known through immersion in the whole biblical tradition. Nothing less than the whole Bible will do, and nothing less than a constant return to it and renewal by it. And for a mature understanding there has to be some sense of the way biblical themes have been interpreted and elaborated through Christian history. It is not a fossilized tradition, but a living one in which criticism and development are the signs of vitality. Christianity is particularly resilient to this kind of treatment because, as Pannenberg has put it,

> in Christianity the history of religious experiences and their changing forms has itself become the theme of religion, the sphere of divine self-revelation. This is the source of the ability of the biblical religions to survive the experience of their own historical change. Whereas religions which are dominated by the idea of an allegedly unsurpassable mythical Golden Age and a corresponding world order are swept away by the changes produced in them in the course of history, the Jewish and Christian religion, because it is a religion of history, can integrate changes in itself and see them as divine guidance.[11]

Nevertheless, the problem remains of sustaining this constant process of re-evaluation, of growth in understanding through dialogue, in a world where religious and intellectual traditions have become attenuated, by reason of the fact that the only language on offer for cross-cultural exchange is the neutral language of a pluralist society which tends to reduce basic religious insights to their secular counterparts. I have already fallen into this trap earlier in this lecture in referring obscurely to God, through a bloodless abstract concept, as 'a focus of meaning'. I now want to suggest that perhaps one way of strengthening the sense of belonging to a tradition, while at the same time exposing it to questioning from a coherent alternative tradition, is through inter-faith dialogue. My hope is that it may in time provide us with just that kind of cross-checking, that complex network of interrelated experiences and interpretations, which gives strength and stability to scientific thought. Could a more comprehensive religious map help us to find our bearings? I speak here from very little experience, but it seems to me that inter-faith dialogue has rightly been moving centre-stage, not just for social or missiological reasons, but because theologians have begun to perceive that the integrity and credibility of Christian faith depends in part on its ability to define itself in relation to other faiths.[12]

Dialogue is more than talking. It is about the meeting of minds and people in their total cultural context. It entails the learning of the other's language in the broadest sense, to the point at which it is possible to think and feel in and through the other's language. Macintyre writes about 'second first languages', which imply much more than the ability to translate one sentence into another. He asks us to imagine by contrast a dialogue conducted solely in sentences from phrase books, a recipe for farce. Inter-faith dialogue entails an openness and a willingness to learn of the kind which Gadamer described as essential to his hermeneutics. It is very demanding and threatening. At first sight it also seems to under- mine the very notion of reliability which I have tried to locate within the experience of belonging to a mature and tested tradition. How can we assert the reliability of our own knowledge when faced with an alternative mature and tested tradition?

I am told, however, that the experience can be just the opposite of what might be feared. In a minor classic written twenty years ago Klaus Klostermaier described his own deeper conversion to Christ through dialogue with Hindu friends.[13] He began for the first time to see Christ in India, not as a stranger who had come from Europe, but as one who had been there from the beginning.

This was a discovery of oneness and reinforcement. But even when dialogue only serves to expose differences there can be a kind of rein- forcement through the recognition of a certain commonality in difference. Surely the most dramatic encounter between different faiths took place in 1519 when Cortez anchored off the Mexican coast and two religious traditions which had been isolated from one another since the dawn of human history met for the first time, like aliens from outer space. There are records of the meeting from both sides, and though Aztec religion was terrifyingly different from Spanish Christianity, even as it was then in its most bloodthirsty phase, these aliens recognized religion as religion. Cortez knew where to set up his first images of the saints – on sites which were already religiously significant.[14]

It is not wise to conclude too much from the apparent universality of religion, though again and again there is fresh evidence of it even in our own country, as the most recent opinion polls demonstrate. Gods, as Mencken said, can die. But while the questions, the feelings, the hopes, the needs, which seek religious expression, may be frustrated and distorted when there is no adequate vehicle to carry them, nevertheless they do not seem to disappear. The religious impulses of humankind have an astonishing record for reliability. And the fact that over thousands of years only a small number of great traditions have survived, and are now finding it possible to talk with one another to their mutual benefit, is at least an indication that religious responses are responses to some coherent, though ultimately hidden reality.

Beyond that we can only rely on our traditions and see them as containing within themselves the roots of an understanding which goes deeper than present day secularisms. And we can go on talking, as Gifford lecturers have talked for a hundred years; and we can go on acting together for the world's good, as increasingly it is possible to do across the barriers of different beliefs. And who knows, one day we might find each other closer than we imagined, in the place where the world's suffering is most fully exposed. As Brunner said in commenting on the text 'I if I be lifted up will draw all men to myself',

Christ crucified draws us to himself that there we might meet each other.

## NOTES

1   Quoted in Idries Shah's *Darkest England* (Octagon Press, 1987), p. 115.
2   This is 'the experiential – expressive model' as described by G. A. Lindbeck in *The Nature of Doctrine*, (SPCK, 1985), p. 31 ff.
3   Quoted in John Bowker's *The Religious Imagination and the Sense of God* (Oxford, 1978), p. 1.
4   John Ziman, *Reliable Knowledge: An exploration of the grounds for belief in science* (Cambridge, 1978).
5   Howard Root, 'Beginning all over again', in A. R. Vidler (ed.), *Soundings* (Cambridge, 1962), p. 19.
6   The key work is, of course, Gadamer's *Truth and Method* (English translation 1975). I have also relied on Georgia Warnke, *Gadamer: Hermeneutics, Tradition and Reason* (Polity, 1987); Richard J. Bernstein, *Beyond Objectivism and Relativism* (Blackwell, 1983); W. Pannenberg, *Theology and the Philosophy of Science* (Dartman, Longman & Todd, 1976); David Tracy, *Plurality and Ambiguity: Hermeneutics, Religion, Hope* (SCM, 1987).
7   John Ziman, *Reliable Knowledge*, p. 28.
8   Alasdair Macintyre, *Whose Justice? Which Rationality?* (Duckworth, 1988).
9   Martin Buber, *The Eclipse of God* (New York, 1952), pp. 7–8.
10  *We Believe in God* (Church House Publishing, 1987), p. 24.
11  W. Pannenburg op. cit. (note 6) p. 314.
12  Kenneth Cracknell, *Towards a New Relationship* (Epworth, 1986) spells out helpfully the conditions for successful inter-faith dialogue.

13   Klaus Klostermaier, *Hindu and Christian in Vrindaban* (SCM, 1969).

14   I take this illustration from David Hay, *Exploring Inner Space: Scientists and Religious Experience* (Mowbray, 1987) p. 3 ff. The book as a whole marshalls impressive evidence for the universality of religious experience, as investigated by the Alister Hardy Research Centre in Oxford.

# *Final Thoughts from Muller*

---

*Let us reverence by all means what is called childlike faith, but let us never forget that to think also is to worship God.*

Theosophy, or *Psychological Religion*, p. 523

*It is truth that makes revelation, not revelation that makes truth.*

*Physical Religion*, p. 361

*A clock cannot return to the clockmaker, but a drop of rain can return to the ocean from whence it was lifted, and a ray of light is always light.*

Theosophy, or *Psychological Religion*, p. 515

*What is natural is divine, what is supernatural is human.*

Preface to *Collected Works*, p. xv

# Index